I have been David's pastor for twenty years and can testify to his great love for Jesus Christ. He is well known in our church and appreciated for his beautiful prayers. He has taken that same ability that he uses in prayer and expressed himself in these poems. I am sure that everyone who reads them will be blessed.

-Pastor Michael Collins


This collection of poems is a devotional that is an outpouring of David's spirit through verse. His writings are a reflection of his life's journey and his love and devotion to God. His poems offer hope, insight, and comfort to the reader.

-Brenda Bishop


A common thread throughout David's poetry is God's faithfulness in every season of life. Your spirit will be renewed and you will be encouraged!

-Diane Dalton

# a DAILY WALK WITH THE LORD

# a DAILY WALK WITH THE LORD

## Daily Devotion

David L. Hurst

All scripture is from the King James Version.

Published by David L. Hurst

Cover Design copyright © 2012 by David L. Hurst. All rights reserved.

Interior Design by David L. Hurst

Published in the United States of America

ISBN: 978-0-9855779-0-2

1. Poetry / Inspirational & religious
2. Religion / Christian Life / Devotional

# Dedication

There are some wonderful people in my life whom I would like to honor and show my love and appreciation:  my mother, Agnes L. Hurst, and there is a special place in my heart for my son, Kris M. Hurst.

It is my privilege and honor to dedicate "a Daily Walk with the Lord" to the Hurst family.  My brothers and sisters, I pray that the Lord will bless each of you and keep you in his love and care.

This book is in loving memory of my father, Roy L. Hurst.

# Acknowledgements

I am very thankful to Avery Wilson for reading my poems on his radio program. It is my pleasure to recognize and honor my brothers and sisters, Gordon, Marie, Gene, and Sherry, for the many words of encouragement. My other family members were honored in the dedication. All of my friends and family are greatly appreciated for their kind words and their loyal support. I am thankful for the prayers that ascended to heaven.

With heartfelt gratitude from a sincere heart, I give thanks unto God for the inspiration and the divine guidance in writing a Daily Walk with the Lord.

# January

"Whereas ye know not what shall be on the morrow. For what is your life?  It is even a vapor, that appeareth for a little time, and then vanisheth."

James 4:14

1.   The Old Year Is Passed
2.   From the Miry Clay
3.   Plenty of Time
4.   The Midnight Hour
5.   The Hourglass
6.   Look Up, My Friend
7.   A Little While
8.   Take the Time
9.   It Is Later Than You Think
10.  Here Today, Gone Tomorrow
11.  Surely Goodness and Mercy
12.  The Last Page
13.  A Time to Fast
14.  A New Life in Christ
15.  It is Suppertime
16.  A Time to Rejoice
17.  To Stay or Go
18.  It Is Time
19.  The Train Is Coming
20.  The Journey's End
21.  Solid Rock Foundation
22.  When does life begin?
23.  The Last Amen
24.  Today Is Borrowed
25.  Clouds Pass Away
26.  Heaven or Hell
27.  King's Palace, Poor Man's Table
28.  The Chief Cornerstone
29.  Where will you be?
30.  My Hearts Desire
31.  Where is the cross?

# February

"Jesus said unto him, thou shalt love the Lord thy God with all thy heart, and with all thy soul, and with all thy mind."
(Matthew 22:37, KJV)

1.   Hear My Heart's Plea
2.   Tomorrow, It May Be too Late
3.   Waiting for the Day
4.   White as Snow
5.   Melt the Ice
6.   When the Path Is Hard to See
7.   From His Heart
8.   Open the Window
9.   A New Day Dawning
10.  Resurrection Day
11.  As I Have Loved You
12.  A Beggar Finds Bread
13.  Heaven's Gold Mine
14.  He is worthy of the Honor
15.  Please Forgive Me
16.  Insufficient Love
17.  The Shadow of Life
18.  The Highest Honor
19.  I Can't Do It
20.  Deep Desire
21.  Sunshine of His Love
22.  When Jesus Comes Again
23.  The Trumpet Sound
24.  Our Home in glory
25   Great Expectations
26.  A City in the Sky
27.  A Prodigal Son Returns
28.  Every day with Jesus
29.  Treasure in Heaven

# March

"In my Father's house are many mansions: if it were not so, I would have Told you, I go to prepare a place for you. And if I go and prepare a place for you, I will come again, and receive you unto myself."

(John 14:2,3, KJV)

1.   Sound of the Trumpet
2.   Restore to Life Eternal
3.   A Safe Passageway
4.   Open the Gates
5.   Passing Through
6.   Higher Ground
7.   Almost Home
8.   No Sunday School Today
9.   Patiently Wait
10.  Run to Win
11.  Climb a Little Higher
12.  A Spiritual Journey
13.  This Same Jesus
14.  We Are Almost Home
15.  The Secret of Happiness
16.  Jesus Is Coming
17.  Your Name in Glory
18.  A Refreshing Rain
19.  Break Camp in the Morning
20.  Praise God Today
21.  No Grapes on the Vine
22.  Grafted into the Vine
23.  Gold in the Hills
24.  Break up the Fallow Ground
25.  Carry the Torch
26.  Build a Bigger Barn
27.  Re-Dig an Old Well
28.  Change the Track
29.  From Heaven to Earth
30.  Rain, a Spiritual Desire
31.  No Mountain too High

# April

"Jesus said unto her, I am the resurrection, and the life: he that believeth in me, Though he were dead, yet shall he live:" "And whosoever liveth and believeth in me shall never die, Believeth thou this?"

(John 11: 25,26, KJV)

1. A Living Sacrifice
2. Do you remember?
3. Divine Obedience
4. Honey in a Bear's Den
5. Crucify Afresh
6. A Sacrifice for Sin
7. He Didn't Send an Angel
8. He Didn't Come Down
9. The Tomb Is Empty
10. The Third Day
11. The Grave Is Empty
12. From Death to Life
13. Alive by the Power of God
14. Alive from the Dead
15. I Know Jesus Lives
16. We are Va. Tech. Let's Go Hokies
17. The Debt Is Paid
18. Let the Halleluiahs Rise
19. Meet Jesus at the Crossroads
20. Easter Is Coming
21. The Final Victory
22. It Is Finished
23. Give God the Praise
24. Christ Is Risen, Sins are forgiven
25. Were you there?
26. Faith Never Quits
27. When We Were Enemies
28. If in This Life Only
29. Where is the devotion?
30. Lazarus, Come Forth

# May

"For I am not ashamed of the gospel of Christ: for it is the power of God unto salvation to everyone that believeth;"(Ro 1;16, KJV) "Therefore, my beloved brethren, be ye stedfast, unmoveable, always abounding in the work of the Lord, forasmuch as ye know that your labor is not in vain in The Lord."

(1Co 15:58, KJV)

1.  Come from Behind
2.  The Sword of the Spirit
3.  The Gospel of Christ
4.  Sin in Pencil, Prayers in Ink
5.  A Pen in God's Mighty Hand
6.  The Cross and beyond
7.  A Sharp Axe
8   Revive Us Again
9.  Thread of Life
10. No Talent Left
11. Stop the Train
12. An Empty Lantern
13. Mother's Day
14. The Eternal Summit
15. Gather in the Grain
16. Work in the Harvest Field
17. Strawberry Pie
18. Make Some Bread
19. Weeds in the Garden
20. A Porch of an Idle Life
21. Silver and Gold
22. I Pledge Allegiance
23. Soldier of War
24. Heaven's Treasure
25. God's Search Is Endless
26. The Master of the Clay
27. The Potter and the Clay
28. Deliverance from the Storm
29. Grace Not Yet Found
30. Astray from the Fold
31. God Is Faithful and Just

# June

"Teaching them to observe all things whatsoever I have commanded you: and, lo, I am with you always, even unto the end of the world. Amen."

(Matthew 28:20, KJV)

1. The Shepherd of the Sheep
2. Jehovah
3. A Fresh Refilling
4. Faith Is the Key
5. God Opens the Door, Never Close It
6. The Prayer of Faith
7. He Calls Me, Friend
8. Be of Good Cheer; It Is I
9. A Walk with the Lord
10. A Daily Walk with the Lord
11. When the Path Is Hard to See
12. Greater Is He
13. The Savior's Path
14. A Gentle Shower From Above
15. A Personal Visit
16. Rejoice in the Holy Spirit
17. He Walked among Us
18. Touch the Lord
19. Our Heavenly Father
20. Walking with the King
21. Rescue from the Flames
22. Come and Dine
23. Come unto Me
24. Come and Go with me
25. Trust in the Lord
26. Follow Jesus
27. The Trinity as One
28. Come On In
29. The Lord Be with You
30. Bind Us Together

# July

"If we confess our sins, he is faithful and just to forgive us our sins, and to cleanse us from all unrighteousness."
(1John 1:9,KJV)

1.  A Divine Sacrifice
2.  Final Review
3.  Only by Permission
4.  God Bless America
5.  What manner of man is this?
6.  Who is this man?
7.  Make the Call
8.  Holiness is the Only Way
9.  The Fire Escape
10. Pardon Me
11. Saved from Sins
12. at an Old-Time Altar
13. Blind, but Now I See
14. The Stain of Sin
15. Clay Pits of Sin
16. Have Not Seen but Believe
17. Forgiveness
18. My Confession
19. The Path Less Traveled
20. It is Your Choice
21. Just a Beggar
22. All Have Sinned
23. In the Garden of Sin
24. One Lost Lamb
25. Empty Seats
26. The Path of Sin
27. Sin Was the King
28. A Wasted Life
29. A Blind Beggar
30. Sin Opens the Gate
31. Let Us Reason Together

# August

"For the wages of sin is death; but the gift of God is eternal life through Jesus Christ our Lord.

(Roman 6:23, KJV)

1. Left Town, No Regrets
2. One Word Assignment
3. Jesus Is the Christ
4. The Lord Is My Salvation
5. Grace Abounds
6. Thou Shalt Not
7. The Miry Clay
8. The Verdict
9. The Pathway of Life
10. To Follow a Sinful Path
11. Apples of Sin
12. The Anchor of the Soul
13. A New Image
14. Paid in Full
15. Life Is Worth Restoring
16. I Know What I Need
17. Turn from Sin
18. The Wolves of Sin
19. The Thorns of Sin
20. The Wrestling Match
21. In the Line of Duty
22. The Right Road
23. Safe on the Inside
24. Instant Replay
25. To Be Saved
26. When I Am Weak
27. The Old Sinful Way
28. Christ' Life in Review
29. The Stream Is Flowing Again
30. Too Late for Heaven's Flight
31. The Storm Is Over

# September

"How shall we escape, if we neglect so great salvation."
(Hebrew 2:3, KJV)

1.  A Broken Vessel
2.  Road to Destruction
3.  The House of Neglect
4.  Drifting Away
5.  An Old Fire Escape
6.  In the Fire
7.  A Runner Has Fallen
8.  Oil for the Lantern
9.  Throw out the Lifeline
10. A Thief Comes to Destroy
11. Little Foxes Spoil the Grapes
12. Through the Grapevine
13. Depart from Me
14. Slow the Wagon Down
15. A Walk in the Dark
16. Time to Repent
17. In the Lions' Den
18. Take Away the Pain
19. Oil in the Lamp
20. This Old Train
21. Lion on the Prowl
22. Thin Ice
23. Abandoned
24. Too Close to the Edge
25. Self-Inflicted Wound
26. This Old House
27. Too Close to the Fire
28. Drifting Away, Not Anymore
29. Fire on the Mountain
30. What would we do?

# October

"But if we walk in the light, as he is in the light, we have fellowship one with Another, and the blood of Jesus Christ his Son cleanseth us from all sin."

(1Joh 1;7,)

1. Tomorrow's Victory
2. Dig a New Well
3. God Will Bless
4. Tear the Old Fence Down
5. Prepare to Meet Thy God
6. Search Diligently
7. A Little Kindness
8. Never Thirst Again
9. In God We Trust
10. Return unto Me
11. Keep the Home Fires Burning
12. Lost More Than Was Won
13. I Will Answer Thee
14. God Answers Prayer
15. Stir Up the Coals
16. Unload the Wagon
17. In His Presence
18. What does God require?
19. Stay on Course
20. In His Hands
21. High Calling of God
22. It is Only a Tree
23. Unlock the Door
24. Strike the Match
25. God Will Supply
26. Go Back to the River
27. Hold On, My Friend
28. Keep the Faith Lines Open
29. Meet Me at the Cross
30. Would you follow Jesus?
31. A Made-Up Mind

# November

"Wait on the Lord: be of good courage, and he shall strengthen thine heart: wait I say, on the Lord (Psalm 27:14, KJV). "Be thou faithful unto death, and I will give thee a crown of life."

(Rev 2:10, KJV)

1.   Early in the Morning
2.   Lovest Thou Me
3.   Keep Going
4.   Live for Today
5.   A Light on a Hill
6.   Till We Meet Again
7.   No Turning Back
8.   One Thing Is Needed
9.   Let Everybody Know
10.  Be Ye Kind to One Another
11.  In a Faraway Land
12.  How much do you love me?
13.  Just a Little Closer
14.  A Day of Haste
15.  Be Still
16.  Keep Running
17.  Onward, Christian Soldiers
18.  My Debt Is Paid
19.  Locked in the Past
20.  Just A Drink of Water
21.  Give What You Keep
22.  A Divine Connection
23.  He Inhabits the Praise
24.  Any good thing in Nazareth?
25.  Tell Me What You See
26.  A Broken Cistern
27.  No Warning
28.  Overcoming Hurdles
29.  Picking up Pebbles
30.  Wings as an Eagle

# December

"For unto you is born this day in the city of David a Saviour, which is Christ the Lord"

(Lu 2:11, KJV)

"Behold, now is the accepted time: behold, now is the day of salvation."

(2Co 6:2, KJV)

1. A New Life Living
2. A New Candle
3. Confidence
4. Praise, Glory, and Honor
5. Faith Comes by Hearing
6. Praise God Today
7. My Father
8. Peace Be Still
9. Peace in the Shadows
10. Peace on Earth
11. Peace in the Storm
12. My Peace I Give unto You
13. A Brand-New Slate
14. This Gift is for You
15. A Reflection
16. The Gift of God's Love
17. What can I give?
18. An Open Window
19. The Birth of God's Son
20. God's Gift to Us
21. Countdown for Christ
22. Let's Say We Start with Ten
23. How about nine?
24. Do Not Forget Eight
25. Christmas Past, Think About Seven
26. What about six?
27. Now We Come to Five
28. There Is Only Four
29. Then We Come to Three
30. Don't Forget the Number Two
31. Then There Was One

# The Old Year Is Passed
## January 1

No turning back to the ways of the old.
The new-year has begun.
There is nothing left to hold.
Even the shadows disappear in the evening sun.

The days are gone.
They will never return.
Perhaps you would try to reclaim just one.
The calendar page has already been turned.

The old year is a thing of the past.
You cannot go back, even if you wanted to.
December 31st was the last.
This New Year God has a special blessing just for you.

Show a little kindness to your brother,
Give a lot of love,
Someone will meet the heavenly Father
And feel the hand from above.

The days are gone, please don't worry, fret or sigh.
About the things you should have done.
The gentle Savior is passing by.
Follow Him; a crown of life will be won.

Look ahead my friend.
This is a new year.
You have the hope of going to heaven.
The way of peace is made clear.

Give your heart to Jesus, love Him, too.
Trust Him all along life's way.
He goes before you.
And God hears you when you pray.

There is no looking back to the old—
The past is forgotten.
Follow Jesus, you will see what the future holds.
A home is in glory for the forgiven.

The new-year has begun.
Sing a new hymn.
Keep pressing on!
Soon, you will be with Him.

# From the Miry Clay
## January 2

A lowly gift to give
From the deep miry clay,
The heart cries for God to forgive.
A sinner is at the throne room of grace in disarray.

Unclean hands and an impure heart,
They hold a life with bonds of grief and despair.
The stronghold of sin God can break apart.
A grieving heart is a heavy weight to bear.

Just as you are with an open plea,
Don't worry about the mud and the grime.
Jesus died on the cross for you and me.
Life won't be the same

When you love Him with heart, soul and mind.
Though your transgressions are many,
At the cross you can leave them all behind.
A multitude of sins, now there are not any.

God's grace is sufficient
For a poor wretched sinner.
He knows those who are repentant
And He will not hesitate to deliver.

Come into His presence.
You will find that He is holy beyond compare.
Let go of all your worldly resistance.
At the cross, God will meet you there.

A sinner of disgrace
Stands before a holy and righteous God.
Jesus, "I'm sorry;" God gives an abundance of grace
To all those who plead His Son's blood.

Sins are forgiven.
A life is transformed by the power.
Soon you will be called up to heaven.
Rejoice this is your salvation hour.

So what can I give
From the miry clay of sin?
Give Him your heart if you want to live.
Jesus will enter in.

# Plenty of Time
## January 3

I have plenty of time,
Eat, drink, and be merry.
These are the thoughts of a careless mind.
Live for God later in life, what's the hurry?

Well you don't know how long the day will last
Or when the shadows of darkness will cross your path.
There will be great sorrow if your day of grace is past.
A sinful life is ended in death.

My friend would always say,
"I have plenty of time."
I wish he were alive today
To serve God and sing a beautiful hymn.

But to everyone's dismay,
The call came at the midnight hour.
His day of grace has passed away.
No hope of the resurrection power.

There'll be no tomorrow,
No glorious hymns,
In that land of sorrow.
When death called for my friend,

It was too late for him to pray.
Today is the day of salvation.
When Jesus speaks to your heart, don't turn Him away.
Repent; let heaven be your destination.

Many cries from the grave,
The Lord could have been accepted.
Where is God's Grace?
Jesus Christ was rejected.

Thoughts from the grave, "I wish I had time.
But the days are gone.
I would like to change my mind
And believe in God's Son."

"Choose you this day,
Whom you will serve"(Joshua 24:15).
It's not too late to pray.
You can know of God's great love.

# The Midnight Hour
## January 4

The day is approaching.
A grand and marvelous event,
The Lord of glory is coming.
You still have time to repent.

Would you be ready
To leave this world of sin?
A new home is waiting in glory.
Entrance will be granted to the forgiven.

If the oil in the lamp is running low,
Or if the fire of life has gone out,
Repent, a new flame will glow.
You will leave this earth with a shout.

When Jesus comes again
The sweet harmony of hallelujah will rise.
The gates will open in heaven.
This could be the day you meet the Lord in the skies?

No one knows when He is coming.
Suppose He comes at the midnight hour.
Would He find you spiritually sleeping
Or wide-awake to rejoice in the resurrection power?

The final hour of destiny draws near.
Darkness covers the earth as a heavy blanket.
The sleepers are unaware that Jesus will soon appear
And the kingdom of God they will forfeit.

Arise, oh faithless generation.
Join with the saints and martyrs of old.
Today is the day of salvation.
Confess Jesus Christ as Savior and Lord.

He is coming!
Now, I don't know exactly when.
Please allow me to give a fair warning.
A decision for Christ will open the gates of heaven.

It is getting very close to midnight.
This could be the hour
When the saints of God take flight
And feel that resurrection power.

# The Hourglass
## January 5

The hourglass:
For every particle of sand,
Time will pass.
The day will come to an end.

The glass needs to be turned
Each and every hour
So the sand will return,
Or else it will lose its power.

Watch the sand as it falls.
From the top to the bottom,
Every last grain, one and all.
Soon it is a life of boredom.

Let us watch and prepare
To live our lives daily
To meet the Lord in the air.
Make sure the soul is ready.

Let us watch for the coming of the Lord.
Make sure we redeem the time.
He is coming back according to His Word.
Look up; He will return in the clouds of glory divine.

He tells us to watch and pray,
To be ready when He comes,
The Lord could come today.
He wants to welcome us home.

The particles of sand slowly pass.
Soon they will be gone.
The day is nearly past.
There is much work to be done.

The day is far spent.
It's time to look up, my friend.
God requires us to repent.
The day is coming to an end.

Beware the sand in an hourglass.
A strong ticking heart grows fainter.
Look back; it's hard to believe time went so fast.
Now it is time to stand before the Master.

# Look Up, My Friend
## January 6

We have a heavenly vision
To rise up high.
Our hope is in a Savior, risen.
We will meet the Lord in the clouds of the sky.

From that first emotional prayer
When the Lord took our sins away,
He turned us from a life of despair.
Heaven is promised, if only we will obey.

He is coming in great power,
The Lord of glory.
I don't know the day or the hour,
But we need to be ready.

A blessed day that will be.
We learn from the Holy Word
The kingdom of God we shall see.
Our hope is to be forever with the Lord.

The Lord is coming,
Not just for me,
But to all who love His appearing!
Our flight to glory begins on bended knee.

Just a few simple words
From a repentant heart,
All of glory unfolds;
The riches of heaven He imparts.

Look up, my friend!
The day of redemption draws nigh.
Jesus forgives sin.
Receive the blessing from on high.

Let us watch and pray.
When the Lord descends,
I do not know the day
The saints of God will ascend.

The graves will open.
The dead and the living shall rise
To begin a new life in heaven.
We'll meet Jesus in the skies.

# A Little While
## January 7

In just a little while
Christ would go away
That last long mile.
A life would end at the closing of the day.

A time of sadness and sorrow
As He carries the cross up the hill,
From a distance the disciples follow.
The heavy weight of grief they could feel.

Many people crying
For Jesus, whom they loved,
But soon they would be rejoicing
In the mighty working power of God above.

In a little while,
Sorrow would be turned into praise,
Grief and mourning replaced with a smile.
From the grave, Jesus was raised.

No longer in the tomb,
The earthly grave could not contain.
But in His heavenly home,
No suffering or pain.

"Weeping may endure for a night,
But joy cometh in the morning" (Psalm 30:5, KJV).
Patiently wait for that heavenly flight.
The Lord is returning.

Keep holding on,
Let no man take your crown.
Live for Jesus, God's Son
Until victory you have won.

The Lord is coming back for us.
Hear the saints as they cry.
"Even so, come, Lord Jesus" (Revelation 22:20)
He will come in the clouds of the sky.

In just a little while,
Christ is coming.
It may be your last long mile.
Keep the faith; joy comes in the morning.

# Take the Time
## January 8

A winter storm is coming.
It's time to make preparation.
I heard the warning.
It came from the radio station.

Snow, freezing rain, and sleet,
They will soon cover the highways.
The roads will be slick.
Airports expect delays.

Hazardous weather conditions,
I know you may have to travel.
Even now I see the clouds' formation.
State trucks are filled with gravel.

Ice covers the windshield
As you travel down the highway.
The car skids and stops in a nearby field.
A safe shelter is very far away.

Do you have a blanket
To keep you warm
Or even a survival kit?
How about a signal alarm?

I know you had time to prepare.
You were told many days in advance.
This is probably not a good time to compare.
Life or death; do you want to take a chance?

I know you have heard the warning
From many people who care.
The Lord is coming.
Want you meet Him in the air?

Prepare to meet thy God.
Oh, that every soul would hear.
In America and abroad,
It is time to draw near.

A life could have been spared.
If a decision for Christ were made.
If only you had prepared,
A soul could have been saved.

# It Is Later than You Think
## January 9

A poem I wish to write
Before I run out of ink
Or the day turns to night.
It is later than you think.

What does that really mean?
Well, I think I know.
The answer is yet to be seen;
It does concern your soul.

I have a watch.
It keeps very good time.
Sometimes it is a stopwatch,
Not worth a nickel and dime.

If the battery dies,
The hands stop moving.
But the hours keep passing by.
My watch shows one thing.

I have to believe
It is telling a lie.
It may even deceive.
A very long hour will pass by.

It is time to go home.
But I'm not yet ready to go.
I know it won't be long.
My watch is running way too slow.

Let us take a look at the spiritual hands.
The midnight hour is nearing.
Watch and pray is the Lord's command.
He is soon returning.

Is it later than what I am thinking?
In a moment, in the twinkling of an eye,
The Lord is coming.
He will come in the clouds of the sky.

Maybe it is time to reset the timepiece.
Restore the spiritual battery.
Wait patiently for the hour of perfect peace.
Jesus is coming, on time, in the clouds of glory.

# Here Today, Gone Tomorrow
## January 10

A beautiful sight to see,
Flowers in the garden,
God has a message for me.
It comes from the throne room of Heaven.

In the spring
See the flowers as they grow;
Listen, to the birds sing
And hear the sweet song of a sparrow.

The bees pollinate the flowers.
Roses and violets I adore.
The Lord sends refreshing showers;
He gives many blessings and much more.

Now it is summer.
I'm sure you will agree
It is a lot warmer.
See the beautiful trees.

The garden in the field,
Tomatoes hang from the vine.
Beans and corn, what a yield.
The harvest is ripe for mankind.

The fall season begins.
The sun is a little farther away.
Summer comes to an end.
The trees have a colorful display.

The last of the season is winter.
Snow covers the ground.
It's nice to have a warm house to enter.
As with all seasons, this one too will be gone.

All the seasons have one thing in common.
Just a little while to stay
But soon they are gone.
And so it is in our lives today.

Here today, gone tomorrow.
We are just passing through.
We have only a little time to borrow.
A decision for Christ, well, that's up to you.

# Surely Goodness and Mercy
## January 11

When in the valley of despair,
Surely goodness and mercy shall follow me.
Together they are quite a pair.
God will use them to defeat the enemy.

If I look at the situation,
The joy cannot be found.
But I am talking about a combination
Where the grace of God will always abound.

Everywhere I go,
As long as I don't follow the path of sin;
The love of God Iwill know.
Peace and tranquility comes from within.

In the dark hours of the night,
A deep depression will try to move in.
The oppression is blocked by a glorious light.
Shadows fade away at the touch of a friend.

Surely goodness and mercy
Will follow us.
We will dwell in the house of the Lord for eternity.
Our enemy will flee at the name of Jesus.

Rejoice, rejoice, oh Christian.
The light shines brighter still!
We have the hope of the resurrection
When we live according to His will.

When the days are dark and drear.
Go to a friend for an encouraging word.
The darkness of gloom will soon disappear.
Peace will come as we trust in the Lord.

There is no room for defeat or turn and run.
If we happen to fall into the distress chamber,
Call upon God in the name of His loving Son.
His faithful kindness is always a good thing to remember.

"Goodness and mercy shall follow me….
I will dwell in the house of the Lord forever"(Psalm 23:6).
That heavenly home will be a glorious thing to see.
Jesus is coming back for the faithful believers.

# The Last Page
## January 12

The last page,
I know many books have been written,
Stories told down through the ages.
They tell about the aspirations of heaven.

But in my thoughts today,
Are final words in a book,
I just wonder, what would you say?
Suppose the last page were taken by a crook

Now you just have one page.
We don't have time to review your life
Or many chapters to engage.
So please be very brief!

I know it will be just a particle of sand,
So dig deep and search for the right words,
Your life's history will be too much to scan.
The last page, only a few words will be heard.

We are getting close to the end.
I'm sorry if I used too much of your space.
You still have just a few lines
To tell a story of God's grace.

If I have offended you,
Please forgive me!
I certainly didn't mean to.
This is the last page of your story.

I would be thankful
If you would forgive my transgressions.
God's blessings would be bountiful.
I am sorry for taking your last words of expression.

You don't have a lot of room to write.
This is your last page.
I can see only a little bit of white.
I would expect to see rage.

A whole page taken from your life,
Only enough space for two words--
What will they be? The answer is: "I forgive."
Surely this is a good way to end in the Lord.

# A Time to Fast
## January 13

The plate is full.
The cup of blessings is low.
I sit at the table.
Yes, I have plenty of chow.

More than enough
Food to satisfy my appetite;
I hope I didn't overstuff.
The food was such a delight.

I look at the cup of blessings.
I asked the Lord
For a fresh refilling.
He noticed I failed to read the Word.

Not much time in prayer,
He came down to visit.
But I wasn't there.
I could have rejoiced in the sweet Spirit.

He went back to heaven.
I continued to indulge.
The food from the kitchen,
It was delicious, even the fudge.

I really enjoyed the food.
Where are the blessings?
My time spent with God,
My spiritual life was suffering.

I decided to give up a meal
To seek the Lord God.
The Holy Spirit I began to feel.
As I talked with the Lord.

Spiritual blessings came down, my soul to fill.
A day for a fast: leave the plate empty.
The prayer of faith will accomplish His will.
Pray and talk with God earnestly.

Don't be surprised if He pays you a visit.
I know a meal is missing.
You are weak in body but strong in spirit.
A touch of the Master's hand will be gratifying.

# A New life in Christ
## January 14

It's time to build,
A spiritual house to restore,
A life to yield.
The Master is at the door.

Want you please
Invite Him in!
He has a contract to release.
It is a mandate from heaven.

He has a special message to bring.
This is a life-changing construction.
Before the work can begin,
You must follow His instructions.

To be like Jesus you must be conformed
From a sinner of disgrace
To a new life transformed.
This is the work of God's grace.

He can see the sorrow.
He knows when the sin is heavy to bear.
Please, don't wait until tomorrow!
Call upon Him while He is near.

Yield your life to the One from above.
He has all you need
To experience His great love.
Your soul will be satisfied; yes, indeed!

Now don't turn Him away.
It only takes a few minutes of your life to yield.
Maybe the time is now to pray.
Repent, God's love will be revealed.

He hears the heart's cry.
Open the door, my friend.
The cry for mercy He will not deny.
It's time to ask Jesus to come in.

Pray with me; "Come into my heart, oh Lord!
I'm sorry for my sins."
He hears every word.
Let the life-changing process begin.

# It is Suppertime
## January 15

It is suppertime.
Can you hear the Master's call?
It's only a matter of time.
The invitation has been given for one and all.

"Come unto me" the Savior is calling.
All things are ready; the table is spread.
This is the day of great rejoicing.
The saints of God will be fed.

Gather around the table of mercy.
Listen to the angels sing.
Join the heavenly choir with words of "Glory, glory."
Oh, you will be in the presence of the King.

It is more than just a meeting
To gather in the holy place.
It is an eternal greeting
Reserved for the sinners saved by grace.

It is suppertime,
Prepare to meet thy God.
He said for us to love Him with heart soul and mind.
Respond to the invitation and say, "Yes, Lord!

Come into my heart.
I am sorry for my sins."
Jesus said that He would never depart.
At the cross is where a new life begins.

Come to the table, only one thing to bring.
Yes, there is a requirement.
The kingdom of God you can enter in,
But you must have a blood-washed garment.

All things are ready!
The Lord could come any day.
Have you made preparation for eternity?
Maybe it is time to pray.

It is suppertime.
Soon Jesus will come in the clouds of glory.
My friend, I hope you make up your mind
And believe the gospel story.

# A Time to Rejoice
## January 16

The fruit trees are bare.
No grapes on the vine,
Nothing to share,
But there is peace of mind.

"The fig tree shall not blossom...
The labor of the olive shall fail," (Habakkuk 3:17).
Best to go back home,
Even with an empty pail.

"The fields shall yield no meat;
The flock shall be cut off from the fold" (3:17).
Scarcely anything to eat,
The pockets are empty of silver and gold.

The labor of our love is not in vain.
Whether we are rich are poor,
He loves us all the same.
Just give what we have and He will bless us more.

He gives us a spiritual blessing.
The cupboard of the heart is full.
God in our lives is a good reason for rejoicing.
His Spirit refreshes the soul.

Thou we are hungry and thirsty,
God wants us to cast all of our cares upon Him.
He fills each waiting vessel with mercy.
Rejoice in His glory and sing a new hymn.

Our life consists not in the abundance
Of the things we possess.
But we have the blessed assurance
Of life eternal when our sins we confess.

We will rejoice
In the God of our salvation.
No need for sadness or remorse,
Soon we will feel the power of the resurrection.

To be forever with the Lord,
Keep holding on my friend.
The trumpet of the Lord will soon be heard.
From earth to glory we shall ascend.

# To Stay or Go
## January 17

When my work on earth is done,
The hand of the Lord I grasp.
At the setting of the sun,
The saints of God pray and fast.

Yes, my time has come to an end.
The choice is not mine.
I'm going to heaven.
I will live in glory divine.

I would like to stay awhile,
But it is time for me to go.
I have walked that last long mile.
The love of God I know.

Please don't ask me to stay.
The sun is shining.
It is a bright and glorious day.
Soon, it will be morning.

To stay or go,
The choice is not mine.
Jesus, the Savior of my soul,
He is calling me home; it is time

To walk the streets of glory,
To hear heaven's choir.
The angels sing in eternity.
Yes, I want to go there.

When they open the windows of heaven,
I'll be looking for you, my friend,
In the clouds of glory to ascend!
Into God's kingdom we shall enter in.

Till we meet again,
Watch and pray.
Let a new life begin.
The Lord may call you home just any day.

Well, it is time for me to leave.
Jesus has come.
Remember, salvation for all who believe.
The Lord is taking me home.

# It Is Time
## January 18

I want to tell an imaginary story.
To look into the future
Of God's eternal glory,
Through the eyes of faith, you see the Rapture.

The Lord is coming soon!
Oh, to hear the words which were spoken.
With love and concern, God speaks to His Son.
It is time; go get my children!

Bring them to their home in Heaven.
To an eternal resting place,
To live in the land of the forgiven,
Bring all the sinners saved by grace.

Listen very closely
To the words of God,
Draw near to Him, very close!
You will be blessed indeed to hear the word.

A message to hear,
You certainly can't miss
Words spoken loud and clear!
Life eternal, enjoy everlasting bliss.

The angels prepare to sing a new song.
God speaks to His Son; "It is time!
Bring my children home.
They will spend eternity in glory divine."

Oh yes, down through the ages,
Christians have been watching and waiting,
Reading the Bible and searching the holy pages.
Jesus is coming!

He is coming to take His children home.
Can you hear that trumpet sound?
All of your fears and cares are gone.
A born again Christian is heavenward bound.

When God turns to His Son,
Perhaps He will say, it is time;
My children have suffered way too long.
Bring them home to glory divine.

# The Train Is Coming
## January 19

Down at the old train station,
I will meet the rest of the family.
Loved ones from the entire nation
Prepare for a journey into eternity.

Family members have gathered around.
They patiently wait.
The old train is coming to town.
It will not be late!

There stands mother and father,
Together once again,
And look: all the sons and daughters
Will soon be at home in heaven.

But there seems to be one family member missing,
And the train is about to leave.
Down the track a person is running.
"Don't leave without me!"

The conductor shouts, "All aboard!"
But will this person make it
Before they shut the door?
His journey to eternity he may have to forfeit.

The father reaches for his son's hand,
One last desperate attempt.
He will try to save this young man
Before his life becomes extinct.

Now, the son is with the family.
He made it just in time.
The train to eternity
Is coming down the railroad line.

Now I told this imaginary story
To maybe help you understand.
One day Christ is coming in the clouds of glory.
God the Father is reaching down His hand.

He wants to save you from your sins.
The conductor shouts, "All aboard!"
If you want to go to heaven,
Take hold of God's hand before He closes the door.

# The Journeys End
## January 20

The end of a life is only hours away.
Dark shadows move in.
The sun will not rise another day.
A life on earth is coming to an end.

Friends and loved ones gather around.
It is time to say goodbye.
Soon only memories will abound.
A faithful servant of the Lord will die.

The grave will hold him for a little while
Until Jesus comes in the clouds of the sky.
From the deathbed each visitor is met with a smile.
In the resurrection the saints of God will fly.

A life is at the journey's end.
No more roads to travel,
The angels of God descend.
Our heavenly Father awaits his arrival.

What kind of advice would you leave for us?
We too would like to look upon His face.
"Well, there is one thing; believe on the Lord Jesus."
God will save you by grace."

Before you close your eyes for the last time.
Please tell us what does God require?
"He wants you to love Him with heart, soul, and mind.
Follow Jesus all the way; soon you will meet Him in the air."

Last words from a departing friend
As his eyes begin to close.
The Savior is now holding his hand
The words softly spoken from a dying man, "Jesus arose!"

Faith is the grip in the Savior's hand.
He will never let you go.
The promise is to enter the glory land.
To be forever with the God you know.

Well, Jesus is here.
Till we meet again!
When our time comes we will meet you over there.
Goodbye, my friend.

# Solid Rock Foundation
## January 21

Forever it will stand,
The solid rock foundation,
It is not built on corruptible sand
Nor is it a figment of the imagination.

The waves of time
Will not weaken or destroy
God's salvation plan for mankind.
All will be fulfilled for His glory.

Christ is the rock of ages
He died of an old rugged cross
His death is recorded in the holy pages
Salvation in any other, we would be lost.

Nails in His Hands and feet,
A crown of thorns on His brow,
He would not accept defeat.
Death in obedience was for Him to humbly bow.

Oh, how great the love, the man of Galilee,
His life to give
On Calvary's dark hill for you and me.
His death was by crucifixion; He died so we can live.

The solid rock foundation,
Steadfast, unmovable, Jesus Christ is our Lord.
He lives by the power of the resurrection
And we live by faith in the soul cleansing blood.

Touch Him now; ask Him to forgive,
He will come into your life as Lord and Savior.
We must die to sin before we can live.
Life eternal is promised to every believer.

Let us pray.
"Lord Jesus, come into each heart.
We are sorry for our sins; forgive us this day.
We claim the promise; you will never depart."

On the solid rock we stand;
Safe and secure for Jesus is the foundation.
We are not building on sinking sand.
Our lives exist in the resurrection.

# when does life begin?
## January 22

When does life begin?
Many people would say at birth.
At a hospital, born therein,
A little child takes its first breath.

A child is born.
Life is given.
Nice clothes to adorn,
At birth a new life came into being.

Life is a wonderful thing.
Many years pass.
When life comes to an end,
Is there something else to grasp?

I am happy to say
The wonder of the Creation,
It goes beyond the grave.
A life in Christ has the hope of a new destination.

When does life begin?
Well, first of all this life is only temporal.
When Christ forgives us of our sin,
We have the hope of life eternal.

His forgiveness is not automatic.
If we do not have a repentant heart,
The consequence of sin is dramatic.
If we believe in Christ, salvation He will impart.

Let me warn you my friend.
Sin is a dead man's game.
Until a life with Christ begins,
You will live a life of shame.

There is only one life to live
With the reward of eternity,
A committed soul to give,
God has promised us a home in glory.

When does eternal life begin?
Well, it begins at birth.
When we have been born again,
A glorified life will ascend from earth.

34

# The Last Amen
## January 23

The last amen,
No longer to be heard.
The day has come to an end.
A person's Bible is closed, God's holy Word.

The pages will not be turned
As in the days of old.
A new life has been confirmed,
The kingdom of God to behold.

The Bible lies silently
With the words in red.
It waits patiently.
The souls of humanity will be fed.

The book is not dead
As some might suppose.
With a few words to read,
A life of sin it will expose.

It reveals the heart of man,
The great plan of salvation,
The Lord's nail-scarred hands.
The Bible shows the awful crucifixion.

If you take a closer look,
A glorious transformation,
The power of life is in this book.
From death to life is the resurrection.

Maybe you have heard
Your last good-bye,
But now it is time to meet the Lord.
Go to be with Him in the clouds of the sky.

A Christian's life ends in prayer.
The King calls for the faithful and true.
"Come, ye blessed of my Father,
Inherit the kingdom prepared for you" (Matthew 25:34).

The last amen,
The final word was spoken.
Jesus forgives sin.
Give God the praise; the gates of heaven are open.

# Today Is Borrowed
## January 24

Hear the Lords plea.
A call from the Master,
Come unto me.
You may need to walk a little faster.

I hope you realize
Today is only borrowed.
Just a moment to visualize
There may be no tomorrow.

The Lord is calling.
I know you can hear.
To receive salvations blessings,
I hope you say, "I'm sorry," loud and clear.

Your words ascend to heaven above.
The answer is quickly given.
He fills each sincere heart with His love
And you will know your sins are forgiven.

I see the sun is beginning to set.
The Lord's hand,
Can you reach it yet?
Darkness spreads across the land.

A few hours to remain,
Can you hear the Lord's plea?
I believe He is calling your name.
Come unto me.

Oh, it is a glorious day.
When you answer heavens call.
He hears you when you pray.
Forgive me, Lord, Jesus says, "I will."

Well, it's time to go to sleep.
When you awake,
My Savior to seek,
Morning comes. Is it too late?

There may be no tomorrow.
It is time to move a little faster.
Remember, your days are borrowed.
"Come unto me." Heed the call of the Master.

# Clouds Pass Away
## January 25

Clouds gather in the morning
When the dew is on the ground.
There is a gradual disappearing,
Soon the condensed vapor cannot be found.

Like a puff of smoke
From a chimney,
It covers the cedars and the oak.
Soon there is not any.

Sunshine today,
If I could only borrow
Before the night steals the day,
Just give me a glimpse of tomorrow.

My life to plan
In a far different way,
To set my sights on the promised land,
I would walk the glory-land way.

Oh, that I had time
My life to commit.
I would walk a fine line.
The light of His love I would transmit.

Just as the clouds, I can relate.
The days have come and gone.
The days of my life they quickly evaporate.
Oh, that I could say, "I am going home."

Well, listen, my friend!
A new day is rising.
The clouds of glory descend.
The sun is still shining.

The Lord is waiting
To open up the gates of glory!
He is looking for a soul repenting.
He will hear the hearts plea. Lord, I am sorry.

Forgive me, please!
Remember, life is as a vapor.
But there is everlasting peace
When you know the Savior.

# Heaven or Hell
## January 26

I remember the day I was saved.
Christians gathered around.
Together we prayed.
Joy and mercy was found.

The preacher was going to end the service.
He preached about heaven or hell.
Well, in my soul there was no peace.
I was far away from God's will.

The preacher made it quite clear.
Heaven or hell, it would be my choice.
All of a sudden the Holy Spirit was near.
I realized I had to change course.

From the path of destruction,
From the broad road of sin
To the way of salvation,
Where eternity begins.

The preacher had a countdown for Christ.
From sixty seconds back to zero.
For me to be blessed,
I had to turn from sin; the Love of God to know.

I made my way down the aisle
I knelt in prayer.
I stayed there for a while,
And Jesus met me there.

Heaven or hell,
I heard the preacher say.
The Holy Spirit I could feel.
I made my decision that day.

I chose Jesus;
He gave me mercy.
He appointed me to a life of service.
Now I'm on my way to glory.

Heaven or hell, it's your choice.
The countdown has begun.
Maybe it is time to change course,
Receive eternal life; believe on God's Son.

# King's Palace, Poor Man's Table
## January 27

The king's palace
And the poor man's table--
Let us visit both places.
Make yourselves comfortable.

Let me remind you,
We have a spiritual treasure to find.
We may stay an hour or two.
Before we leave I hope we have peace of mind.

Where can God's grace be found?
Perhaps in fellowship with the king,
An abundance of wealth abounds.
The king talks about his many gold rings.

All of his earthly possessions,
With an arrogance of pride, all of this is mine!
He loved his treasures with an obsession.
To live and serve God he had no time.

The Grace of God was not found.
But what about the poor man's table?
Does God's grace abound?
Well let's see; there is God's Holy Bible.

It tells of God's love and mercy,
About a man named Jesus,
How he died for you and me.
If we believe, He will save us.

God's grace can be found,
Not at the table of the king.
At the poor man's table, grace abounds.
The love of God descends.

Let us review this imaginary story.
The rich man held close to his heart
His most prized possession--his money.
From his earthly treasures, he would not depart.

The poor man was richer, yes indeed!
God's grace can be found; I think I know the place.
More than just a few crumbs to feed,
At the poor man's table, is a sinner saved by grace.

# The Chief Cornerstone
## January 28

Allow me to use my imagination.
Travel with me back in time.
Workmen begin the construction.
Huge rocks are rolled up a steep incline.

The workmen continue to build at a steady pace.
The rocks are carefully designed.
Now each stone has a special place.
But why has the chief cornerstone been declined?

I know it is a good structure, yes, indeed!
But would you live in a building,
With all of its beauty to see,
Where the chief cornerstone is missing?

Let me tell you, my friend.
I hope you understand.
A lot of people have already moved in,
But this building will not stand.

It will not be a house strong and sure.
If the foundation is weak,
In times of storm the house will not endure.
I pray to God the Lord you will seek.

Jesus Christ, the chief cornerstone,
In the heart, a special place,
His precious blood to atone,
I am thankful for His grace.

The stone the builders rejected.
The house will not stand.
A soul will perish if Jesus is neglected.
So please don't reject God's redemption plan.

Without Jesus, the house is empty.
Soon it will come crashing down.
No hope of glory,
Only a shattered life can be found.

Where is the stone?
The rock of my foundation,
It is Jesus, God's beloved Son.
He is my hope and the joy of my salvation.

# Where will you be?
## January 29

A decision for Christ, what will it be
Righteousness, peace, joy, or complete denial?
The clouds of death overshadow thee
And the grave awaits your arrival.

Is your heart right
With the Lord of Glory?
Does the Son of righteousness shine bright?
He gives a blessed hope for eternity.

What is your hearts condition
If Jesus Christ is your Lord?
It is free from all sinful transgressions.
Corruptible sins are cleansed by the blood.

Where will you be my friend,
When the sun goes down,
When you come to the journeys end?
Does the grace of God abound?

When your faith touches God,
Sins are forgiven.
Your life is purged by the blood.
If death comes, it can be a gateway to heaven.

Where will you be?
Like the criminal on the cross, you must believe.
The Lord said, "Today shalt thou be with me (Luke23:43)."
By faith in Jesus, heaven you shall receive.

Where will you spend eternity?
Jesus gave His life's precious blood.
He died for you and me.
Receive peace and joy, rest in the arms of a loving God.

Where will you be?
When in the valley of decision,
He asks that you only believe.
Christ from the dead has risen.

Where will you be?
In the eternal heavens above?
If Jesus says, "This day thou shalt be with me."
You shall be with Him in His everlasting love.

# My Heart's Desire
## January 30

A devotional book will inspire
True faith and unconditional love.
To help others is my desire.
Let the sparks of a loving heart rise to God above.

All praise and glory belong to Him.
Use me, oh Lord, with the words I write.
The anointing of God is required on all of them.
A holy touch will guide someone through the night.

A blessing for the day,
Show a little kindness, God's love and mercy to share.
Today is all we have, no time for delay!
It is best to put another log on the fire.

Go and gather some wood.
Call upon your friends to work together.
The flames of love and compassion are good.
The sparkle of life will revive if we help one another.

No one is called to work alone.
God will help us to keep the fire going.
He has given a special talent to each one.
As we labor together, the flames are growing.

Bind us together in the Spirit
With cords of love that cannot be broken.
A soul saved is the kingdom of God to inherit.
Heaven is gained when sins are forsaken.

Remember the strength of a fire,
The comfort and love for a neighbor,
God has given us a talent to inspire.
He wants us to help someone know the Savior.

Don't let the fire fade away.
If only a few embers are glowing,
The flames of life will rise when we begin to pray.
Work together, the high hopes of heaven are rising.

My heart's desire
Is the same as yours, my friend!
Love God with heart, soul, and mind, a soul to inspire
Is salvation for the lost and a home in heaven.

# Where is the cross?
## January 31

In the eyes of a sinner,
Lost and undone,
The kingdom of heaven to enter,
A soul can be won.

Where is the cross?
Please show me the way.
I am lost!
Salvation is needed today.

Only a little time,
Soon it will be too late.
The cross I must find
Before God closes heaven's gate.

Is the cross on a hillside
In a faraway land?
Do I need to sail the ocean deep and wide?
Perhaps it is across the desert sand.

Where can I find Jesus
With no money to pay?
Salvation is free; He does not charge us.
He is not very far away.

But I cannot afford
To travel in a faraway country,
I must find the Lord.
My search is for eternity.

Let me tell you my friend,
You don't have to cross the crystal sea
To find forgiveness for sin.
You can kneel at the cross of Calvary.

Right here and right now, this day,
The cross of Christ can be found.
From a sincere heart, let us pray.
The glory of God comes down.

"Lord Jesus, I am a sinner.
Please forgive me for all of my sins.
Come into my heart as Lord and Savior."
The cross is found and a new life in Christ begins.

# Hear My Heart's Plea
## February 1

Lord, fill me with the Spirit.
Hear my hearts plea.
I desire a little visit.
I want a closer walk with thee.

Refresh my soul in the sunshine of your love.
A revived spirit will show.
The dark shadows of sin please remove!
A light on a dark path is the only way to go.

Hear my request, oh Lord,
Give me a new desire
That I may study your Word
And be filled with the Holy Spirit and fire.

Yes, Lord, I want to draw closer today.
You are welcome
In my temporal house made of clay.
Prepare me for that journey home.

On my knees in prayer,
with my hands raised,
There is a sweet fellowship there
When the Lord of glory is praised.

Lord, there are loved ones in my family.
They need to be saved.
A special request for mercy,
The flag of truce is waved.

Send down a blessing,
A soul stirring conviction.
Yes, we need a good Holy Ghost refreshing.
My loves ones need salvation.

Hear my heart's plea
For loved ones I cry today.
Touch my friends and family.
Keep them in your care every day.

Draw them by your Spirit,
Fill each waiting heart with love.
Salvation will come when they believe it.
So please, touch them with the hand from above.

# Tomorrow It May be too Late
## February 2

A man went to church
Seeking something far more precious than gold.
This would be his final search.
In my own words, the story is told.

The minister preached the sermon.
He gave an altar call.
He preached about God's Son.
Jesus Christ loves one and all.

Now I don't remember the message.
It could have been "Today Is the Day of Salvation."
Maybe that was the sermon from the gospel pages.
Oh, to hear the story of redemption.

Well, several people came to the altar,
Each one with a special need,
But one man earnestly sought God the Father.
His heart was very heavy indeed.

He was on his knees in prayer.
Meanwhile, the other folks went home.
But this man prayed for many hours.
He gave a desperate plea for his sins to atone.

"Please, forgive me!"
Words from a repentant heart,
The Lord hears the cries for mercy.
He responds with salvation to impart.

Finally, the man arose to his feet
With joy unspeakable and full of glory.
He gave his life to the Lord, his soul to keep.
He went to work that day and told the gospel story.

Remember, last night at church he felt the need to repent.
The Lord gave an invitation to follow Him.
A decision was made for Christ before the fatal accident.
He made peace with God just in time.

Thank God he was saved last night.
Today is all you have; please don't hesitate!
Even these hours, they quickly fade out of sight.
Tomorrow it may be too late!

# Waiting for the Day
## February 3

Waiting for the Day,
Holding on to the promise.
Christ will come and take us away.
Our hope is in Jesus.

He said he would rise from the grave.
We are his witnesses; He is alive!
Let each one testify, the power of God to save.
Christ would die so we could live.

From the grave He would rise.
Gather around my friend.
A living Savior now abides.
Death to life, Jesus forgives sin.

Our faith is not in vain.
He has risen!
Glory to God; bless His name.
Alive forevermore, our sins are forgiven.

He gave a promise to rise from the dead.
Well, the tomb is empty.
Isn't it time to believe what He said?
He is coming back in the clouds of glory.

"Ye men of Galilee,
why stand ye gazing up into heaven" (Acts 1:11)?
A message from the angels is for us to believe.
This same Jesus is coming again.

From heaven to earth He will descend.
We shall be changed in the twinkling of an eye.
Heaven is waiting!
Jesus will meet us in the sky.

So keep on watching,
He may come as a thief in the night.
The midnight hour is approaching.
Are you ready for that heavenly flight?

Waiting for the day,
The trumpet of the Lord will sound.
Be vigilant in prayer all the way.
Keep the faith, soon we will be heaven bound.

# White as Snow
## February 4

Just look out the window.
A heavy snow is falling.
Tree branches hang low.
A northwest wind is blowing.

Everywhere you look a beautiful picture to behold.
The ground is covered.
Aren't you glad, you don't have to get out in the cold?
Then you wonder how's the driveway going to get shoveled.

But for now just enjoy the scenery.
God is painting a picture of His delight.
This one is in early February.
The snow began to fall last night.

A few brush strokes by His mighty hand;
He moves the crystal white flakes around.
Each snowflake obeys His command.
After a while the snow completely covers the ground.

Please tell me what you see
As you look at the snow covered mountains,
The crystal white flakes are on every tree.
A sparkle of God's love is seen in the hills and plains.

Look closer, that same sparkle is in a person's life.
No spots or blemishes, sins are forgiven.
God can change a corruptible life to pure white
And you will know life is worth living.

Look out across the field,
A snow-covered earth, marvel at the place!
The inner glow of the heart is revealed.
A sinner is saved by grace.

Look out the window.
Your sins, thou they are many.
Jesus precious blood makes them as white as snow.
Sins are gone, now there's not any.

It's beginning to snow
Pure and white, undefiled, as a touch from heaven above
An inner peace of the heart begins to glow.
You have a new life because of His great love.

# Melt the Ice
## February 5

The lake is frozen.
The hills reveal a sparkling glaze.
There is a wintry mix of snow, ice, and freezing rain.
The clouds are twilight gray.

In the midst of this winter show,
There is a strong north wind.
The earth is covered with a fresh blanket of snow.
From heaven the snow keeps falling.

Icicles hang on the trees.
The branches hang low.
An icy cold winter breeze,
It continues to blow.

Now I know it is very cold.
The snow has to be removed.
A snow shovel is very hard to hold.
The ice is nearly impossible to move.

It's best to go back inside.
Warm your hands by the fire.
It is just too cold to be outside.
There is a bitter chill in the cold winter air.

Many days have come and gone.
There is a wonderful peace on the inside.
A fresh pot of coffee has been turned on.
A good warm feeling is by the fireside.

Life is like this winter scene.
To break the ice away,
The earth needs a little sunshine.
The ice melts more each day.

On the outside distress and turmoil,
The sun gradually melts the ice.
On the inside, peace and joy for the soul,
There is sweet fellowship with Christ.

Lord Jesus, on this weary soul of mine,
Break up the frozen ground.
With a plea for mercy, let the Son shine.
Melt the ice that grace may abound.

# When the Path is Hard to See
## February 6

Directions for the day,
We will find them in the holy pages.
Divine guidance will come when we pray.
The readers' delight is the rock of ages.

The pages are worn,
Like footprints in the sand.
The tracks are filled in as the wind is blown.
When the path of life fades, keep holding His hand.

The Master of the storm,
The words will fade and footprints vanish.
When He speaks there is a deep spiritual calm.
It is not God's will that any should perish.

Sometimes the word is forgotten.
As the years go by, the memory is not the same.
Jesus said He would go with us to the end.
When our strength begins to fail, remember Jesus' name.

He loves us and He will never let us fall.
His promise is to go all the way.
No matter if we are weak and frail,
The days of our youth are not meant to stay.

Days of our lives, so quickly they are gone.
There has never been a day,
Jesus has left us all alone.
He will not start now; let us pray.

"Our kind and gracious heavenly Father,
We come before your presence in the name of your Son.
Help us just a little while longer.
Precious Lord lead us on."

Words will fade
And the pathway will grow dim.
But the decision to live for Christ was made.
We made a commitment to follow Him.

On the wind-blown sands of time,
The pathway of life is hard to see.
Love Him with heart, soul, and mind.
Jesus is still calling: "Follow me!"

# From His Heart
## February 7

The door of the heart is wide open.
A special visitor is coming.
He wants us to go on a little errand.
To serve Him we know it is a great blessing.

Listen, as He gently whispers.
The words He speaks for us to share.
Our eyes fill with tears
As we think about the cross He had to bear.

He offers peace.
The calling for all of us is to go
Tell others of God's grace.
His great love is a wonderful thing to know.

An open door He will enter.
The Master will most certainly stay a while.
A grateful heart may hear a whisper
To help a poor lost soul that last long mile.

Give a lot of love.
As Christ loved us, so should we love one another.
Help someone grasp the hand from above.
In prayer we may hear them say, "Our heavenly Father."

The visitor that is coming by our house today,
Open the door of the heart wide.
Sweet fellowship with God comes when we pray.
So please invite Jesus to come inside.

The gospel message is for us to proclaim.
Eternal life is promised to the believer.
Go forth in Jesus' name.
Our God is able to deliver.

Oh, just one more thing!
Spend time with God in peaceful meditation.
The hand of mercy to cling.
Give hope, peace, and love, for this generation.

The Lord came for a visit
And He shared with us His heart.
Feel the sweet Holy Spirit?
Now God wants us to do our part.

# Open the Window
## February 8

The windows are closed,
Shades are drawn,
A sinful life is exposed.
God's love is basically unknown.

The heart is a desolate place,
Empty and void of God's love.
Curtains are pulled to keep out His grace.
In a dark room you cannot see the sunshine from above.

If you walk and live in darkness,
The rays of hope will never shine.
Your days on earth will be filled with sadness.
In the heart's dark dungeon, is this where you want to resign?

You have a choice, my friend!
Live in the darkness of the night
Or with a motion of the hand,
You can open the window of light.

Look at the spiritual side of this story.
The window of your heart is tightly closed.
Sunshine from heaven will come when you say, "I am sorry!"
All of your sins will be immediately decomposed.

Emotional cries from the heart,
God will not despise.
A bond is made in heaven that no one can break apart.
Pull back the curtains; you will see the sunrise.

Open a window.
Let the sunshine of His love come in.
Don't worry about tomorrow.
Be content for Christ dwells within.

Open the window of the heart.
Allow the rays of mercy to shine through.
Salvation for the soul is the best part.
Forgiveness is promised for you, too.

The sinner's prayer, "I am sorry for my sins.
Please forgive me!"
A little light from heaven shines in
And a poor wretched sinner can see.

# A New Day Dawning
## February 9

The bounty of God's love the day is filled.
Life's treasure chest is full.
If another blessing is needed,
One touch of His hand will supply the soul.

His goodness and mercy extend
As far as the eye can see.
The vastness of His love no one can comprehend.
A special blessing is promised when we believe.

The blessings of God overflow.
A day past brings forth a new day dawning.
Another day of grace is a good thing to know.
God's deep love is always overflowing.

Each day He fills with hope and wonder.
Everyday a new light is shining.
Now this is a very important thought to ponder.
Ready or not, Jesus is coming.

May God give us another chance to learn?
Light the candle of our love
That our hearts fire will forever burn.
One day we will be with Him in heaven above.

Our days on earth are only a few,
But God fills each one
With hope, faith, and mercy, too.
The blessings will come when we believe in God's Son.

Now is the time to serve.
Live for God every day.
May the emotions of our heart be as a vibrating nerve?
Every throb of the heart intensifies when we pray.

God's blessings are in abundance.
He supplies all the needs of the heart.
Let us be thankful today for divine deliverance.
Jesus said that He would never leave or depart.

The day is full.
So let us do good; our faith to share.
Let everyone know we are thankful.
Help someone along the way; show them that we care.

# Resurrection Day
## February 10

God's beloved Son,
He gave His life the world to save.
Victory at Calvary was won.
A divine sacrifice He gave.

Blood of calves would not do.
This offering for sin
Had to be Holy and true.
Jesus was the one chosen.

He was as a lamb without blemish,
Led to the slaughter.
His life was faultless,
Always holiness unto the Father.

Jesus died to save the lost.
Sin had a high price to pay.
God gave the one He loved the most.
Tears filled His eyes on crucifixion day.

A Son was given
For a blood sacrifice.
Without Him no one would be forgiven.
He was the only one who could pay the price.

It was mercy divine
That compelled Jesus to give.
Love for God and mankind
Radiates in the heart for every believer to live.

Hope in Him goes beyond the grave.
The stone was rolled away.
Life exists by the one who came to save.
Joyful hearts sing on resurrection day.

Dead but now we are alive in Christ the risen.
Our hope is to meet Him in the clouds of glory.
The Son of God will descend
As revealed in the Gospel story.

Christians will ascend
To a home far beyond the sky.
Behold, the gates of heaven!
Look up, redemption draws nigh.

# As I Have Loved You
## February 11

A Father's love for His Son,
Don't be alarmed, but this story is true.
God and Jesus' love combined as one.
"As the Father hath loved me, so have I loved you" (John 15:9).

"As I have loved you" (John 13:34):
Now that's something to think about!
After all He went through,
There should be no doubt.

A crown of thorns upon His brow,
The whip that tore the flesh of His back,
"Crucify Him," shouts from an angry crowd.
They watched the brutal attack.

Even when He was being crucified,
He prayed that God would forgive.
He bowed His head and died.
His life He gave so you could live.

Jesus died in your place.
He died for your sins.
The Lord offers salvation; receive His grace.
A new life begins.

God's Son—no crime was committed
He was innocent of all the false accusations,
But He was horribly executed.
He died for the sins of the entire nation.

He gives a new command:
As I have loved you, love one another.
Behold, the nail prints in His hands!
There is no salvation in any other.

You must love God first and foremost!
But to love as Jesus loved,
He came to save the lost;
His life on earth, God approved.

Love is the calling,
The fulfillment of God's plan.
Reach out, receive a blessing,
Touch someone with a loving caring hand.

# A Beggar Finds Bread
## February 12

Just a beggar on the sunny-side of town,
Good news to share for the world to hear,
The bread of life can be found.
Peace and joy in the heart when Jesus draws near.

A beggar can tell you where to find some bread.
Please gather around.
A spiritual soul will be fed.
The grace of God will abound.

Satisfaction for the soul,
Please pay attention.
The God from heaven you can know.
Jesus even gives the invitation.

Come unto me all ye that are heavy laden.
Jesus will satisfy the longing heart.
Bread for the soul, your sins are forgiven.
The Savior promised He would never depart.

If you know where to find the bread,
The water of life for the thirsty,
Don't you think this message needs to be heard?
The bread of life is for the hungry.

Without Him the soul will perish,
There will be a spiritual starvation.
The hope of heaven will vanish.
Without Jesus there is no salvation.

Remember when you were a sinner of disgrace,
Another beggar told you of God's love.
Now you are saved by grace.
Be thankful for the blessings from above.

Just a beggar holding up the cross,
This is God's chosen work for you.
Share the gospel message with the lost.
The bread of life is for them, too.

Food for the soul, just ask a beggar.
Where to find some bread?
When you tell others, Jesus is Lord and Savior,
Souls around the world will be fed.

# Heaven's Gold Mine
## February 13

Go and search till you find
In the glory hills
Heavens gold mine.
A treasure, it is so real.

I know you've heard the story
From rags to riches.
But have you heard of God's glory?
Your sins you must confess.

So kneel at the cross.
Your soul will be blessed.
As the glory stream flows,
The heavenly gold mine you can posses.

Now I'm not speaking of earthly gold,
Which is very valuable indeed.
But I'm talking about faith in God.
Receive a new life in Him if you will concede.

This treasure cannot be found in an earthly mine
Or in a mighty rushing stream.
But it can be found in the mind.
It's more than just a dream.

Let me tell you, my friend,
I found something better than gold.
Jesus forgave me of all my sins.
Let the story of faith be told.

Faith is better than gold.
Faith in Jesus you'll find,
A kind and loving God.
At the foot of the cross, there is glory divine.

Just believe in Jesus' name.
The blood flows from His veins.
You don't have to stake a claim.
He owns the deed to the mind.

Kneel at the cross.
The glory of God to find,
Jesus came to save the lost.
Welcome to heaven's gold mine.

# He Is Worthy of the Honor
## February 14

Give honor where it is due.
From a life that was misspent
To Christ who is faithful and true.
He is the one we represent.

He is worthy of our praise
For the life He gave.
Rejoice every day with holy hands to raise.
He would die for us, many souls to save.

Who deserves the honor,
The crown of glory from on high?
Well, the one who became a blood donor.
On a cross, they would crucify.

Where can this honor be found?
I believe it is in Jesus.
His love always abounds.
He wants to forgive us.

Even when He was beaten,
He prayed, "Father, forgive them."(Luke 23:34)
His back had just been smitten.
He offers forgiveness if we ask Him.

I'm beginning to see
At the cross of Calvary
Where the honor should be.
It is in the man of Galilee.

Jesus came to honor God,
To forgive those who dishonored Him
By the giving of His life's blood.
Listen closely, "Father, forgive them."

I just felt a touch from heaven.
Jesus forgave me!
My sins have been forgiven.
Thank God for His mercy.

The praise and honor belong to Him.
At Calvary He took our place.
Worship with a new hymn.
Now we can sing, "Amazing Grace."

# Please Forgive Me
## February 15

Forgiveness came
When I knelt upon my knees
And I called upon His blessed name.
I longed to say the word please!

When the heart is heavy laden,
Grief and sorrow to bear,
A new layer of sin,
It is certainly a time of despair.

Sin is a reproach.
It is a disgrace.
The Lord patiently waits our approach.
The gift of mercy comes with grace.

God is faithful and just.
Oh, blessed redeemer is He.
He forgives the past.
I'm so glad He forgave me.

The Lord listens attentively.
One word He wants to hear.
Come into His presence sincerely,
Let the word please enter into His ear.

That may not be sufficient
For the dishonor brought to His name.
Truly there are words more efficient
That can erase the shame.

Please forgive me!
The gates of heaven swing wide.
A plea for mercy,
The Lord gives His reply.

"I will!"
A sinner's prayer,
It will not lose its appeal.
God is still our heavenly Father.

Please forgive me!
Teardrops on every word,
A plea for mercy,
It will touch the heart of God.

# Insufficient Love
## February 16

Let us go to the imagination.
There are two letters from heaven.
The first letter concerns your salvation.
The letter is very well written.

It has been proof read.
There are no errors therein.
Hear what the Lord said:
"Ye must be born again" (John 3:7).

Well, that letter was received.
Grace and mercy was found.
Salvation came when you believed.
Soon sin called and you left town.

While you were gone
Another letter came and the fate of sin was revealed.
Urgent! Please read this one!
Your trip to heaven has been canceled.

The words you read over again.
Truly there must be a mistake!
The angels of God will soon descend,
Sinners cast into the fiery lake.

"But Lord, remember, I confessed.
I asked you to forgive.
My soul was most certainly blessed.
A new life I received."

"Well, let's see what the records hold.
I commanded you to love me.
But I see here that you loved the world
And walked away from my mercy."

"Not everyone that saith unto me, Lord, Lord,
Shall enter into the kingdom of heaven" (Matthew 7:21).
To hear and obey God's word,
You must love and serve Him, turn from a life of sin.

I know this letter is make-believe.
But what if your trip to heaven was canceled?
Insufficient love you failed to give.
Now the wrath of God is revealed.

# The Shadow of Life
## February 17

Everybody has a shadow.
They don't cause any trouble.
On the ground it always lies low.
Sometimes it hides under the table.

A faithful follower is the shadow.
It never seems to leave.
Wherever you go I'm sure it will follow.
It touches the rocks and the trees.

Every place you go,
All the things you do,
You will certainly know
This shadow is for you.

No matter how hard you try,
It will always be with you,
Even until you die.
You cannot separate the two.

Your life and the shadow
They are always together.
So don't worry about tomorrow,
One won't leave without the other.

In life you need a companion
So strong and true.
You need one of compassion
That will be with you the entire journey through.

Jesus is the one
That is closer than a shadow.
He will never leave you alone,
Nor will He lead you on the path of sorrow.

So everywhere you go
The Lord will be by your side.
He is far better than a shadow
That in the darkness of the night will hide.

A shadow is always close by.
It is hard to find at night.
Jesus is forever at your side.
His glory always shines bright.

# The Highest Honor
## February 18

I wrote a poem one day
For hearts stricken with sorrow.
God blessed me in His own special way.
A blessing from heaven, this I know.

Yes, I wanted the Lord to use me
To tell of His great love,
To let others know of His mercy
So they might feel His presence from above.

I wish to tell of a special blessing,
The highest honor in the land.
I don't know where to begin.
But when God stretches out His hand.

The angels of God descend.
The glory of the Lord comes down.
Just a little closer to heaven,
God's grace abounds.

This highest honor can be found
When God's will is done,
His love spread all around
Many souls will be won.

Sing a new hymn.
Speak and preach the Word.
Give glory to Him.
Magnify the Lord.

Pray without ceasing.
Work while there is day.
God has a special blessing.
He wants to send our way.

The highest honor in the land,
It will come when we obey.
God is reaching down His hand.
A poem I wrote, God blessed me today.

Whatever our talents may be,
Let us give our very best.
God wants to be glorified in thee.
He will do the rest.

# I Can't Do It
## February 19

Some interesting words came to my mind.
There was some doubt about a certain review.
It seemed as though courage was hard to find.
The day was approaching for the big interview.

Oh for more confidence,
Stronger faith to stand,
Just a little more assurance,
Guidance comes by His almighty hand.

The words I heard one day.
"I cannot do it."
Now, God touched me in His own kind of way.
Reassurance came by the Holy Spirit.

God knows some things are hard to do
Fear can hold us back; no victory to claim.
Real faith can see us through.
We must really believe in Jesus name.

I cannot do it, but God can do it through me.
The things that are impossible,
Faith opens the heart to believe.
With God all things are possible.

Strength for the day, courage for the night,
We are not alone.
The glory crown is in sight.
Keep the faith in God's Son.

He stands beside us.
Every day to lead,
We are not alone in His service.
Our cries for help, He will intercede.

The Holy Spirit dealt with me one day
When fear was the overpowering force.
God touched me in His own kind of way.
Don't turn and run, stay on course.

I can't do it, but God can.
We are not alone my friends.
Take hold of the Master's hand.
He will be with us all the way, even to the end.

# Deep Desire
## February 20

Give us a deep burning desire,
A longing in our hearts to serve you.
Faith as an unquenchable fire
That lasts throughout the night too.

Oh, to be in your presence,
To feel the hand from above,
Give us the assurance
Of your great love.

Fill our hearts with praise
As we walk the straight and narrow way.
Rejoice in the mercy and thank you for your grace.
Give us a touch from heaven we pray.

We desire to be led by the Spirit
Through this corruptible world of sin.
A life is void and empty unless you fill it.
Give us eternal peace within.

We want you to stand beside us,
To lead us through the valley,
Bind us together to follow Jesus.
Give us a deep desire to follow Him daily.

A Holy Ghost visit is what we need.
A good old fashioned cleansing
Will purify the soul, yes indeed!
Give us a spiritual refreshing.

If need be, lift us from the miry clay.
No sin can hold us down.
Give us the victory every day.
We know the grace of God will abound.

Strength for the day and courage for the hour,
Our hope and desire is to be with you.
We know you are coming in great power.
Give us joy, peace, and love, too.

We have a strong burning desire,
A few more days to wait.
We will meet Jesus in the air.
God will open heaven's gate.

# Sunshine of His Love
## February 21

Sunshine of His love,
It shines upon the soul.
Radiant beams from above,
Peace with God you will know.

Open up the window,
Unlock the door so He can enter.
Tears of a repentant soul begin to flow.
You are in the presence of God the Father.

Open the shutters of the heart.
Invite the Lord to come in.
Peace and joy He will impart
And He will forgive you of your sin.

Let the rays from heaven
Illuminate the inner most being.
Sins are forgiven.
You are in the presence of the King.

The sun is beginning to shine
Overcast clouds disappear at the first sign of light.
Darkness of the past is left behind.
A soul is delivered by His power and might.

On an old rugged cross,
He proved His love for you.
He gave His life to save the lost.
Died, buried, now, He is resurrected, too.

If you were the only one,
He would have died just for you.
Salvation for the lost is not for you alone.
Every believer has the hope of life eternal, too.

Open your heart to receive
Jesus Christ as Lord and Savior.
Salvation is promised if you will only believe.
The light of His love will shine forever.

This is the place
where the sunshine of His love
Will fill your heart and life with grace
And you will be touched by the hand from above.

# When Jesus Comes Again
## February 22

The first time He came,
In a stable He was born.
Jesus is His name.
Mary gave birth to her first-born Son.

The angels sang,
"Glory to God in the highest" (Luke 2:4).
A sweet melody over the mountains rang.
Shepherds came to worship the Christ.

The first time He came,
He walked upon the earth.
The world has never been the same.
He offered to mankind a new birth.

He came riding on a small donkey
The people offered glory, praise, and honor.
He spoke of eternity.
The people gave praise to the Savior.

He came as the meek and the lowly one.
Let me ask you my friend,
Do you remember how they treated God's Son?
The nails they drove in.

The first time He came.
Jesus was crucified.
He endured the pain and the shame.
On an old rugged cross, Jesus died.

They mocked Him and made fun.
They made a crown of many thorns.
Yes, this was God's Son.
Remember how His back was torn.

He came as an obedient servant.
On earth the people cried, "crucify."
He arose from the grave triumphant.
The strong bonds of death He would defy.

When He comes again,
"Glory to God in the highest,"
As King of kings and Lord of lords, He reigns.
Every knee will bow to Jesus Christ.

# The Trumpet Sound
## February 23

There's coming a day—
I don't know when—
The Bible tells us to "Watch and pray" (Matthew 26:41).
The Lord will descend.

He will return in the clouds of heaven.
He said in his Word,
"I will come again" (John 14:3).
Are you looking for the Lord?

He will come; hold fast.
In other words keep the faith.
"Hold that fast which thou hast" (Revelation 3:11).
Be faithful unto the end, even unto death.

Christ is our Savior,
Keep holding on.
Redemption last forever.
We are almost home—

A crown of righteousness we shall win.
Let "No man take thy crown." (Revelation 3:11).
From earth to glory, we shall ascend.
Sins are forgiven; God's grace abounds.

The trumpet shall sound.
We will be raised incorruptible.
The saints of God will be heavenward bound.
This is the message of God's Holy Bible.

Read and believe the gospel stories.
The Lord is coming!
Christ will appear in all of His glory.
Be ready; He will come without warning.

Oh, want it be a glorious day
When we hear that trumpet sound.
Be ready when He comes; Watch and pray."
Soon we will be heavenward bound.

When we hear that trumpet,
Saints of God, we'll be gone
Far away from this earthly planet.
Keep the faith in God's Son.

# Our Home in Glory
## February 24

Our home upon this earth,
It's just a temporary dwelling place.
A home in heaven awaits those who have a new birth.
Everlasting life is for the sinner saved by God's grace.

We are traveling through this land.
Walking with the Lord,
He is our friend.
He guides us by His Holy Word.

Our new home is in heaven.
On this earth we are just passing through.
The gates of heaven will open for the forgiven.
Jesus, we thank you!

We know that beyond the sunset,
Our new home is waiting for us.
No need to worry or even fret,
Soon we'll see the face of Jesus.

Someday our journey will end.
The gates of heaven will open.
Life in heaven will begin.
From earth to glory we will ascend.

To hear God say, "Welcome home, my daughter and son!
Enter into the glories of the Lord."
So, my friend, keep holding on.
Travel with dignity the gospel road.

Up ahead to see
A glorious sight to behold,
The mansion the Lord has prepared for you and me
Where the streets are pure gold.

Heaven is a magnificent place.
Its splendor no one can compare.
At the end of this earthly race,
All the saints will meet up there.

Home at last, home at last!
Now we will live eternally.
The earthly journey is in the past.
God welcomes us to our home in glory.

# Great Expectations
## February 25

Look up, my friend.
From the clouds of heaven,
Jesus will come again.
He will descend.

It will be a glorious day.
If we're looking for the King
And walking the straight and narrow way,
Maybe today we will be leaving.

Going to a place,
Far beyond the skies,
A soul saved by grace,
Set free from all earthly ties.

No longer bound
Or enslaved by the chains of sin,
Nothing to hold them down,
Saints of God will ascend.

This could be the hour.
Remember, Jesus' blood was shed.
To forgive sins He has the power.
He arose from the dead.

We have a glorious expectation.
Jesus said, "I will come again!"(John 14:3).
We also will feel the power of the resurrection.
Jesus forgives sin.

Every soul that is covered by the blood,
Their sinful nature is purified.
Each one receives a bounty of God's love.
We have hope of life eternal in Christ the crucified.

Paul said," I am crucified with Christ.
Nevertheless, I live."(Galatians  2:20).
Truly, a life is blessed.
Salvation is a wonderful gift to receive.

Look up, my friend.
In the twinkling of an eye
To heaven we shall ascend.
We will meet the Lord in the sky.

# A City in the Sky
## February 26

I'm going to take a trip,
Not on a slow-moving train.
I'm going to a city,
Not on a high-flying plane.

I don't have much money,
But I'm going to a place
Where I don't need any.
Entrance is gained by grace.

I'm going to a city
Far beyond the sky,
Past the Statue of Liberty,
Where the torch is held high.

I won't be going on a 747,
Or a rocket in the sky.
I'm going to heaven
When Jesus comes in the sweet by-and-by.

I'll be heavenward bound.
I'm going to a city that needs no light.
At the trumpet sound,
Soon I'll be wearing the crown of life.

I don't know the day or the hour.
"In a moment, in the twinkling of an eye," (1Cor. 15:52).
I will feel the resurrection power
And be in that city in the sky.

This trip will not be complete
Unless, my friend, I extend an invitation.
My Savior I want you to meet.
You can make your own reservation.

I'm sure you will meet the qualifications.
No salvation by grace until you believe it.
There is a need for a life changing transformation.
You will receive conviction from the Holy Spirit.

Please go with me
To that city in the sky!
Receive His mercy.
A repentant heart He will not deny.

# A Prodigal Son Returns
## February 27

A prodigal on the run
From a time of contentment.
The good life to shun,
He goes to the back streets of resentment.

Where the dark shadows loom.
No place for a poor, hungry soul,
To leave the comforts of home.
Walk away from the peace and love you know.

To go to a faraway land
Where you have no real friends,
Only a lot of pretends;
They leave quickly when the money ends.

You are left all alone
In the barn yard of mire,
Faraway from your peaceful home,
Oh, how you wish that you were there.

Now you suffer the consequences of sin.
You left a home of delight
To wallow in the pigpen.
It is your darkest night.

When you turn from the good path
To the way of the world,
You can expect to wallow in the sins of wrath.
It is disastrous when you walk away from God.

God is a loving Father with much concern.
He cares very deeply for His daughter or son.
He patiently waits for their return.
Their sins He will atone.

If you meet a prodigal son
That seems to be in a hurry,
He just left the pigpen of sin.
Please don't worry!

I believe he is going home.
Don't be alarmed!
He answered the Saviors call, "Come!"
Soon, he will be back in his Father's arms.

# Every day with Jesus
## February 28

Every day with Jesus
The love of God grows stronger.
He is a Savior that stands beside us.
He is not a stranger.

He knows us by name.
His love is unchanging.
Every day it is the same.
The affection of His heart is always caring.

When trials and troubles come our way,
Give us grace to keep pressing on.
Jesus is not very far away.
We are not left alone.

Jesus will go with us every day,
No matter how much it cost.
Suffering for Him was the price He had to pay.
He was crucified on an old rugged cross.

Every day we live,
Not in the shadow of the grave.
We know Jesus Christ is alive
And those who believe will be saved.

Every day is the promise,
He would never forsake or leave.
Life with Jesus is joy and peace.
Salvation comes when we believe.

He does not save for a day or two
And then leave us to fall by the wayside.
He will lead us safely through.
His promise is to be forever at our side.

The way of life is before us.
The invitation is given.
Heaven will be our home if we follow Jesus.
The choice is ours, my friend!

Life with Jesus is a blessing every day.
We know He's not a stranger
As we walk the straight and narrow way.
With Him our love for God grows stronger.

# Treasure in Heaven
## February 29

The days on earth are past.
A quick review of the days and years gone by,
Earthly treasures were not made to last.
In the dust of the earth they solemnly lie.

Things of metal rusted away.
You see the devastating effect of Corrosion.
Wood is no different, only decay.
A mansion lies in rubble in extreme deterioration.

Flowers and fruit trees planted in a row.
Now because of erosion in the field,
They will no longer grow
And the harvest is an empty yield.

An earthy treasure is here just for a season.
Even If you have plenty of money
The banks will close without a good reason
And leave you without any money in the treasury.

The days on earth are gone.
All of your earthly treasures left behind.
How many valuable assets are in the grave? Not even one!
Search if you must, there will still be nothing to find.

"Lay not up for yourselves treasures upon earth,
Where moth and rust doth corrupt" (Matthew 6:19).
A treasure in heaven will be of a greater worth.
The blessing's bank of heaven will never be bankrupt.

Rewards will be given for each deposit.
Abundance of grace is given with all earthly transactions.
This exchange will be verified by the Holy Spirit.
No investment will be made without complete satisfaction.

A treasure in heaven
It will not disappear or be destroyed by corruption.
The pure in heart will have access to the rewards therein.
The righteous will enter the pearly gates of incorruption.

When God opens heaven's treasure chest,
A crown of life will be given
For eternity's reward, it's time to invest.
Repent, sins will be forgiven.

# Sound of the Trumpet
## March 1

When I hear a jet,
The sound barrier to break,
Just as the sun begins to set,
The windows of my house begin to shake.

Quickly I run to the door
For a glimpse into the sky.
I wonder how many more.
So quickly the jets pass by.

Usually, I look far beyond the sound.
With an all-searching eye,
Sometimes the jet is found.
It flies low in the sky.

There is a sound I want to hear.
I don't want to miss it.
Not a jet passing far or near,
The sound is a trumpet.

Even if I am in the grave,
No more jets to hear.
I'll rise from the earthly clay.
I will hear the trumpet loud and clear.

"The dead in Christ shall rise first" (1Thess.4:16).
I know what I will do.
My departure is not rehearsed.
I will go to heaven. What about you?

When I hear that trumpet sound,
"In a moment in the twinkling of an eye," (1Cor.15:52),
I'll be heavenward bound.
I'll meet Jesus in the sky.

You may be wondering
How I know to heaven I will ascend.
Knowing and receiving all comes with believing.
Jesus forgave me of my sin.

I'm listening for that trumpet sound.
The dead and the living shall rise.
No need to look around,
Just look up; the Lord is coming in the skies.

# Restore to Life Eternal
## March 2

A time to imagine or remember,
In the store window a brand new Chevrolet;
Many years ago in late December
A 55 Chevy was on display.

Oh, a beautiful thing to behold.
The color a bright blue,
The car would soon be sold.
This beautiful vehicle was made just for you.

But you know the story of a car mighty and fine.
A few years of bad weather
An automobile will lose its shine.
This temporal thing will not last forever.

Imaginary thoughts of an old car to restore;
Patiently it waits for fresh paint.
The owner makes a quick trip to the store.
His hard earned money will soon be spent.

This project is very time consuming.
It takes a lot of hard work to refinish.
Well, it's time to begin!
From the old to the new, you have a lot to accomplish.

Just like the restoring of a car; this work is only temporal.
Your life is pretty much the same,
Except God is preparing you for the eternal.
You can have a complete restoration in Jesus' name.

"Old things are passed away;
Behold, all things are become new"2 Co 5:17).
Remember the old life when you knelt to pray.
Maybe you were sitting on a church pew.

The Savior passed by.
A soul was saved that day.
You said you would follow Him until you die.
Somewhere, somehow, sin brought a life of dismay.

Is there any hope for a sinner of disgrace?
God is in the business of restoration
And He will save you by grace.
Repent this is still your obligation.

# A Safe Passageway
## March 3

On life's stormy sea
When the strong wind blows—
It's not a very safe place to be.
If on the ship, the waters overflow.

In the darkness of the night,
Huge rocks are a very present danger.
Oh, for a guiding light.
Help us to see past the waves of anger.

Surely this is a time to pray,
To escape the wrath of the storm.
Lord, show us the way.
A light from heaven will reveal the jagged rock forms.

A radiant beam is seen
In answer to our prayer.
A glorious light to shine,
The Lord provides a safe passageway on the water.

Shouts of joy arise!
A lighthouse, a wonderful thing to see,
Thankful tears fill the eyes.
The journeymen move safely through the sea.

Through this imaginary story,
I just want us to visualize.
We are on a journey.
We have very important things to realize.

Jesus is the way, the truth, and the life.
He is the only way to heaven.
As long as we follow the light,
Stay clear of the rocks of sin.

The celestial land is in sight.
The light of His glory,
It will shine through the darkest night.
Press onward; look for the shore of eternity.

Let us keep our eyes on Jesus.
Through the storm of night
He will go with us.
He gives a safe passageway to eternal life.

# Open the Gates
## March 4

Just a glimpse into the future,
Along the path of my imagination,
We are going to take a tour.
We will travel to an eternal destination.

Let's say Jesus comes at midnight.
This is a time when many people are sleeping.
No preparation for the final flight,
Now they stand before God weeping.

This is the spiritual side of the story.
Spiritually asleep,
When the Lord comes in the clouds of glory
An unrepentant heart will weep.

The pleas for mercy will not avail.
On earth Christ was rejected.
There was no desire to do God's will.
It's too late to be accepted.

The blood was not applied.
Sin was the game.
Entrance to heaven is denied.
There is no reward to claim.

Let's go back to a different time.
We knelt at the cross of forgiveness
And we loved God with heart, soul, and mind.
Our life with Christ brought peace.

Before the throne we stand.
The blood of Jesus is our plea.
All doubt is removed in the nail-scarred hands.
Blessed are they who believe.

.
Open the gates of heaven.
Let them swing wide.
A sinner has been forgiven
And the Lord Jesus abides.

The pearly gates are open.
Truly this is a beautiful place.
Jesus told us about heaven.
Now we stand at the gate, saved by grace.

# Passing Through
## March 5

A small town comes into view.
It is a beautiful place to see,
Maybe we will stop for a day or two,
Rest beneath the colorful trees.

Now let me remind you,
I know you would like to stay longer,
But we are just passing through.
Let us walk by the crystal blue water,

The mountains to climb,
Pictures to take of the beautiful sky.
I know we don't have much time.
The day is gone; my how time flies.

Only one day remains;
Soon it will be gone.
Time to pack our clothes and things.
We are going home.

Our journey upon this earth,
The beautiful things to see and do,
The days of our trip began at birth.
But let me remind you!

We are just passing through.
The end of a journey,
The days left, maybe just a few.
Where will you spend eternity?

In the dark shadows,
Or in the glorious light?
The love of God you can know.
You can be delivered from the night.

We are just passing through,
In this earthly town,
Maybe just a day or two.
Soon we will be gone.

At the end of our journey,
What are we holding on to?
I pray it is the hope of glory,
For in this life we are just passing through.

# Higher Ground
## March 6

In the valley low,
The rain is coming down.
The river overflows.
It is time; go to higher ground.

With each passing hour,
The torrents of rain descend
To torment and devour.
A good shelter is hard to find.

A strong and mighty wind
Sweeps across the land,
Peace and safety to apprehend.
Shelter is on the mountain.

The raging river continues to rise.
Men, women, and children,
They all run for their lives.
Try the best you can to save the perishing.

An arm to extend
For those too weak to climb,
Give a helping hand.
It's only a matter of time.

Men's hearts fail for fear.
Across the land they are dying.
The roads and houses disappear.
The watery grave keeps rising.

High upon the mountain,
The place of safety is higher ground.
The violent storm comes to an end.
But there's not much left of the town.

Many souls are dying.
The Lord is reaching down His hand
To save and rescue the perishing.
He brings conviction across the land.

He came to save, not from a watery grave,
But from the eternal flames.
Salvation of the soul requires God's grace.
It is time; go to higher ground in Jesus' name.

# Almost Home
## March 7

Many years have gone by,
God was with us all along life's way.
Jesus (the Savior) was always at our side.
Our joy was walking with Him each day.

Now the hope of heaven is our final destination.
Soon we will cross the crystal blue sea.
A life in review, we are forever thankful of His salvation.
Our lives have been changed because of His mercy.

Oh, we have a blessed hope, yes, indeed!
Our days are past; we are going to our home in heaven.
Come and go with me; this is my heartfelt plea.
The gates of heaven will swing wide for the forgiven.

We will meet the Savior face to face,
Our expectations shall be fulfilled.
Since we have been saved by God's grace,
The Holy Spirit, we can feel.

There may be many miles
Or maybe just a few,
But we know it will be worthwhile
When we see the kingdom of heaven come into view.

When our journey on earth ends,
Or we cross over destiny's hill,
The King of glory will descend:
The glory of the resurrection, what a thrill!

Yes, my friend, from this sinful earth
We will enter the glories of heaven.
When we take our final breath,
From death to life, we will live again.

Death may claim,
Or the trumpet will sound.
We are going home in Jesus' name.
God's grace always abounds.

We are almost home.
The glory land we will see.
It won't be long.
My friend, want you come and go with me?

# No Sunday School Today
## March 8

This is a very special day.
Many years have gone by.
I want to bring my imagination into play.
Now don't ask me why.

I waited for so long;
The time has finally come.
I'm going to meet God's Son.
He has promised me a new home.

He touched me many times
And called me to repent.
He told me to leave my sins behind,
But in the pleasures of sin I was content.

So now I wait patiently.
I have decided to give my life to Christ
And join the ranks of the heavenly.
A sanctified soul is blessed.

The church is not open.
Where is the pastor?
I want to turn from my sins.
Let Jesus Christ be my Savior.

The parking lot is almost empty.
There is no preacher,
No one to tell me about eternity.
Where are the Sunday school teachers?

This is my day for heartfelt praying.
As I sit in my car and wait
To find forgiveness of my sins,
I realize it is too late!

I heard the gospel story.
Many times I walked away
And rejected the Lord of Glory.
No time to pray.

There'll be no Sunday school today.
The Rapture took place.
The saints of God were called away.
All the born-again believers saved by grace.

# Patiently Wait
## March 9

Be patient, just a little longer.
The Lord is coming.
Be a faithful soldier,
Keep on marching

Up the steep hill,
Across the lonesome valley!
Be obedient to God's will.
Fight for the eternal victory.

From the cross of repentance,
Walk with the Lord; take a detour from sin.
The war will be won by your persistence.
The battle against corruption you will win.

Don't give up or turn and run.
Just hold the cross high.
Keep the faith in God's Son.
Let the Christian flag fly.

In just a little while,
The Lord will come again.
You may be traveling that last long mile.
Fight to the very end.

Be patient, He will come without delay.
In the clouds of glory the Lord will appear.
No one knows the hour or day.
He could come this year.

Trust in the Lord every day,
Resist the tempter (Satan) of his evil corruptions,
Follow Jesus all the way.
Rejoice in the Lord of your salvation.

Patiently wait; the Lord is coming
In power and great glory
For the saints of God, He is returning.
Sinner, friend, it's not too late to say "I'm sorry."

Jesus will forgive sin.
The command is to "watch and pray."
The Son of God will descend
Rejoice His coming could be today.

# Run to Win
## March 10

The race has begun.
Now this is not your ordinary race.
First you must talk it over with God's Son.
To be a runner you must be saved by grace.

A sinner at the cross is where it all begins.
To be a participant you must be accepted.
It only takes a few minutes to confess your sins.
An unrepentant sinner will be rejected.

Now let's just say you have made things right with God.
You told the Lord you were sorry.
The stains of sin were covered by His blood.
As the tears flowed, you felt the hand of mercy.

Now you are qualified
In the spiritual race for eternity.
Keep your eyes on the one who was crucified.
Soon you will be with Him in your home in glory.

The length of the race is not the same.
Some people will cross over early, and other's late.
I have to remind you, this is not a game.
At the finish line you will enter heaven's gate.

Keep your eyes on Jesus.
Live each day for Him.
Be obedient in His service,
Obey His commandments, yes, all of them.

Run to win!
You have a cross to bear.
Just ahead is the finish line.
In just a little while a crown of life you will wear.

With a strong heart and a made-up mind
The victory will be won.
The weight of sin has been left behind.
A life in Christ has begun.

A sinner saved by grace,
Faithful to the end,
This person will win the race.
A life in heaven will begin.

# Climb A Little Higher
## March 11

Climb a little higher
The time is near.
We are going to meet the Lord in the air.
In the clouds of glory He will appear.

Remember the cross He bore,
Why He was crucified,
The crown of thorns He wore.
For you and me He died.

Climb a little higher,
Think about His great love.
Each step we are closer.
Soon we will be with the good Lord above.

Be determined to make it.
Keep pressing on!
Be led by the Holy Spirit.
We are almost home.

We'll walk the golden streets.
See the walls of jasper.
Our heavenly Father to meet,
We'll stand beside the Master.

Our time is drawing near for us to go.
Whatever the day or the hour,
The promise is for us to know
When He comes we will feel that resurrection power.

It won't be long
Till we enter the pearly gates
And walk around our brand-new home.
Until the time comes, let us patiently wait.

After all, He is preparing us a place,
A mansion in the sky.
For the sinner saved by grace,
He will come in the sweet by-and-by.

Climb a little higher; we are almost there.
Walk daily with the man of Galilee.
Don't turn back to the valley of despair.
Jesus is coming for you and me.

# A Spiritual Journey
## March 12

A Spiritual Journey,
What exactly does that mean?
Friends gather around from all over the country.
They talk about a place we have not seen.

The joy overflows as my friends speak of heaven.
It is always a pleasure for them to share,
To help someone know they can be forgiven.
A word of encouragement is given so we can go there.

We are walking this path together.
Although we have never met,
Our deep desire is to help others
Inspirational words are given by the Holy Spirit.

We are separated by many miles.
The distance of time has no barriers to separate us.
Frowns of sorrow turned into joyful smiles.
We are drawn closer still when we talk about Jesus.

We are friends on a journey.
We will probably never meet face to face
Until we meet in eternity.
The time is now for us to share God's grace.

We all know that friends will go for a morning walk.
This is always a good thing to do.
We can just imagine they love to talk.
We have a friend who walks with us, too.

He is ever at our side,
A friend closer than a brother,
As we journey through this land, He is our guide.
Jesus always speaks reverently of His Father.

He brings us into a closer relationship with God.
Now Jesus prayed, "My Father, and your Father," (John 20:17)
What a deep spiritual blessing we find in the Word.
A spiritual journey is to share, love, and help each other.

As we walk this earthly path below,
Help us to encourage, show kindness, and be a blessing.
We want the whole world to know:
Salvation for the soul is for the believing.

# This Same Jesus
## March 13

This same Jesus
Left His home above,
Came to earth, to show us,
To tell us God is love.

This same Jesus
Turned the water into wine.
All the vessels filled up,
He invites us to come and dine.

This same Jesus,
He walked upon the sea.
Simon Peter He lifted up.
With Him to forever be.

This same Jesus,
He sets the captive free,
For by His justice
We have divine liberty.

This same Jesus,
He suffered with great pain
And died on a cross for us.
He ascended to heaven, but He's coming again.

We shall be changed in a moment,
In the twinkling of an eye.
Until He comes, be patient.
Our hope is to meet Him in the sky.

The Lord is coming for the chosen.
He will recognize the blood applied.
It will be a blessed day for the forgiven.
The gates of heaven will swing wide.

This same Jesus,
Now we see God with grace to impart.
God loved us
With all of His heart.

This same Jesus
In the clouds shall ride.
It is alright to be anxious.
With Him we will forever abide.

# We Are Almost Home
## March 14

My God will make a way.
When the heart is heavy laden
And the soul filled with dismay,
Look up toward heaven.

God is on the throne.
He has the power.
He will give us strength; keep pressing on.
Be as a vigilant soldier in the final hour.

He will help us
The barriers of life to overcome.
Trust and believe in Jesus.
We are almost home!

When the day is dark and drear,
The shadows of darkness fall.
Remember, the Lord is always near.
His love touches one and all.

If we are in the valley of despair,
A good thing for us to know,
God loves us and He cares.
He will never let us go.

I know words cannot express
When our life is full
Of sorrow and distress.
Be assured God cares for each soul.

Hold on a little while longer.
Keep the faith in God's Son.
We will always grow stronger
But we must continue to go on.

Don't look back to the days of the past.
Our heavenly home is in sight.
Keep holding on; the days of sorrow will not last.
A time of rejoicing will come in the morning light.

The Lord will never leave
Or let us stand alone.
A crown of life to receive,
We are almost home!

# The Secret of Happiness
## March 15

Listen closely, my friend.
A sweet voice is calling.
The words of peace ride the wind.
The day has come for rejoicing.

Tell me what you hear.
The world would like to know.
In the shadow of death, no fear;
Tell me the secret of your soul.

Please tell me
So I can wear a smile!
At the end of my journey
When I walk that last long mile.

Words of a greeting,
They travel through the air.
A soul receives a blessing.
Soon a crown of life he will wear.

A familiar voice in the distance,
He speaks the words loud and clear.
The gates of heaven open for a grand entrance.
The angels in white appear.

Before you go
Into that eternal resting place,
The words you hear I have to know.
The love of God I want to embrace.

He spoke softly; "Jesus set me free."
The Holy Bible contains the words for all to hear.
The Savior gave a command, "Follow me."
Obedience is required of us for Him to draw near.

The words that brought such joy
I'm glad you revealed.
Before the end of this story,
The mystery is unveiled.

A soul saved is peaceful bliss.
As the eyes begin to close,
The secret of his happiness is this:
Jesus Christ arose!

# Jesus Is Coming
## March 16

Look across the fields.
As far as the eye can see.
Past the harvest yield,
Come and travel with me.

We are going to a faraway land,
To a place in the great beyond.
There is a mansion prepared by God's mighty hand.
We'll be there in less than a second.

That great and wonderful day is approaching.
I hope you have made preparation.
The Lord is coming.
The dead will rise first on the day of the resurrection.

Jesus is coming!
I do not know the hour.
Maybe this morning,
He is coming with great power.

Think about the day
Are you prepared to meet thy God?
Still a little time to pray,
A sinful soul can be purged by blood.

Give God the praise.
We are going to meet the King.
Let us rejoice in God's grace.
Someday soon, we will hear the angels sing.

"Glory to God in the highest"(Luke 2:14).
A heavenly message relayed:
"Believe on the Lord Jesus Christ" (Acts 16:31).
A soul will be saved.

The Lord said, "I will return again"(Acts 18:21).
Don't give up, but patiently wait!
The King of Glory is about to descend.
Be ready when He opens heaven's gate.

I hope I have given you fair warning.
Ready or not!
The Lord is coming
For all the souls His blood bought.

# Your Name in Glory
## March 17

An earthly contract is binding.
Everyone agrees to the rules and regulations.
The transaction will be complete at the signing.
The name on the page fulfills all the obligations.

At the stroke of a pen,
The writing of a name,
A way of life will end.
Days ahead will not be the same.

It is really quite amazing
When the signature is complete.
Whether it is for loss or gain,
Joy or sadness, it's too late to delete.

Let's take a quick look at heaven's contract.
Life begins at Calvary.
Remember the whip lashes on Jesus' back.
He bled and died so your name could be written in glory.

Jesus forgives sin.
All blemishes of the past fade out of sight.
The believers' hope is that Jesus will come again.
A new day is dawning at the beginning of light.

No need for delay,
The opportunity may pass if you hesitate.
Bright hopes of joy and peace can be claimed today.
Friends and loved ones will meet at heaven's gate.

The time of the spiritual signing is at hand.
Belief and acceptance is the clue.
Obedience to God is His command.
Your name in glory, that's up to you.

Heaven's contract is for today; this may be the final hour.
Faith in a risen Savior begins here.
You will be resurrected by God's mighty power.
It's only a matter of time, Jesus will appear.

When God writes your name,
Eternal in heaven, forever to stay,
You will have a crown of life to claim.
Be ready when He comes; watch and pray.

# A Refreshing Rain
## March 18

Give us, we pray,
A wonderful refreshing
In your own special way.
A spiritual rain is desired from heaven.

Our hearts will rejoice.
The rain comes down
To fill the well with joy and peace.
His abundance of grace always abounds.

Give us a fresh supply,
A heart felt blessing,
A sweet outpouring from the sky.
We need a holy arm embracing.

Let the rain of your glory descend
To accomplish your will.
Precious water from heaven
Our longing hearts it will fill.

Draw us closer to thee
In this waiting hour.
Your glorious face to see;
Saturate us with a gentle shower.

As a well needs water
For a dry and thirsty land,
Like a mighty rushing river,
We need the touch of the Master's hand.

The Holy Spirit to guide,
A refreshing shower of His love,
The Lord Jesus will abide.
We need a sweet blessing from above.

Let the rain descend,
The spiritual rain from the sky;
Our praises to ascend,
Thank Him for the fresh water supply.

Give God the praise!
Our worship is not in vain.
With holy hands raised,
It's beginning to rain.

# Break Camp in the Morning
## March 19

How short are the days:
So many minutes in an hour,
Only a little while left to pray
Before the Lord comes in mighty power.

We are only passing through.
As a camper sets up for the night
To break camp at the morning dew,
We will leave at the first sign of light.

The tent is taken down,
So neatly packed away.
We are going to a new town.
We will spend another day.

We won't stay long,
Just a short visit;
Soon the time will be gone.
We may have to make a quick exit.

On the road again,
A new destination is in sight.
Pitch camp at the top of the mountain.
We are only going to stay for the night.

So is the life of man.
We are here for a short stay.
We are just passing through this land.
Soon to pull up stakes and we will move away.

The choice is not always ours to make.
The shadow of death passes by.
The Lord decides a soul to take.
No time to say good-by.

This can be a time of rejoicing.
Peace with God, everything is all right.
Break came in the morning.
Heaven is in sight.

We are just passing through.
Life eternal awaits!
God may call us home in a day or two.
He will open the pearly gates.

# Praise God Today
## March 20

In the presence of God,
Let us worship Him.
We receive inspiration from His Word.
Sing a new hymn.

The time is now to give honor and praise.
Rejoice in His great love.
Reverence Him with hands to raise.
Let the words of a joyful heart ascend to God above.

Enter into the holy place.
Kneel at the altar.
Seek the glory of His face.
Give praise and honor to God the Father.

Come before His presence.
Rejoice and sing today.
We will feel the power of deliverance
When we kneel to pray.

His love is great toward us.
He hears the heart's cry.
God's only Son, Jesus,
He comes walking by.

Touch the hem of His garment.
The virtue flows.
From a sinful heart repent!
The love of God we will know.

He will not turn away.
God loves us and He cares.
He hears us when we pray.
All of our burdens He will bear.

Talk to God in prayer.
Go to a special place.
I know He will meet us there.
Feel the spirit of His grace.

Jesus prayed, "Our Father and our God."
Let us worship Him with holy hands raised.
May we be joined together in one accord.
Our God is worthy to be praised.

# No Grapes on the Vine
## March 21

No grapes on the vine,
No fruit to yield;
It's harvest time.
Workers are in the field.

From sunup till sundown,
They labor in the vineyard.
Many grape vines all around,
No need for a guard.

The harvest field abounds,
But some vines have died,
No grapes to be found.
The dead vines in bundles tied.

A fruitless vine,
Many a wasted day.
The labor is all in vain;
Withered vines hauled away.

If I don't see
Grapes hanging on the vine,
Or fruit on the tree,
I get discouraged some of the time.

God has a blessing for you and me.
He wants us to keep on working,
A great harvest to see.
A soul saved is a marvelous thing.

Work in the vineyard of His mercy,
In the harvest field.
Souls will be prepared for glory,
The fruit of our labor will yield.

For as much as we know,
Our labor is not in vain,
The Word of God to sow.
Soon there will be an abundance of rain.

We need to be faithful all the time.
Our labor of love is no disgrace.
Be steadfast and love God with a made up mind.
Continue in the Lord, a soul will be saved by grace.

# Grafted into the Vine
## March 22

Our relationship with Jesus,
He is the vine.
His love is great toward us.
We love Him with heart, soul, and mind.

We cannot bring forth fruit
Until the limb is grafted in.
Afterwards, He will prune it.
Take away the branches of sin.

Thank you, Jesus,
For our lives you saved the limb.
Your love is great toward us.
There were more than a few branches to trim.

You could have cast them away
Or placed them in the pile to burn.
But Lord, you had mercy when we knelt to pray.
This is a spiritual lesson we all need to learn.

He spared the limb.
Our souls He grafted in,
Gave us a new life in Him,
We are joined together; He is the true vine.

We are one with the Father
Joined together by His Son.
Our salvation was not obtained by any other.
Faith in Him makes us as one.

It was a blessed day
When Jesus grafted us into the vine.
We made peace with God that day
When we surrendered to Him, heart and mind.

Jesus is the mercy vine.
We know it is true.
His love and our souls combine.
An old life is replaced with the new.

Jesus said, "I am the vine,
Ye are the branches," abide in me (John 15:5).
He will be with us all the time.
He gives us a blessed hope for eternity.

# Gold in the Hills
## March 23

Gold in the hills,
It has just been discovered.
Run with the news across the field,
Bright shiny nuggets uncovered.

Now this gold is free.
Bring your wagons.
An invitation for you and me:
The ore will soon be gone.

Search till you find.
Stake a claim if you must.
It's your gold mine.
But you have to be first.

I must remind you
It's only a temporary thing.
A pot of gold or a nugget or two,
Certainly the heart will sing.

But its value will not last.
An earthly treasure—
It can be spent very fast.
There are many wonderful pleasures.

When the gold is gone,
The pockets are empty.
A broken-down home,
A morsel of bread will feed the hungry.

A treasure to be found,
It is far better than gold.
The wealth always abounds.
It is the love of God.

The gold mine of faith is free.
All you have to do is receive
A lasting treasure indeed,
Eternal riches, when you believe.

Faith and love in God's Son,
Receive glory divine,
The earthly treasures are gone.
The hope of eternity is yours and mine.

# Break Up the Fallow Ground
## March 24

Take the bridle from the rack.
It's time to plow.
Place the harness upon the horse's back.
The season is now.

The plow cuts deep into the earth.
Remove the earthly sod.
The topsoil must go first;
The horses gently trod.

Make straight the furrows,
For a narrow line is better.
You can have more rows.
Let the horses work together.

Break up the fallow ground,
Bring forth the harvest.
Let the fruit of the earth abound.
You will bring forth the very best.

Take the Bible from off the shelf,
Harvest time is now.
In your labor of love, God will help.
Put your hand to the harvest plow.

Work for the Lord while there is day.
Break up the fallow ground.
Walk with Him the straight and narrow way.
May the salvation of souls abound.

Break up the fallow ground.
Plow the earth all around.
One day you'll hear the trumpet sound.
In heaven you'll be found.

Let the plow of mercy dig deep
With the labor of love.
Soon the harvest you can reap.
Work with the good Lord above.

Dig deep and plough straight.
The narrow way is forever.
The time is now to cultivate.
You will be rewarded for your endeavors.

# Carry the Torch
## March 25

God lights the fire,
A work in your heart.
It is His desire
That you never depart.

God has a calling.
He has a job for you to do.
Only a few are chosen.
It is a special work for you.

Running is required,
A torch needs to be held and passed to a friend.
Tell others Jesus is coming in the air.
This is a strong flame burning.

The torch is passed
From one hand to another.
From the first to the last,
All must work together

To accomplish God's will,
A mission to complete,
Even over the desolate hills
Until a crown of life you keep.

Work while there is day.
Up ahead is the finish line.
Carry the torch all the way.
Give God the glory all the time.

Love keeps the flame burning bright.
Carry the torch every day.
Be ready when He comes, day or night.
Please don't forget to pray.

The high calling of God,
When He hands the torch to you,
Let His love be spread abroad.
Let your light shine too.

Run the race all the way through.
There is a torch to carry.
Each person depends on you.
Now is the time to tell the gospel story.

# Build a Bigger Barn
## March 26

Build a bigger barn.
Work on it today.
Not enough room on the farm,
There is an abundance of hay

A small barn cannot contain.
Even the silos are full.
No place to put the wheat and the grain,
More ears of corn you need to pull.

A bigger barn to build,
The harvest comes at the end of the year.
Work and labor in the harvest field.
I hope you realize the time is near.

Work on the barn, but don't forget about the house,
The place where you live.
A home to build please don't refuse!
God offers a blueprint of eternal life.

The foundation is laid.
A new house to build,
The cost of the home has been paid.
You continue to work in the field.

Every day you turn away
To build a bigger barn.
Your house can wait another day.
Just make room for more corn.

The work on the barn is finally done,
But what about the house you neglected?
The foundation stands alone.
Jesus Christ you rejected.

The barn is full, cares and pleasures of sin.
A life is empty, no Savior to represent.
You still have time to be forgiven.
It's not too late to repent.

When you come to the journeys end,
No time for Jesus or the love of God to know,
An empty house is in ruin.
A bigger barn is the only thing that will show.

# Re-Dig an Old Well
## March 27

Remember the day,
A fresh water supply,
When you knelt to pray.
Only God you would glorify.

Time has gone by,
To your deep regret.
No spiritual rain from the sky,
The well is full of neglect.

Salvation so full and free,
But you walked away,
So many other things to see.
Now your heart is filled with dismay.

The days have come and gone.
It is a dry and thirsty land.
You stand all alone.
Oh, for a touch of the Master's hand.

No need to despair,
Go back to the place
Where you talked with God in prayer.
Seek His face!

He loves you and He cares.
Back on your knees,
He will meet you there.
He will give you joy and peace.

Re-dig an old well.
Go back to the first love.
Living water to fill.
It comes from the fountain above.

It is beginning to rain.
The water begins to flow.
A touch of God's almighty hand,
The well of life overflows.

Give Him your heart.
Dig the well deep.
A committed life will be our part.
God has the power to keep.

# Change the Track
## March 28

I know you like to travel.
Let us go down the imagination railway.
Take along the Bible.
Read its pages along the way.

A fast-moving train,
Many passengers on board,
It is going down the railroad line.
Let me remind you, sin is a heavy load.

Disaster is at the end.
A terrible fire is burning.
Hear the words from a friend,
Make sure you heed the warning.

Give your heart to the Lord.
Before it's too late,
Read and believe the Holy Word.
There is a new course to take.

Up ahead there is a switchman.
He can change the track for you.
Jesus is the only one who can.
What are you going to do?

Keep following the railway of sin
Or get on the glory train.
The railway leads to heaven.
Invite Jesus to come in.

At the very moment
When you believe and confess,
The day you repent,
God will most certainly bless.

The track is changed.
You are saved just in time.
Eternal life is gained.
Life or death, it all depends on the mind.

It is your decision my friend.
Only Jesus can change the track.
If you ask Him, He will forgive you of all your sins.
Heaven is waiting; please don't turn back.

# From Heaven to Earth
## March 29

Let me tell you the story.
I don't know exactly where to begin.
So let us start at the Portals of Glory.
Jesus left His home in heaven.

He came down as a servant.
To do Gods will,
His message was to repent.
He had to carry the cross up Golgotha's hill.

The place of His execution,
An innocent man would die
On an old rugged cross by crucifixion.
His death sentence was pronounced, "Crucify."

Jesus walked among men.
His life He would give.
A divine atonement for sin,
He would die so we could live.

I'm glad He came.
The way of life to show,
Salvation is in Jesus name.
The love of God we can know.

Soon, on a cross He would hang.
Sins of the world to bear,
He would endure the unbearable pain.
His life on earth would expire.

For our sins to atone,
The heavy weight upon His shoulders,
He would carry the burden all alone.
Remember His words; love one another.

He came down,
To walk among us,
A message to bring in every city and town,
God sent His Son; a man named Jesus.

Salvation to bring,
His life to give,
Forgiveness of our sins,
Our Lord came to forgive.

# Rain, a Spiritual Desire
## March 30

Rain from above,
We are in need of a spiritual blessing.
Fill each waiting heart with love.
Give us the anointing.

Open the windows of grace.
We desire to be in your presence.
With Jesus in the heart there is peace.
Fill our hearts with that blessed assurance

That we may know everything is all right.
No sin to burden us down,
Give us a renewed hope for that heavenly flight.
We are going to leave this earthly town.

A spiritual rain is desired for the soul.
A touch of your hand will calm life's sea.
Rain from heaven, everybody will know.
Goodness and mercy come from thee.

Walk among us.
Speak to every heart.
Give us peace as we walk daily with Jesus.
We know that He will never depart.

A gentle shower is good.
It is a quick refreshing,
Sometime just a little rain will change the mood.
A downpour from heaven is a greater blessing.

Is there anything we can do?
Our life is so barren today.
God will send the rain, spring flowers too.
The clouds start to form as we begin to pray.

We can feel a gentle breeze from heaven's sky?
Oh, yes, there are even a few drops of rain.
Jesus is walking by.
The rain is coming, no need to complain!

Just rejoice in the Holy Spirit.
We are in the presence of a Holy God.
A longing, sincere heart, He will fill it.
The rain will come if we wait upon the Lord.

# No Mountain too High
## March 31

Keep going, we can cross over the mountain.
From the valley of sorrow,
Slowly climb the rugged terrain.
Don't worry about tomorrow.

Victory will come when we pray.
Christ is our Savior.
The time is now to live for Him. Don't delay!
Heaven is waiting, so climb a little higher.

God is reaching down,
A holy arm outstretched.
To save a poor lost sinner, His grace will abound.
Take hold of His hand, be blessed.

He will give strength and courage each day.
When the path is dark and dim,
Even through the darkest of night,
He will make a way to cross over, just call on Him.

We do not know what each day holds.
But we know who holds us.
The glories of heaven we will behold.
Keep going, it's all a matter of trust.

He will not let us fall or slip
He loves us too much to let go
Our God has a very strong grip.
He can keep us from falling to sins valley below.

Just to make sure we make it,
God sent His Son to show us the way.
He also gives us the Holy Spirit.
If we want to go higher, take the time to pray.

Soon we will cross over this mountain.
One day, the lights of home grow brighter.
The summit of glory we will attain.
The direction of our life is always higher.

There is no mountain too high
That will hinder or turn us away.
Our Savior draws nigh.
His grace and strength is sufficient all the way.

# A Living Sacrifice
## April 1

A divine sacrifice was given.
God gave His Son
So our sins could be forgiven.
No salvation by any other, He was the one.

A man called Jesus,
A sacrifice He gave.
Oh, how He loved us.
He gave all He could give.

He was lead "As a lamb to the slaughter" (Isaiah 53:7)
Without spot or blemish;
At the cross, there was sorrow and laughter.
Jesus last words; it is finished.

With a big hammer, the nails were driven.
A crown of thorns He wore.
A sacrifice was given.
The weight of the cross He bore.

The sacrifice for sin was His to give.
His precious blood for the ones He loved,
Salvation for all, He died so we could live.
His great love for us, God approved!

We talked about His sacrifice,
How He bled and died.
His death would suffice.
For our sins He was crucified.

Jesus wants us to love God,
To live in such a way
That the sacrifice of His blood
Will compel us to live for Him each day.

To walk uprightly day or night,
To live holy, this is our reasonable service.
He requires us to do the things that are right
And to present our bodies a living sacrifice.

Holy, pure, undefiled, with love every day,
Love God with heart, soul, and mind.
To walk the straight and narrow way,
He wants us to be faithful all the time.

# Do you remember?
## April 2

Do you remember
A child who was born
In late December?
Mary gave birth to a Son.

Do you remember
When in the garden
Jesus was agonizing in prayer?
What a heavy burden.

He wanted His disciples to pray one hour
They fell asleep before the time was complete.
Soon the world would see God's mighty power.
Death, the grave, and hell, He would defeat.

Jesus died for your sins and mine.
Do you remember?
"Not my will, but thine." (Luke 22:42).
The weight He had to bear.

Remember the day Jesus died.
He hung on an old rugged cross.
He was crucified.
The price of our sins, see what it cost.

When it comes times for you and me to die,
When you have to tell your loved ones good-by,
Do you remember why He died?
He hung on a cross with His arms held wide.

How great the love for sinners of disgrace.
Faith in Him, sins are forgiven.
This is the miracle of God's grace.
From the cross to the grave, He has risen!

May this be our hearts plea!
Remember me when you come into your kingdom.
Listen, "To day shalt thou be with me"(Luke 23:43).
It will be a glorious day when the saints are called home.

Do you remember when life began?
On your knees in prayer
You felt a touch of His nail scarred hand.
A life was reborn in Jesus the Savior.

# Divine Obedience
## April 3

One wooden cross to bear,
Christ never gave up or quit.
No life can compare;
His life He did commit.

He carried the cross.
He walked Up Calvary's dark hill.
To save the lost.
He was obedient to do God's will.

A crown of thorns was forced upon His brow.
The blood dripped from His cheek.
His head hung low.
Nails were driven into His hands and feet.

"Behold, the Lamb of God" (John 1:29).
Our sins to atone,
He takes away the sins of the world.
Yes, on the cross, God's Son,

He died for you and me.
His blood was spilled;
He offers divine mercy.
God's plan of salvation was fulfilled.

His beloved Son, Holy and Divine,
He prayed "Thy will be done,
Not mine, but thine."
Come down from the cross if you are God's Son.

"He saved others, Himself, He cannot save."
A faithless generation in His dying hour,
But a quick visit by faith to an empty grave
Will prove without a doubt, God's resurrection power.

He was laid in the grave.
Death came to claim.
He had no intentions to stay.
Only His death clothes remain.

Jesus is risen
He is the hope of all the nations.
Faith in Him, sins will be forgiven.
This is the joy of our expectations.

# Honey in a Bear's Den
## April 4

The old ways of life beckon us to return.
The lure of honey is in a bear's den.
Now, this is a painful lesson to learn.
We may not escape this time, my friend.

A sinner returns to sin,
The sweetness and joy are for the moment.
In reality Christ is crucified again.
Grace restored, peace as before, repent.

Great drops of blood dripped from His brow.
The Son of God was crucified.
In a sorrowful distress, His head was bowed.
Along time ago Jesus died.

For the sins of the world
He came to forgive,
To bring us back to God.
He has a new life for us to live.

Turn from sin, Christ love is greater still!
His love will prevail.
A sincere longing heart desires to do God's will
And to know His love will never fail.

Pray from a repentant heart.
The promise is given.
He will never depart.
Old returning sins are forgiven.
.
Listen, It is the Savior, "I forgive."
Oh the joyful words to hear.
Rejoice, we have a new life to live.
The Son of God is near.

Sweet honey is a deceitful lure.
Resist the temptation.
Avoid the sinful pleasure.
Crucify again will lead to devastation.

"He is faithful and just to forgive us
And to cleanse us from all unrighteousness" (1 Jo 1:9)
Blessed be the name of Jesus.
He still offers forgiveness.

# Crucify Afresh
## April 5

Remember how He died?
God's only begotten Son,
He was crucified.
Our sins He came to atone.

Let me tell the story again.
Mary could hear the hammer?
As the nails were driven in,
The spikes pierced the hands of the Savior.

A crown of thorns
Placed upon His brow.
His back was torn
As furrows of a plow.

To forgive us of our sins,
His life He had to give.
So please don't drive the nails again!
But continue to live.

By the grace of God, stand,
On the cross Jesus died.
Never let go of His hand.
Turn loose, Jesus will no longer abide.

A back-sliding sinner fades away.
Fellowship with God is gone.
There is no peace in the old sinful way.
Come back to Christ; don't wait too long.

Jesus died for our sins,
So don't pick up the hammer
And start all over again.
With a confession of sins He will deliver.

 If we return unto sin,
Think about the crown of thorns.
They pierced deep into His skin.
The cross held His earthly form.

So listen, my friend,
For our sins Christ died.
Please don't crucify Him again!
But let Him be glorified.

# A Sacrifice for Sin
## April 6

A young man was chosen.
His life was without spot or blemish.
A sacrifice for sin, He would be given.
Death on the cross was a horrible way to punish.

Jesus would die that day
For sins He never committed.
This was the only way
Our sinful lives could be acquitted.

A sacrifice was given.
For the sins of the world,
Christ gave His life so we could be forgiven.
The believer has life by His precious blood.

Before the cross, Jesus endured a whipping.
Attached to a whip were pieces of metal and bone.
His back was lacerated; blood was dripping.
Our salvation was in Him alone.

Most people died just from the beating.
I cannot even imagine the pain.
His commitment to God was unwavering.
He was led as a lamb to the slaughter to be slain.

His love was stronger than the suffering.
An innocent man was dying in our place.
We know who should have been on the cross dying:
The unholy, unrighteous, sinners of disgrace.

Only one man could die for all—
Jesus Christ, God's only begotten Son.
He was obedient to the heavenly call.
His love for us compelled Him to go on.

From the cross to the grave,
Faithful to the end,
All who believe will be saved
He was buried but now He is risen!
.
A divine sacrifice was given.
A resurrection from the dead took place.
Sinners confess Christ and sins or forgiven.
Now we can sing "Amazing Grace."

# He Didn't Send an Angel
## April 7

God looked upon the earth.
He saw that it was corrupt.
Great sorrow filled His heart.
It seemed no one was looking up.

He didn't send an angel
The world to save,
For mankind was filled with anger.
But His Son He gave.

He didn't send a king
Or give Him a crown of pure gold.
Jesus came to save us from our sins.
In God's Word the story is told.

"For God so loved the world,
He gave His only begotten Son"(John 3:16).
Read His divine holy Word.
Jesus is coming soon!

In the clouds of glory,
Meet Him in the air.
What a wonderful story,
We will be with Jesus over there.

God looked upon the earth and it was corrupt.
He didn't send a holy angel to save the lost.
But now His people are looking up.
Jesus saves to the uttermost.

He didn't send an angel,
But on a cross
His Son did hang
So we would not be lost.

Many angels came.
They had a special mission.
Salvation only Jesus could claim.
God gave His only Son.

An angel on the cross would not suffice,
But the death of His own Son,
He gave the supreme sacrifice.
Now the heart of the sinner is won.

# He Didn't Come Down
## April 8

He didn't come down.
On the cross He would stay.
God's only Son,
He took the time to pray.

It was not the nails or spikes of lead
That held Him to the tree.
I know why His precious blood was shed.
He loves you and me!

For your transgressions and mine,
Jesus bowed His head and died.
A witness to all the earth of glory divine,
The Son of God was crucified.

I hope you understand.
Jesus stayed on the cross; sin demands a sacrifice.
The nails were driven into His hands,
The price of sin so high, only God's love would suffice.

The pain would be gone.
If Jesus came down from the cross,
Sinners would return to their homes,
No one could sing "Amazing Grace." All would be lost!

No hope of heaven.
The Christian life would be in vain.
We would still be in our sins.
Jesus endured the pain.

On the cross to stay,
His love is greater than the pain.
Jesus took the time to pray,
"Not my will, but thine" (Luke 22:42).

He didn't come down,
Committed to stay on the cross.
His love abounds.
He came to save the lost.

He endured the pain and the suffering.
He stayed on the cross for your sins and mine.
Forgiveness of sins He is offering.
Let us love Him with heart, soul, and mind.

# The Tomb Is Empty
## April 9

Three old nails
Held Him to the cross.
The story I must tell:
Jesus came to save the lost.

He was bruised and beaten.
Oh, the suffering He had to bear.
With a whip He was smitten.
A crown of thorns He was forced to wear.

On a cross made of wood,
The horrible death of a man,
Behold, the Son of God.
Spikes were driven into His hands.

He paid the price.
The debt we owed, He paid it all.
He gave the supreme sacrifice,
The penalty for sin paid in full.

Please do not walk away
From the cross where He died!
Take a few minutes to pray.
For us He was crucified.

Our payment has been made.
Take heed of the warning, my friend.
Repent or the hope of heaven will fade.
We must be born again.

Let us visit the grave
Where the body of Jesus was laid.
Remember, for the debt of sin, His life He gave.
Our redemption has been paid.

There is the sepulcher.
By faith let us look in.
If Jesus is there,
We are still in our sins.

The tomb is empty.
He has risen!
Give God the glory.
Our sins are forgiven.

# The Third Day
## April 10

On a cross He died,
A man called Jesus.
He was crucified.
He gave His life for us.

He came to save us from our sins.
He was buried in a borrowed grave.
Soon He would be leaving.
He had no intentions to stay.

Jesus gave a promise.
He would surely keep His word.
On the third day, "I will rise" (Matthew 27:63),
Thus saith the Lord.

A sacrifice He gave
In complete obedience to God's will.
Our souls He came to save.
Deliver us from the fire pits of hell.

In the grave He lay,
A lifeless form,
But on the third day
The power of God would transform.

He was dead.
But now He is alive!
His blood was shed.
For our sins He had to die.

If He is still in the grave,
Our faith is in vain.
What good is the life He gave?
Remember the suffering and the pain.

We have good news, my friend,
No longer in the grave,
Jesus has risen!
All who believe and repent will be saved.

Our faith is in a risen Savior.
We too shall rise.
We will be with Him forever.
Soon we will meet Him in the skies.

# The Grave Is Empty
## April 11

"He lives, He lives,"
The church choir sings.
I want to know what I can give.
My desire is to honor the King.

What special gift can I bring?
Silver and gold have I none.
He requires none of those things,
But He asks me to come alone.

By faith to see an empty tomb,
Where our Savior would not remain.
His grave clothes folded in a vacant room,
Let me explain!

Now this is what I see:
Yes, Jesus dying on a cross.
He was dying for you and me
So we would not be lost.

To save us from our sins,
His precious blood was applied.
I invited Jesus to come in.
For our salvation He was crucified.

He suffered and He bled.
Death claimed the Son of God.
His body was placed on a deathbed.
Remember the verse" God so loved the world" (John 3:16).

His Son He gave.
Three days later His Son was raised.
He is not in the grave.
Give God the praise.

Let us go to the gravesite.
I want you to go with me
Through the vision of faith.
Tell me what you see.

If He is in the grave,
We are still in our sins.
Glory to God, He has the power to save.
Jesus Christ has risen.

# From Death to Life
## April 12

In the grave He lay.
He was not asleep
As some people might say.
But at the cross His mother did weep.

She wept for her beloved Son.
She saw the suffering.
He was the only one,
God's divine offering.

A sacrifice He gave
To forgive us of our sins.
Believe on Him; we can be saved.
But if He's in the tomb, this must be the end,

Our faith will not open heaven's gate.
Christ was laid to rest in the earth.
From death to life, there is no debate.
If Christ is in the grave so is our faith.

If Jesus is still in the grave,
Our faith is in vain.
Forget about the life He gave,
Disregard the suffering and the pain.

If Jesus is in the grave,
The hope of all the nations
Lie with Him in the cave.
Our hope of eternal life is a false expectation.

Be not dismayed.
The grave for Him was not the end.
He arose from the dead.
We too shall live again.

In the grave He lay,
But never again!
He had no intentions to stay.
From the grave to glory He did ascend.

"Jesus said, "He that believeth in me,
Thou He were dead, yet shall He live."(John 11:25).
From death to life, He will set us free.
Receive from Him everlasting life.

# Alive by the Power of God
## April 13

They took Him down
From the cross where He was crucified.
Great drops of blood fell to the ground.
On Calvary's dark hill Jesus died.

Joseph begged for His body for a burial.
He wanted to give Him a proper resting place.
Christ in the grave was only temporal.
With the mighty hand of God He would raise

His Son to the throne.
The sepulcher was sealed.
The entrance was blocked with a huge stone.
In the tomb of the dead, God's Son was concealed.

Angels came down from heaven,
And the stone was rolled away.
Christ of Calvary has risen.
He arose from the dead the third day.

No mortal hands could open
The grave that was sealed.
Jesus in the grave, how could we be forgiven?
But the glory of God was revealed.

Soldiers of war barricaded the tomb with a heavy stone.
No one was allowed to even get close.
Nothing could stop God from getting to His Son.
The power of the enemy defeated, and Jesus arose.

The strong hold of death,
Who is that God who can deliver from the dead?
Remember, Jesus took His last breath.
My God is able to deliver; think about what Jesus said.

The third day He would rise again.
In a sealed tomb, death held Him as a prisoner; but God,
No power on earth could stop Him from coming in.
The grave was opened and Jesus arose as Savior of the world.

As God loved Jesus with all of His heart,
His great love for us is the same.
With loving kindness, always He will impart.
We are alive by the power of God in Jesus' name.

# Alive from the Dead
## April 14

Jesus was crucified.
The spikes were driven in.
For you and me He died.
The world had forsaken.

The Son of God they denied.
They took Him down from the cross.
But soon He would be glorified.
The guards did boast.

"Behold your King."
They saw a lifeless corpse.
Tears ran down the cheeks of those mourning.
Some of the people felt no remorse.

But others realized
This was no ordinary man.
It was God's Son they crucified.
His blood was on their hands.

One guard spoke in solemn words.
I believe from a heart of repentance.
"Truly this was the Son of God" ( Matthew 27:54).
At that moment he felt the power of deliverance.

Oh, truly it is a blessed day
When we find out about Jesus.
The Holy Spirit touches us as we pray.
He offers salvation for all of us.

In the grave He lay,
Jesus of Nazareth,
But on the third day
He conquered death.

It is true; God's Son was crucified,
The Lord of lord's and the King of kings.
The strong hold of the grave was denied.
He arose from the dead; upon the throne He reigns.

Let us love Him with heart and soul.
This is the day and hour.
A new life in Christ, we can know.
By faith in Him we will feel the resurrection power.

# I Know Jesus Lives
## April 15

You ask me how I know
Jesus lives.
Well, there are many things to show.
I would like to tell you He forgives.

I know He lives!
Yes, it is true.
In my heart He abides.
My sins He forgave; I'm quite sure.

There is a sweet, sweet spirit.
He meets me at a holy place.
The presence of the Lord, I can feel it.
There is no doubting His saving grace.

He wakes me up in the morning,
At the rising of the sun,
When the clouds are forming.
He stays with me until the work is done.

He walks with me.
Throughout the day,
I feel the hand of mercy.
He shows me the way.

He is my light
That keeps me from falling.
In the darkness of the night.
With Him I just keep on walking.

I talk with Him in prayer.
I read about Him in the Word.
He always meets me there.
He is my Lord.

If you want to know more,
The grave is bare.
The stone rolled away from the door.
Jesus is not there.

I know Jesus lives.
In my heart to stay,
Sin He forgives.
Salvation comes when we pray.

# "We are Va. Tech." Let's Go Hokies."
## April 16

"We will prevail."
From the dark shadow
Our spirit will avail.
We will live through the sorrow.

Precious memories held close to the heart,
We make a solemn promise,
A sincere message of hope and love to impart.
We pray that God will bless the families with peace.

With each passing day,
A new light shining,
The memory of life to stay,
God's holy arms are extending.

He sends down His love,
A strong and loving embrace
From the throne room above.
He gives an abundance of grace.

His love grows stronger still
As we hold one another.
With deep, sorrowful emotions to feel,
Let us be kind to each other.

The voice of Virginia Tech was heard that day.
It was the sound of triumph and victory,
Even in the midst of sorrow and dismay.
Let us hold fast the love of life in our memory.

Keep them in our hearts forever to stay.
They have a place in glory to claim.
Hold them close with each passing day.
I am sure they would loudly proclaim:

"We are Va. Tech." "Let's go, Hokies."
It is the victory sound.
Keep holding on to the memories.
The grace of God always abounds.

The memory of life forever to stay,
The strong bond of love
No one can ever take away.
Gentle peace comes from God above.

# The Debt Is Paid
## April 17

It is time to make a payment.
Now days, living expenses are quite high.
I hope your exchange will be sufficient
Or the officer in charge will deny.

Money in the bank
Will purchase just about anything
Or you can leave the check blank.
The cashier will do all the investing.

But what if you have no money to buy?
Lack of funds can be disturbing.
The purchase price is just too high.
A rejection is really discouraging.

Is there something that cost more than you could pay?
Well, how about peace with God, forgiveness of sin,
These things can only be obtained when you pray.
Come to the cross; payment will be made then.

Believe in Jesus and you will be saved.
The debt is paid, the full amount.
God heard the words that were prayed.
'Go thy way, no sins in this account."

Settlement for sin was made.
Only the blood of Jesus would suffice.
The supreme price was paid.
He is the only one who could pay the price.

If you have empty pockets or money to spare,
Salvation is needed, how can you afford the cost?
.At the cross you will meet Jesus there.
Payment is made in full for the lost.

Unable to pay for salvation so free,
The price was too high.
Jesus paid it all at Calvary.
The high cost of sin, He had to die.

It is not too late to realize
Christ paid the debt for sin.
He will forgive if you accept His sacrifice.
The debt is paid; He has risen!

# Let the Halleluiahs Rise
## April 18

The darkness fades away.
Morning comes with a joyful sound, halleluiah!
Oh, they worshiped the Savior that day.
Praise was given to the Messiah.

It was a day of rejoicing.
The Lord was passing by.
It was a time of spiritual blessings.
Holy hands were raised to the sky.

The Savior they would magnify.
In the early hours of the morning,
A lot of voices would amplify.
"Hosanna: blessed is the King (John 12:13).

The people heard that He was coming to Jerusalem.
This was a day of praise and honor to Jesus.
A lot of people when they heard came to meet Him.
Also, some of them wanted to see Lazarus.

"Praise ye the Lord."(Ps 104:35)
The mountains seem to echo.
A glorious sound to be heard,
The love of God they would know.

The days and months have gone,
Also, the worship and the praise,
The adoration for God's Son,
An old rugged cross is raised.

Once the day was bright.
There was rejoicing throughout the land,
Now, the day has turned to night.
Nails were driven into His hands.

Darkness covers the souls of men.
Lightning flashes across the sky,
There is deliverance for sin,
The Son of God had to die.

I have good news to bring
Let the glory halleluiahs rise.
Look up my friend,
The risen Savior is coming in the skies.

# Meet Jesus at the Crossroads
## April 19

The GPS system will not help you this time.
Even the maps are useless for spiritual guidance.
Your destiny will be controlled by your mind
And your desire to go the entire distance.

Many life-saving decisions were made at the Crossroads.
A wrong turn has led to many miles of grief and despair.
No way to get home as long as you follow these roads.
Go back to the crossroads; Jesus will meet you there.

Go back to the place
Where your heart was tender for His love
And there was an abundance of grace.
You will be touched by the hand above.

On a cross Jesus was crucified for your sins.
Perhaps this is your first visit.
This is where the crossroads begin.
The narrow way leads home; will you take it?

This will be your own personal decision.
Christ gave His life so you could be forgiven.
He endured the pain and suffering for your salvation.
The supreme sacrifice was given.

As you think about Him on the cross, He is dying.
A moment of grief overwhelms you.
Teardrops fall to the ground, as you cannot stop crying.
Forgiveness is offered, love and mercy, too.

At the crossroads you met the Savior.
Remember the crucifixion.
At the altar you made peace with God the Father.
The hope of all believers is in the resurrection.

Crucified, buried, and rose again,
He is alive, alive forevermore!
The decision is yours, my friend.
Believe in Jesus and God will open heaven's door.

At the crossroads of life to stand,
This is where life begins.
With one touch of the nail scarred hand
The old ways of sin come to an end.

# Easter Is Coming
## April 20

It is time to make preparation.
We will all gather together.
It will be a wonderful celebration.
Soon it will be Easter.

Go and listen to a sermon.
Hear the gospel story,
A message about God's Son.
Give Him the praise, honor, and glory.

It is true Jesus died,
For the world He bled.
He was crucified.
Take Him down from the cross; He is dead.

In a grave He was laid.
For the price of sin
Our debt was paid.
Soon He would ascend.

To the throne room above,
To reign as an eternal King.
Death was conquered by His love.
Let every person shout and sing.

He has risen!
He is alive, alive, forevermore.
Someday He will be returning,
Perhaps He will come Easter Sunday or even before.

It is time to make preparation
In whatever day or hour.
We too shall experience a resurrection.
Look up, my friend; the Lord is coming with power.

On our resurrection morning
The saints of God will rise.
With robes of white adorning,
We will meet Jesus in the skies.

Easter is coming.
Let us prepare.
It will be a day of rejoicing.
In church I hope to see you there.

# The Final Victory
## April 21

A cross to bear
Up the hill of Calvary,
A crown of thorns to wear,
Jesus will claim the final victory.

The multitude yelled,
"Crucify Him, crucify!"
On a cross He was nailed.
Soon God would be glorified.

But first, an enemy to defeat,
Satan held the death key.
Jesus had a mission to complete.
He would set the captive free.

Now Satan held his captives.
Death was the captain in charge.
There were no pardons or reprieves.
No one was discharged.

The prison walls were fortified,
Imagine Captives held with an unbreakable chain.
To escape many have tried.
All their efforts were in vain.

Soon there would be a dramatic change
From the one who came from heaven's throne.
Death brought forth the chains.
He bound God's Son.

Yes, death came to claim,
To hold in the grave forever.
It was Jesus Christ who was slain.
He is the beloved of the Father.

It is one thing to escape deaths strong hold,
Quite another to defeat the enemy,
To conquer by the mighty power of God.
Jesus gave us an eternal victory.

He defeated the captain of the guard.
He took back the keys of death, the grave, and hell.
Jesus is not in the graveyard.
He won the battle and accomplished God's will.

# It Is Finished
## April 22

The gateway to heaven,
There's only one,
Our sins are forgiven
When we believe in God's Son.

No other name is given.
For us to be saved,
We can enter heaven
By God's amazing grace.

Jesus died on a cross.
A crown of thorns He wore.
To save the lost,
Our sins He bore.

The last words of Jesus; victory was won.
"It is finished" (John 19:30).
Three days later God would raise His Son.
A life on earth had ended.

In the grave His body lay,
The supreme sacrifice was given.
Three days later, Mary heard the angels say,
"He is not here: for he is risen"(Matthew 28:6).

Jesus died and rose again.
Salvation is promised to all who will believe.
He died for us; let life begin.
Eternal life we shall receive.

Believe God's Word.
Jesus will come into a receptive heart.
We are not far from the kingdom of God.
Salvation He will impart.

There was a deep sorrow at His burial.
For three days there was grief and crying.
His temporary grave yielded to the eternal.
On the third day, joy came in the morning.

"It is finished;" He bowed His head to die.
This is not the end of the story.
The angels proclaim He is alive!
This same Jesus will return in the clouds of glory.

# Give God the Praise
## April 23

Give honor to the King.
This Easter morn,
Let all the earth sing.
Let us rejoice at the rising of the Son.

Glory to His name,
Let the halleluiahs ring.
In every heart proclaim,
The Lord has risen.

Give God the praise
For the mercy given
With holy hands raised.
He has forgiven.

Bless Him from the depths
Of the inner most being.
Thank Him for every breath.
He gives us many wonderful blessings.

With a heart of love expressing,
Let us sing a new hymn.
From the tomb He has risen!
The grave could not hold Him.

He is alive!
Let the gospel message be heard.
Jesus has the power to forgive.
Give honor to the Lord.

Come into the holy sanctuary.
With honor and reverence,
Give your life to the King of glory.
Serve Him with complete obedience.

When He comes in the clouds of heaven,
We know not the day or the hour.
The saints of God will ascend.
We will leave by that same resurrection power.

We shall be raised,
Incorruptible and undefiled.
Give God the praise.
Jesus is coming back in just a little while.

# Christ is Risen, Sins are Forgiven
## April 24

Take Him down from the cross.
No more miracles to perform,
He gave His life to save the lost.
Death has come to claim His unsightly form.

Bruised and beaten to die for sins,
The hope of mankind lies in a grave.
Is this the place where our expectations end?
A lifeless body is unable to save.

Jesus spoke of sins being forgiven,
The world would say He lied.
A sepulcher holds Him fast as an earthly coffin.
For the sins of mankind He died.

Turn from the grave and walk away.
Jesus is dead; our sins abide.
If we go too far, we will miss the hallelujah way.
In just three days the Son of God will be glorified.

All of our sins He carried to the tombs retreat.
In just a matter of time, sins will be forgiven.
This is no time to accept defeat.
Listen, Jesus Christ is risen!

I just felt a wave of glory in my soul.
Praise God forevermore, thank you Jesus!
The power of the resurrection is for everyone to know.
He lives! He has the power to deliver us?

The grave couldn't hold Him.
We have been delivered from the strong hold of sin.
Let all the earth rejoice and sing a new hymn.
Sins are forgiven.

The promise of the faithful and true,
Jesus came to forgive sin.
Life eternal is a blessing too.
In Him sins are forgiven.

Jesus Christ has risen.
This could be the day and hour
Born-again believers called to Heaven.
Our hope is in God's resurrection power.

# Were you there?
## April 25

Were you there
When the multitude was fed?
A basket of fish and bread to share
When Christ broke the bread.

Were you there
When Lazarus died?
Jesus eyes filled with tears.
The family members cried.

At the gravesite; a miracle to see,
"Lazarus, come forth"(John 11:43).
Jesus set Him free.
The Lord has power over death.

Were you there when Jesus was crucified,
When they laid Him in the grave?
For the sins of the world He died.
He gave His life, souls to save.

The blood of God's own Son was shed.
He died on a cross made of wood;
For the sins of mankind He bled.
Believe in Him, you will have peace with God.

The days and years have come and gone.
Just one question because I care,
Then I'll leave you all alone.
Were you there?

Take a minute for meditation,
Stand in awe for just a moment; listen!
The angels have a message for the entire nation.
"He is not here: for he is risen!" (Matthew 28:6).

Don't despair
If you failed to see all these events!
Even thou you were not there,
God will save you if you repent.

It's not possible for you to have been there.
That's really ok,
No way to look into the past, Jesus is here.
Faith is better than sight any day.

# Faith Never Quits
## April 26

Why don't you just quit, walk away
From the path of good intentions.
The cross is so heavy today.
Your burden is for many transgressions,

None of them belong to you.
Yet your journey is unwavering,
Oh, that our faith would be as strong, too!
The whelps on your back are from a severe beating.

The lacerations of the whip tore the flesh.
Many people died from the beating alone.
If you turn back, all will perish.
The cross is heavy, but you continue on.

Up the lonely hill of despair,
Each step more painful than the last.
The cross was given to Simon to bear,
But your request is for us to hold fast.

Keep the faith,
Take one day, one step at a time.
Be a faithful servant to the last breath.
Love God with heart, soul, and mind.

Jesus is at the place of the execution.
His hands and feet nailed to the cross.
Angels could have broken the bonds of the crucifixion.
If Jesus came down from the cross, all would be lost.

Why don't you come down?
No more pain to bear.
Love is deep in the heart where grace is found,
Nothing else can compare.

My friend, if the cross you carry today
Seems a little bit heavier,
Don't quit or give up in dismay.
Pray reverently to God the Father.

The way to victory is a made up mind.
Faith never quits even in the dying hour.
Love is stronger than the nails that bind.
An empty grave is a reminder of the resurrection power.

# When We Were Enemies
## April 27

The battle rages on.
War has been declared against the enemy.
Soldiers so valiant and strong,
They fight for their country.

A soldier cries out,
"We can take the hill."
The battle is severely fought.
Men and women die on the desolate field.

Another war continues overseas.
The enemy desperately tries to kill each soldier.
There are many casualties.
Those who fight would die for each other.

They have given the supreme sacrifice.
A life for a life,
They paid the final price
So their friends could live.

Now I can see someone dying for a friend.
To spare him from death,
A fellow soldier to defend,
A dying soldier may need a life-giving breath.

A sinner of disgrace would you die for him?
Even if his life was corrupt with sin,
All sinners, who would die for them?
The battle rages within.

Let me refresh your memory.
At one time we were enemies with God.
His Son died on a hill called Mount Calvary.
They took His life and spilled His blood.

For an enemy He died,
For you and me the sacrifice was given.
Jesus was nailed to the cross and crucified.
He does not hold a grudge; we can be forgiven.

Christ died in our place.
He paid the ultimate price.
Mankind and Jehovah reconciled by grace.
Peace was made with a Holy God by His sacrifice.

# If in This Life Only
## April 28

"If in this life only
We have hope in Christ" (1 Cor. 15:19),
Our home in glory,
Our hope of eternity no longer exist.

"We are of all men
Most miserable"(1 Cor. 15:19).
Still in our sins,
We can close the Bible.

If there is no hereafter,
Our life ends on earth.
Get up from the altar,
No need for the rebirth.

Close the church doors.
From mortal to immortal,
The words of life are no more.
Forget about life eternal.

If this is all there is,
No salvation by grace,
Our hopes of eternal bliss
Are buried with Him in the grave.

We can keep Him in death's prison
With no hope of life going on,
Or believe that Jesus Christ has risen.
God has resurrected His Son.

The hope of the nation,
We have the hope of life eternal.
Oh, the power of the resurrection,
Open up the Bible.

Read the holy pages.
Go back to the altar.
We will live throughout the ages.
This is no time to quit or falter.

We have hope beyond the grave,
To live forever in the kingdom of heaven.
God has the power to save.
Eternal life is for the forgiven.

# Where is the devotion?
## April 29

My God is holy.
He deserves our devotion.
He is worthy.
The earth is His creation.

He is a God of love.
His love is deep as the ocean,
Higher than the mountains above.
He is touched by our emotions.

Our God is holy.
His merciful kindness is great toward us.
Give Him the praise, honor, and the glory.
He has called us to a life of service.

God is great.
He desires our praise.
Our hearts to radiate,
Worship Him with holy hands to raise.

His love was shown
At Calvary's dark hill.
God's beloved Son
An angry mob decided to kill.

Words of hate intensify
As an echo across the land.
"Crucify, crucify."
Nails were driven into His hands.

Remember the God of all creation.
Jesus is hanging on the cross.
Where is the devotion?
He suffers and dies for the lost.

The people mocked and made fun.
A crown of thorns He wore.
Behold God's Son!
A wooden cross He bore.

Where is the devotion, a time of praise?
"As the Father hath loved me, so have I loved you" (John 15:9).
Jesus arose; all across the earth, holy hands raise.
He wants us to love God too.

132

# Lazarus, Come Forth
## April 30

Many years ago
A man named Lazarus,
I believe you know.
His friend was Jesus.

The Son of the Most-High God,
Many people Jesus healed.
Sometimes, He just spoke the Word
And God's power was revealed.

Remember, Jesus is far away,
And His friend, Lazarus, He is a sick man.
Jesus would go to Him but He had to wait another day.
The life of Lazarus was in God's hands.

Jesus said, "This sickness is not unto death,
But for the glory of God"(John 11:4).
Now Lazarus died; He took his final breath.
Jesus came and He spoke the word.

"Lazarus, come forth"(John 11:43).
Out of the grave he came.
Jesus has power over death.
The word of life He proclaims.

When Lazarus died, Jesus was not there.
His absence would help us to believe.
God loves us and He cares.
Faith in Him we will receive.

Salvation for our souls,
Forgiveness of sins,
The love of God to know,
But we must be born again.

Sinner, come forth.
Now, we were dead in our sins.
Jesus breaks the hold of death.
A new life has been given.

Jesus spoke the word to come.
He calls us by name.
Soon it will be time to go home.
Eternal life is for us to claim.

# Come From Behind
## May 1

The race has begun.
Faith or good deeds will win.
In our earthly race a trophy will be won.
A reward will be given at the end.

Let's take a quick look at our competitors.
With faith we can move mountains.
This is a favorite choice of the spectators.
The race is more exciting if we hold the reins.

Another wonderful choice is good deeds.
Its special desire is to feed the poor
And with intercessory prayers it intercedes.
I am sure you would like to know a lot more.

Well at one time this was a perfect team.
They could not be separated by anyone.
The multitudes of people held them in high esteem.
Not anymore, this race is for only one.

Both participants are highly qualified.
As a team they were favored to win.
In their disrespect of others, they should be disqualified.
The race has begun; no one was forbidden.

But wait, they have not yet won the victory.
A new arrival has just entered the scene.
This one is known by the name of charity.
We know it is peaceful and very serene.

 Faith and good deeds tremble at the name.
They cannot run at the same pace.
All of their mighty acts are worthless and vain.
They tried to win without grace.

Love comes from behind.
The three runners become as one.
All joined together with heart, soul, and mind.
Now the race can be won.

We can move mountains and feed the poor.
Together we make a great team.
I can tell you more.
Without love it is impossible to please Him.

# The Sword of the Spirit
## May 2

On the battlefield
A soldier stands.
He is obedient to yield.
He hears the command.

Fight on!
A sword has been given.
Make sure it is drawn.
He has a victory to win.

War has been declared
Against a mighty foe.
Now it is a spiritual warfare.
The Lord has commanded us to go.

Be faithful to the end.
A crown of glory to wear,
Angels of God descend.
We will meet Jesus in the air.

God has given to us
A powerful weapon,
In the name of Jesus,
Fight on till the victory is won.

The sword is God's Holy Bible.
As a war against Satan,
We can win the battle
And be victorious over sin.

Inspiration from God above,
Victory is promised by the Word.
Be a faithful warrior, carry the cross with love.
The enemy is defeated by the one who holds the sword.

"Who is he that overcometh?"(1John 5:5)
Search the holy pages
And we will see he that believeth.
The cross bearer continues on, even as the war rages.

The word is quick and powerful.
It is the sword of the Spirit.
Open up the Bible.
Triumphant in life are those who believe it.

# The Gospel of Christ
## May 3

The mountain is not too high
That we cannot climb.
Our Lord we will magnify.
Let us give glory to Him.

Nor is the ocean too wide,
A soul so deep in sin we cannot reach.
Let us cross over to the other side.
We have a gospel to preach.

From the valley below,
Let our voices be heard.
Jesus has commanded us to go
Share the good news of the Bible; speak the Word.

Souls need to be saved.
The captive to be set free,
The great commission the Lord gave.
A commitment to serve comes from you and me.

He has called us
With an high calling.
We are to follow Jesus.
Speak the word; rescue the perishing.

Go into the cities and the towns
That all may hear
The blessed gospel sounds.
The word of life needs to be heard.

Go forth in Jesus name.
Good news to bring.
The word of salvation to proclaim,
A joyful heart will sing.

The great commission is to go.
The gospel of Christ is the power of God unto salvation.
Everybody needs to know,
God's love for sinners is without exception.

If the Gospel we hide,
It is hid to the lost.
Whether in the valley low or the mountain high,
The message we bring: Jesus died on the cross.

# Sin in Pencil, Prayers in Ink
## May 4

Sins written in pencil
They are only temporary.
A page of white the words will fill.
A quick review will tell your life's story.

A pencil is a good way to write
Especially if you need to make a few corrections.
Your sins may have led to a corruptible life.
Now the page is full of imperfections.

Please don't despair!
Even thou every page has a blemish,
The marks of a sinful life are there.
A good eraser will cause them to vanish.

On paper the pencil marks gradually disappear.
Corrections are made to your satisfaction.
Wait another day; words of life will reappear.
Take away the bad; now look at the page transformation.

Corruptible sins are gone at last.
So my friend, write your sins in pencil.
In comparison, prayers in ink, sin fades into the past.
Ink is a lasting impression of the eternal.

You can erase sin on paper
But you still have it in your life, my friend.
When you talk with God in prayer
You will know He permanently forgives sin.

The table of the heart is a good place to write.
See how quickly the prayers ascend.
God's gentleness and loving care is your delight.
The marks of faith are written in heaven.

Your words in ink, God will not erase.
He holds them in His heart with all spiritual things.
He answers every prayer with a touch of grace.
Peace and joy He always brings.

Sin in pencil
You can erase or take it away.
Prayers in ink are for the eternal.
The grace of God abounds when you pray.

# A Pen in God's Mighty Hand
## May 5

I am just a little pen
In the hands of a mighty God.
He gives me a message to send.
I try to reveal the truth in every word.

Now I don't know what I am going to write.
Inspiration comes in many different ways.
When a heavenly thought comes I know it is right.
God blesses me with a poem; I am simply amazed.

One sentence begins to form,
After a little while there is another.
Each word I use, God will bless to transform.
I give glory and honor to my Father.

God is pleased when I mention His Son.
He knows I will recall a special place
Where I met the Holy One.
Jesus forgave me, now I am saved by grace.

It is my pleasure to write.
The blessing God gives is not for me alone.
For Christians around the world it is their delight
To help someone make it home.

The words appear on paper from His heart.
A little pen has a love letter to share.
So let us write with His love to impart.
A love for others is the cross we bear.

The words we write, God gives to us.
People of all nations, He will use us to tell them
About His Son, Jesus.
By our faithfulness, others will know and love Him.

We thank you Lord for the words that inspire,
For the grace to help someone along the way.
In our hearts, we always want you to be there
And we want to serve you every day.

Just a little pen
In the hands of a mighty God,
We have a love story to send.
Bless us as we write; anoint every word.

# The Cross and Beyond
## May 6

This will be a long journey
As we go back in time.
Let's begin at the cross of Calvary.
The past and the future we will combine.

God's Son is dying.
The pain is unimaginable.
Many people were crying.
Suffering was unbearable.

Dark clouds filled the sky.
Great teardrops came from above
God's beloved Son would die
In obedience of His Father's love.

Jesus was buried in a borrowed grave.
God knew He would rise to live again.
At His death, mourners felt sorrow and dismay.
On the third day Jesus was risen.

Well the cross is gone.
Towns and cities may occupy the place
Where they crucified God's Son.
But nothing can hide His grace.

It is vast as the ocean,
As far as the East is from the West.
His love always prevailing,
God gave His very best.

No longer in the grave.
Jesus is alive.
He has power to save.
Heaven is promised to all who will believe.

Even thou the cross is gone,
It remains forever in our hearts.
Faith in God's Son
Holds on to the promise; He will never depart.

The cross and beyond
As recorded in the holy pages,
A loving Savior lives on
And Christians are steadfast on the Rock of Ages.

# A Sharp Axe
## May 7

Go into the woods.
Take the best axe.
Cut the trees for firewood.
You may want to apply a little wax.

But before you leave home,
Take a little extra time;
Go to the tool room.
The axe has a dull edge that a file will refine.

It doesn't matter about the shine,
The most important thing
Is to have a sharp edge, very fine.
More firewood you will obtain.

A friend will meet you there.
His axe he did not sharpen.
Soon the chips fly into the air.
The day comes to an end.

They both gather the wood.
The man with the sharp axe,
The winter supply is good.
It's time for him to relax.

But what about the other man?
It looks like he has to return.
Back into the woods, his work was vain.
Not much wood to burn.

In our Christian walk with the Lord,
Take a little extra time.
Go home and study the Word.
You will have a sharp axe of a keen mind.

"Study to show thyself approved" (2 Timothy 2:15).
Your labor of love will not be in vain,
The hard edge of sin removed.
Souls can be won in Jesus' name.

With a sharp axe, the trees lay on the ground.
Take the Gospel of Jesus Christ.
The Grace of God abounds,
Make sure you pray first.

# Revive Us Again
## May 8

When the fire is burning low,
A new log will restore
A bright and glorious glow.
Wood on the ground: let us gather more.

When the fire begins to sputter and spout,
I hope it is understood.
The fire will go out.
Please add more wood.

To save the fire,
Add a few pieces of kindling,
The flames reach into the air.
A new log will keep the fire burning

To restore an old flame.
Once it was glorious and bright.
High hopes to acclaim.
Now a few dying sparks drift aimlessly in the night.

Do not despair!
The flames reach higher
With each new log on the fire.
Each day the fire burns a little bit brighter.

So it is in life.
When the firewood is burning low
And we are burdened down with strife,
A new log will set the flame aglow.

Flames reach into the sky,
The soul to restore.
When the Word of God is applied,
Peace with God forevermore.

Revive us again, oh Lord!
A new log on the fire,
Inspiration from the Word,
Let this be our hearts' desire.

To live and serve God,
A flame that grows brighter,
Let us study the Word.
The bright flames of love will reach higher.

# Thread of life
## May 9

It's not too late my friend,
But if you continue to travel
The path of sin,
The threads of life will unravel.

Just a small thread
No damage is done.
If the Bible is not read
How close are you to God's Son?

Faith, hope and love create a strong bond
Think about a weaver's beam,
The thread so tightly wound.
So is your bondage with Christ; He came to redeem.

To restore fellowship with God,
His life to give
It is very important to read the Word
And to know that He will forgive.

If the thread should break
I know you cringe at the thought,
But a new life He came to remake,
With a supreme sacrifice a soul is bought.

On a cross to die
His precious blood was spilled.
In a grave He would lie.
The love of God was revealed.

For a life that is broken
He came to restore
Sins of the past can be forgiven
A day of repentance leads to life forever more.

Call upon the Lord today,
It is time well spent.
It's not too late to pray
But today may be your last chance to repent.

A weaver's beam so strong,
Threads of life are woven together.
Keep the faith: it won't be long
Christ will come and you will be Him  forever.

# No Talent Left
## May 10

In the beginning,
Strong words to embrace, repent!
You received a spiritual blessing
And God gave you a very special talent.

The anointing of God was upon you.
This gift was not given to another.
He knew that you would be faithful & true.
This call of grace was not for any other.

A Lot of your friends hold the same title.
Maybe a singer in the church choir
Or a preacher of the Holy Bible,
All the gifts given, none can compare.

This talent was specially designed.
God even placed your name on it.
No contract was signed.
The endorsement came by the Holy Spirit.

Use the things that God has given.
Go forth in Jesus' name.
Hold the cross up high; you are one of the forgiven.
Many gifts He gave, but yours is not the same.

A Christian in His service;
God will multiply the blessings.
He will honor the name of Jesus.
But God wants you to use the talents given.

Use it now; please do not delay!
Negligence may be your downfall.
I hope you can say:
No talent left, I used it all.

When it's time to stand before God,
The talents of a life are exposed.
A crown of life will be given according to the word.
Inheritance into the kingdom; your place is reserved.

At the end of your journey
May there be nothing left to give.
You gave it all for His glory.
With Jesus you will forever live.

# Stop the Train
## May 11

Many passengers on board,
Friends and family you adore.
The old train moves quickly down the railroad.
Loved ones wave good-by from the old country store.

This seems to be an ordinary day.
The sun is shining bright and fair.
No trouble is expected along the way.
The hope of the big city, soon they will be there.

A long time has passed
Since they left the peaceful valleys and hills.
The scenery all around is completely unsurpassed.
Wild animals scurry across the track to the open fields.

There are some very high mountains to climb.
A storm moves in with very strong winds.
Ever so slowly this wonderful trip begins to decline.
Lightning flashes across the sky as the rain descends.

Part of the bridge is washed away.
The flood waters intensify.
A watery grave will claim lives at the end of the day.
Stop the train or many will die

Unless someone can warn them of their fate,
A messenger of hope is running down the line.
A delay in time could be a fatal mistake.
It is not too late to stop the train.

The death train is moving on.
Sinners on board, please give the warning.
A tragedy can be prevented by faith in God's Son.
By God's grace sins are forgiven.

This imaginary story was told for a reason.
Loved ones are on a perilous journey.
Their only hope is in God's Son.
We are the messengers of hope for friends and family.

The Gospel of Christ proclaim it aloud.
Let the sound travel through the air-waves.
Souls saved will meet Jesus in the clouds.
Stop the train; tell them Jesus saves.

# An Empty Lantern
## May 12

Lord, fill our lives with concern.
A deep burning flame,
May the love radiate in our hearts as a lantern.
We have a gospel message to proclaim.

A touch from heaven
Will ignite the flame to burn.
Wait a little longer, keep the light shining.
Soon He will return.

If we allow the lantern to burn low,
We pray for a fresh anointing.
A rekindle of the Holy Spirit will show.
Help us to keep the fire burning.

Many souls need to know
The wonderful salvation story,
A touch from heaven; watch the flames grow.
A Christian life shining; God gets the glory.

Let the lantern shine bright.
The pathway of life is clear.
To serve you is our delight.
Our hope is to help others draw near.

Do you remember the day?
An empty lantern before the Lord,
Faith was ignited when you knelt to pray.
Forgive me Lord; aren't you so glad He heard.

A sinner is saved!
So hold the lantern up high.
God answered the prayer you prayed.
A repentant heart, He will never deny.

Salvation came when you believed in Jesus' name.
Keep the lamp trimmed; the Lord will return.
We have a gospel message to proclaim.
A light for His glory, may it always burn.

Lord, fill our lives with a spiritual burning
We want to be saturated with your Love.
The time is near for your returning.
An empty lantern is filled with mercy from above.

# Mother's Day
## May 13

A day to remember,
Think about the many blessings.
This day we honor a special member.
A mother's love is never ending.

Always caring,
A gentle hand to touch,
She has a warm heart for sharing.
She prays for her children to go to church.

Her love grows stronger still.
Every day that she lives,
Her hope and desire is to do His will.
Joy and peace she always gives.

This is a special day.
It's not like any of the others.
Bless her today; in Jesus name we pray.
Lay your holy hand upon all the mothers.

Their lives are filled with giving.
A mother's caring heart
Makes life worth living.
A kind gentle spirit is hers to impart.

A mother holds her children.
She draws them close to her side.
A mother so dear, we also call her friend.
Faith, hope, and love, always abide.

She always gives hope for tomorrow.
The lessons of life, she has taught us well.
Her Lord and Savior, she wants us to follow.
Commit our ways to Him and do His will.

A mother holds her children.
I just want everyone to know,
She keeps on giving
And she will never let them go.

She always holds them in her heart
A special thanks on this Mother's Day,
We are thankful for a love that will never depart.
May God grant you peace all along life's way.

# The Eternal Summit
## May 14

Go a little higher.
I know it is a steep hill to climb.
With every step you draw nearer.
Closer to heaven, it's just a matter of time.

Don't give up my friend.
The glory land is in sight.
A crown of life to win.
Everything will be all right.

Keep your eyes on the cross
And your faith in God above.
Don't worry about being lost.
Jesus will guide you with love.

Over the treacherous terrain,
Up the steep mountain slopes.
Keep on climbing.
Hold secure to the lifeline.

His grace is sufficient
He will keep you from falling.
The journey of life begins, but you must repent.
Eternal life, this is your hope in believing.

Take hold of the Savior's hand.
He will lift you from the miry clay.
To the rock of ages you will stand.
A decision for Christ, no time for delay.

God is attentive to the heart's cry.
He is very sensitive to a plea for mercy.
Remember, it was for you He died.
Your hope in Him is for eternity.

Just a few more weary days
A crown of life to wear.
Give Him the honor, glory, and praise.
The coming of the Lord is near.

Are you ready to meet the Lord?
To reach for the eternal summit,
Prepare to meet thy God.
Be led by the Holy Spirit.

# Gather in the Grain
## May 15

No one will sleep-in this morning.
A lot of work needs to be done today.
This job calls for an early rising.
Before the day begins take the time to pray.

There is a special work to do.
Gather in the grain.
Help with the other jobs, too.
Please don't complain.

Out in the fields,
The volunteers work today.
To do God's will,
There is no time for delay.

Some people plow, others glean.
They gather the grain left behind.
All must work together to bring the harvest in.
Grain will be sent to the mill to grind.

The fields are ripe for harvest
And the laborers are few.
Work for God today and do your very best.
A reward in heaven is promised for you.

Now you can labor in the field all day,
Work until the sun is gone.
Load the wagons and take the grain away.
Work in God's harvest field is never done.

The harvest field is the world.
Gather in the grain, the souls of mankind.
In the furrows deep, sow the Word.
Be a faithful servant all the time.

Go and glean in the field.
The harvest field is white.
God will give an abundant yield.
Go quickly! The day will turn into night.

The time is drawing near.
Your labor of love is not in vain.
In the clouds of glory, Jesus will appear.
Gather in the grain; heaven's gate will open.

# Work in the Harvest Field
## May 16

Christians work in the harvest field.
They know the coming of the Lord is near.
They labor to do God's will.
Soon the Lord will appear.

The harvest is white,
Much work to be done.
A labor of love is the Christians' delight.
Their faith is in Christ alone.

Before the harvest ends,
Take the time to commit.
God is faithful to forgive sins,
A wonderful blessing, God will transmit.

It is not too late to pray.
A new life He will give.
Work for Him all day.
Eternal life is promised, only believe.

Be ready when He comes,
Before the threshing is done.
Soon it will be time to go home.
Patiently wait; it won't be long.

Look up, redemption draws nigh.
The Lord is coming.
From the throne room on high,
He will be returning.

Work in the harvest field.
"Watch and pray!"
Bring loved ones to Christ, what a yield.
Work while there is day.

There is coming a time
When laborers in the field will be idle all day.
Just a reminder, this job is not part-time.
A faithful servant will always pray.

Be ready, my friend.
Work in the harvest field.
When the Lord comes again,
A mansion in glory will be revealed.

# Strawberry Pie
## May 17

Strawberries a plenty,
They hide beneath the colorful green leaves.
Now don't pick too many.
Take caution; the leaves may deceive.

Please be aware:
The leaves of three,
Poison ivy may be there.
It lies silently in the shadow of the tree.

The vines cover the ground.
But all I can see,
Ripe strawberries all around,
And they all belong to me.

I pick up the strawberries.
Leaves of poison also to pull.
I don't have to worry.
The basket is now full.

But what is that I feel
Between my fingers and toes?
Strawberry pie has lost its appeal.
Poison ivy now over me flows.

It spreads like a wild fire
In the strawberry field of delight.
I wish I did not go there.
Warning signs were in plain sight.

The pain and itching
I had to bear.
Strawberry pie was not worth the suffering.
Poison ivy; please beware!

We may have to suffer the consequences
If we are in the poison ivy of sin.
It is certainly not worth the expense
If our souls perish in the end.

Stay away from sin's poison ivy.
It is not worth the suffering.
But live a life that is holy.
Only by grace will the gates of heaven open.

# Make Some Bread
## May 18

Awake from thy sleep,
A poor, hungry soul is crying.
Sow the word; soon it will be time to reap.
A little bit of bread will be most satisfying.

So rise up early,
Many souls need to be fed.
The word of God is for the hungry.
Get out of your slumber's bed.

It's time to make some bread.
There is much work to be done.
Before the long winter ahead,
Summer will soon be gone.

Awake, oh sleepy eyes!
You've been asleep way too long.
Friends and family, hear their despairing cries?
They need to hear about God's Son.

Awake, out of thy sleep,
Stir up thyself in the morning hour,
Stand upon thy feet,
Begin each day with prayer.

There are many souls to be saved.
God's love and mercy is for all of them.
When the bread is made,
Souls will be fed and nourished in Him.

Stir up thyself,
Feed the rich and the poor.
Even if you must deny yourself,
Give and God will bless a whole lot more.

Arise from your sleep.
Be up and about your Father's business.
Emotions of the heart run deep.
The harvest is ripe, many souls to bless.

The time is far spent.
Go and share the bread.
The gospel message is for all to repent.
Nations around the world will be fed.

151

# Weeds in the Garden
## May 19

The sun is shining.
It's such a beautiful day.
The birds are singing.
Field mice are playing in the hay.

It's time to plant the seed.
The ground is fertile.
You have a large family to feed.
Now this will certainly take a while.

But, please be patient!
Soon you will have a beautiful harvest.
There are many different types of plants.
You want to use the very best.

The days and weeks have gone by.
Some of the plants have lost their form.
The fruit seems to wither and die,
What is the problem?

Oh, it's very plain to see
The plants cannot breathe
Surrounded by so many weeds.
They grow in the soil of the earth.

The plants will grow
Only if you remove the weeds.
Sometimes you can use a hoe,
Or you may have to get on your knees.

When the work is finally done,
The garden brings forth a beautiful crop.
All the weeds are gone.
Dinner is on the countertop.

In life's garden,
Sometimes there are many weeds.
You can call them sins.
God will restore a garden if you get on our knees.

God will take away all the sinful deeds.
Just like in the garden of the earthly soil
A life will grow once it has been freed,
God removes the weeds of sin in the heavenly soul.

152

# A Porch of an Idle Life
## May 20

Just imagine no work required, not even a prayer,
Just sit on the porch,
Not a worry or a care.
Watch the people; they are going to church.

Wave as they pass by.
This has been your friendly greeting for many years.
My how time flies.
The days are gone when you sat in church with many tears.

You had a sorrowful heart and a gentle spirit.
Your love for others was beyond compare.
The Christian life you chose to live it.
If someone needed a visit, you would not hesitate to go there.

The days have come and gone.
Now you just rest peacefully in the shade.
Jesus and you, what a team, now there's only one.
The memory of the good life, even that begins to fade.

Think about the time many years ago,
As a follower of Christ, you would always attend church.
When Jesus came by, you were eager to go.
Now you just sit on the porch.

Wave at the people as they drive down the road.
Remember the good old days when you were like them,
Trusting, loving, faithful to a kind, loving God.
There was joy unspeakable when you worshiped Him.

No one can live in the past.
You can recall a lot of wonderful memories.
But treasurers in heaven are the only ones that will last.
Sometimes it is good to think about the old stories.

Well, the people who go to church, they drive by.
There are no friendly waves anymore.
Did the man on the porch die?
No, Jesus came into his heart just as before.

The Lord came by today for a visit.
The man who sat on the porch,
He was touched by the Holy Spirit.
Where did he go? He went to church.

# Silver and Gold
## May 21

"Silver and gold have I none"(Acts 3:6),
Just empty pockets.
Faith in God's Son
Is better than a gold locket.

The disciples carried neither silver nor gold.
They did have something better to offer;
Their faith was in God.
They put their Trust and belief in the Savior.

"Such as I have
Give I thee"(Acts 3:6).
What a wonderful blessing they gave.
Salvation will set the captive free.

Silver is a worthless thing,
No value to behold.
A wooden cross the death of a man was seen.
His life was more precious than all the gold.

Money cannot buy,
Your eternal salvation,
Or a home in the sky.
A new life in Christ is a divine transformation.

Jesus paid the price
For sinners of disgrace.
He gave the ultimate sacrifice
So the unrighteous could be saved by grace.

His life He gave
At the cross of Calvary.
He was laid in a grave
Faith in Him opens the door to eternity.

All hope is given.
The price is paid, only believe,
Christ the Savior has risen.
Forgiveness is yours to receive.

Silver and gold,
Though I have none.
These are precious stones, the value to behold.
The debt for sin was paid in full by God's Son.

# Allegiance
## May 22

I pledge allegiance
To commit my soul, heart, and mind,
To live in complete alliance,
And give God the praise all the time.

I solemnly pledge from the depths of my heart
To follow Jesus all the way.
Never to stray or drift apart,
My commitment is to always pray.

Never turn and run,
Always obey His command,
Fight until the battle is won.
I promise to keep my hand in His hand.

I will consecrate my life to Him.
Always seek His face,
Sing a new hymn,
And rejoice in His grace.

I pledge to be a faithful servant,
To carry my cross,
That I might tell others to repent.
The gospel message I will share with the lost.

I commit to forgive
As Jesus forgave me,
That I may have life
And have it more abundantly.

In this pledge of allegiance,
I just saw the image of Christ.
The life of man and God in alliance.
I know my life is blessed.

I commit to stand steadfast and true,
Faithful to my promises,
He will lead me safely through.
God is not slack in His faithfulness.

The blessings God has promised me,
He is well able to perform.
I will love Jesus who set me free
And give my life to Him to transform.

# Soldier of War
## May 23

Many are called but only a few chosen.
Those selected were of a repentant heart.
They were sorry for their sins.
For a new life in Christ, they were anxious to start.

The training would begin.
Each soldier would be trained in warfare.
They would be given the weapons of war to defend.
The armor of peace they would bear.

A shield of faith would be wielded.
Victory is promised to all who believe.
God will reward those who have completely yielded.
A commitment to serve is a life to give.

Faithful in service, victorious in battle!
Every soldier will be solely equipped.
Strength for the day will come from the Holy Bible.
The Sword of the Spirit will be tightly gripped.

Take a stand my Christian friend.
Join the other recruits in the war zone.
Fight against evil and all sin.
No soldier will fight alone.

Jesus is with you.
The Christ of Calvary, He is the one you chose
To follow and trust Him all the life through.
The enemy was defeated when He arose.

Jesus is the commander in chief.
Those who follow Him will never know defeat.
Every soldier will be triumphant by their belief.
The unbelieving will be the first to retreat.

God is looking today for people to enlist.
Obedient to follow Christ all the way
And all temptations resist.
His command is to watch and pray.

It is time to join.
Only volunteers will be accepted.
The decision is yours, my friend.
An unbelieving heart will be rejected.

# Heaven's Treasure
## May 24

In search of heaven's treasure,
Only the sincere in heart will find
The bounty of God's love is beyond measure.
This gift is not far from every soul-searching mind.

Now I am not talking about Gold,
Silver or diamonds in the earth's core,
Precious gems indeed, they are very valuable to hold.
People have died from the heavy weight they bore.

Riches may endure the night,
There is absolutely no guarantee
A person will rise with the morning light
And a new day to see.

Today's wealth is only a temporary thing.
You may be buried in a gold casket,
On every finger a priceless ring,
No hope of heaven, do you want to risk it?

A heart that is void and empty
Is like a treasure chest, dark in every corner.
The hope of the righteous is a different story.
Their life is one of grace and honor.

The treasure they have found,
No corner of darkness and despair,
The gems of faith abound.
The light of His glory always shines there.

Forever in the heart to those who believe.
Eternal life is a treasure that will never fade or die.
The promise of life is to all who receive,
Even the graves will open from which they lie.

At the sound of a trumpet, believers will arise,
Not bound by worldly care, earthly riches or sin.
Watch and pray, Jesus is coming in the skies.
Faith in Him will open the gates of heaven.

Heaven's treasure,
It is not very hard to find.
Sins forgiven is His pleasure
Peace will come with a surrender of heart and mind.

# God's Search Is Endless
## May 25

God is reaching down His hand.
A rescue is in progress.
Deliverance is possible for fallen man.
His search for the lost is endless.

He walks the dark hills.
You will find Him in the desolate valleys.
Quite often He will enter the war torn fields.
He does not hesitate to enter the darkest alley.

He will enter the gutters of despair
Or visit someone who is on dope.
Just to know He is there,
There is always a glimmer of hope.

It is not an uncommon thing to find Him in church
Or in a shelter for the homeless and the poor.
His hand of mercy is extended to the rich.
He will go anywhere there is an open door.

Don't be surprised if He is in prison,
Walking with a friend on death row.
If He is in the dungeon, He has a good reason.
His search is worldwide; He always has another place to go.

Many people have found Him in a hospital room.
His love was beyond compare.
Some of the patients were getting ready to go home.
Their last days on earth, they are glad He was there.

He found them just in time.
This message is not about the place.
It's more about the meeting of the mind:
Souls saved by grace.

He comes down to the altar of the heart.
Many sinners can be found at the cross.
God makes a special visit with His love to impart.
He always honors His Son who died to save the lost.

God is reaching down His hand.
His holy arm is always extending.
He will hear the cries of fallen man.
No matter where He finds you, God is forgiving.

# The Master of the Clay
## May 26

The Master of the clay,
He rises with the morning sun.
A labor of love throughout the day,
His work is never done.

His door is always open
For the visitors passing by.
He likes to have a little discussion.
He is never too busy to hear the heart's cry.

Sometimes a vessel that is in despair,
He picks it up ever so gently
And handles it with loving care.
It is always treated reverently.

The sign on the door says "Come,"
A good invitation for one and all.
To come into His presence, you are welcome!
Can you hear the Master's call?

He never turns a repentant sinner away.
No condemnation is given.
He works in His own kind of way.
A vessel of life is forgiven.

He will create a masterpiece
No matter how long it takes.
Soon a vessel of peace—
It will take its place.

His hand is always firm.
Sometimes a flaw will appear.
But if it is a life to transform,
He will shape the clay until the blemish disappears.

A life that is in disarray,
A special touch of the Master's hand,
He listens attentively as you pray.
The vessel of life is shaped at His command.

The Master of the clay,
He awaits your visit.
Maybe you would like to spend the day.
It is a good time to rejoice in the Holy Spirit.

# The Potter and the Clay
## May 27

The potter and the clay
He works with his hands.
Many long hours throughout the day,
You may not quite understand

Why the artist works so hard.
The clay he will mold and shape.
The beautiful transformation comes from the heart.
Sometimes the model needs to be reshaped.

The master potter will start all over.
He knows what he wants to create,
Even if the model needs a complete makeover.
To shape the clay he will not hesitate.

He knows his work is not in vain.
He can see the finished project.
A work of art was formed in his mind.
It will prove to be a beautiful object.

So it is in the lives of man—
There are many imperfections,
But it is only by a touch of the Master's hand
We can feel a divine transformation.

As the master potter molds and shapes the clay,
God knows what He wants to create.
A life holy and pure, faithful every day,
To be like Jesus, His desire for us is to imitate.

No more a sinner of disgrace,
Each day living by faith in God above,
Saved by His wonderful grace.
A replica was created to live daily with love.

A life is going through the molding process.
The old is replaced with the new.
Only God can mold and shape us by grace.
He knows that we need a lot of love, too.

The potter and the clay,
The work has begun.
God shapes with His hand every day.
The image of Christ in our lives will soon be done.

# Deliverance from the Storm
## May 28

The storm is coming.
Small dark clouds form in the distance.
You still have a little time to give the warning.
To escape the storm there must be complete obedience.

The news has been broadcast in every city and town.
Violent winds are predicted.
The only safe haven is higher ground.
Spread the word so friends and loved ones will be saved.

As time passes, dark storm clouds hover above.
There is the sound of rolling thunder.
No time to waste; now is the time to move.
Soon the small stream will turn into a raging river.

The lightning flashes across the sky,
Strong winds howl through the desolate valleys.
Death is in the shadows; many people will die.
Torrents of rain fall upon the earth, steadily!

Oh, for a way of escape from the turbulent storm.
Is there any hope to rescue the perishing?
Cries of mercy are heard from the impending doom.
There is no remorse in the flashes of lightning.

Oh for a hand to help in time of need,
Rising waters and the torrents of a flood,
There is one who hears the heart's plea.
In the storms of life, you can call on God.

No matter how severe the storm,
God can calm the waters of a troubled heart.
Only believe peace and tranquility will come.
The waves of a restless soul will depart.

He will never turn away
From a distress call.
Just take the time to pray.
Even before the raindrops fall

Or the troubled waters rise,
Pleas for help are heard from a higher power.
Cries for mercy He never denies.
Deliverance will come in your soul-searching hour.

# Grace Not Yet Found
## May 29

God reached way down.
A sinner was perishing.
Grace was not yet found.
He was sinking deeper in sin.

Many years have gone by.
The days of his youth are in the past.
It is time for him to say good-bye.
These final words will be his last.

He lived in a lonely valley
With a spiritual vacancy in his heart.
At times it was a very dark alley.
No fellowship with God, they were far apart.

Many opportunities to make things right,
The call to repentance he rejected
Now he is in the dark shadows of the night.
His salvation was neglected.

Death comes knocking at the door.
God is reaching down His hand
Please don't refuse it as before
And be denied the Promised Land.

A sinner is very close to the end of his journey.
Multiplied thousands of sins abound.
Still no hope of eternity
And God's grace is yet to be found.

The man whispers, "I am sorry."
The time has come for him to die.
Death loses its grip as he opens his eyes in glory.
His pleas for mercy, God did not deny.

God is reaching down
Into the deep places of the heart.
Sins confessed, grace is found.
Salvation to impart.

A decision was made
In the final hour.
A delay could have been too late.
A soul was saved by God's mighty power.

# Astray from the Fold
## May 30

A shepherd is very watchful of His sheep.
He will let no harm come to them.
All of the sheep are safe; now He can go to sleep.
When morning comes they will follow Him.

They respond to His call.
Gather by the river
And lay down by the waterfall.
They drink from the hand of the Master.

Sometimes a hungry wolf will appear.
The shepherd waves the staff in the air.
See how quickly the wolves disappear.
The good shepherd may even fight a bear.

When the time is right,
The sheep move into another field.
To follow the shepherd is their delight.
If a lamb strays, goes too far, it may be killed.

Too far from the fold can be a costly mistake.
As we follow the good shepherd,
Danger lurks just beyond the gate.
Satan runs with fear when the Savior's voice is heard.

We are the people of God's love.
Let us follow Jesus,
Commit our lives to the Lord above,
And be faithful in His service.

A lamb that strays,
Falls victim to the prey.
Our lives are pretty much the same if we go astray,
The enemy comes by if we fail to pray.

The shepherd of our souls is watching.
He will hear the faintest cry.
A soul in distress will bring the Lord running.
See how important it is for Jesus to stand by.

The sheep rest peacefully in the pasture,
Safe in the arms of His love.
The wolves of sin will try to capture,
But the barricade of our heart is from above.

# God is Faithful and Just
## May 31

God is worthy to be praised.
Worship Him in the sanctuary.
Holy hands should be raised.
Join the angel band and sing: "holy, holy, holy."

He is the Lord God almighty,
Which was, and is, and is to come.
Give Him the honor and the glory.
Let the hallelujahs ascend to the throne room.

Love Him with heart, soul, and mind,
He is a kind and gracious Father.
God holds the world in His hands all the time.
He can be found at the altar.

Every day He gives a special blessing
It comes from the throne room above.
He forgives a multitude of sin.
He fills each seeking heart with love.

Peace and joy in abundance,
His love touches hearts across the land.
People come to Him in repentance.
It is a blessing indeed to be touched by His hand.

God is great.
We can all agree
He will not tolerate being late.
A pardon is offered if we come on bended knee.

He is a God who will forgive
His grace is for every sinner.
A new life in Christ, He will give.
He guides the steps of a beginner.

No steps will be taken
Until the work of grace has begun.
His desire is for all sins to be forsaken
And for us to follow daily His beloved Son.

God is faithful and just
To forgive us our sins.
Heaven will be our home if in Him we trust.
At the cross is where life begins.

# The Shepherd of the Sheep
## June 1

The shepherd of the sheep
He protects from harm.
Each one, a promise to keep,
Baby lambs held in His arms.

If a lamb goes astray,
Separate from the fold,
The shepherd will search all day,
Even in the bitter cold.

A lamb may hide
Near the briar patch,
Along the mountainside.
Certainly it would be hard to catch.

The shepherd calls the lamb
With a voice loud and clear.
The little lamb responds to his name
And it comes running, just to be near.

A small lamb is alone,
Now safe in the shepherd's arms,
Soon to be in the fields of home,
Where there is no alarm.

Our Savior has made a promise
Our souls to keep,
Even in danger to give us peace.
He is the shepherd of the sheep.

Please don't try to run
Or find a place to hide.
Backsliders it is time to return.
Stay close to the Savior's side.

He calls us by name.
We can stay in the briars of sin
Or like the little lamb
Sheltered in the arms therein.

No longer to walk the dark. desolate hills,
He is leading us to a place.
His guiding hand we can feel.
Heaven is waiting for those saved by grace.

# Jehovah
## June 2

What is His name?
The God of all creation
Let the whole world proclaim
With love and adoration.

The God of all glory,
Love and worship Him,
Tell the gospel story,
Sing a new hymn.

His children call upon Him daily.
They worship Him twenty-four seven.
The words are spoken very reverently.
"Our Father which art in heaven" (Matthew 6:9).

There is deep reverence here.
When Jesus knelt that day,
"My Father," the words are clear.
Jesus taught us how to pray.

My Father and my God.
Now these words draw us into the fellowship.
Our relationship is by blood.
God requires us to worship.

Well, I would like to know,
Who is the God of the planet?
He is the river of life that ever flows.
God is a spirit.

He is the Father of many children.
He loves with an everlasting love.
He sits upon the throne of heaven.
Showers of His mercy come down from above.

Sometimes we call Him our heavenly Father.
As children adopted into His family,
We worship Him at the holy altar.
He is the Lord God almighty!

God is a Supreme Being.
Let all the earth proclaim,
With the angels worship and sing.
Jehovah is His name!

# A Fresh Refilling
## June 3

A blessing to bestow
From the great warehouse above,
For God's children down below,
His Son came to reveal His love.

Many waiting vessels to fill,
A measure of grace for each one;
Souls who are thirsty to do His will.
They will stand before the throne.

God's wonderful blessings come down.
Soon the cup overflows.
Grace and mercy always abound
When you acknowledge that Jesus Christ arose.

God gives and He keeps on giving,
As a Father so loving and kind.
He has a special blessing every morning.
It was prepared in glory divine.

God pours out a spiritual refreshing
That the earth cannot contain.
Life is given to a sinner confessing.
The hope of glory is in Jesus' name.

Our spiritual vessel, God will fill up.
He will use a life in service.
If we will only hold up the cup,
God gives an abundance of grace.

The blessing will become stale.
Unless we empty the container.
We have good news to tell.
Jesus died for the sinner.

Return unto the Lord;
Bring an empty vessel early in the morning.
Receive inspiration from His Word.
Open the heart to receive a blessing.

Take the time to pray.
Use all the blessings given.
A Holy Ghost anointing will come each day.
Yield to Him, a fresh refilling is coming.

# Faith is the Key
## June 4

Many years ago I met the man of Galilee.
I was just a young man twenty-one years old.
I didn't have to travel to a faraway country.
My pockets were empty of silver and gold.

Just imagine, no valuable riches to pay,
Surely it would cost a lot for my freedom.
Sin and corruption was the host for the day.
Without any money, how could I enter the kingdom?

Security at the kingdom was really tight.
No one was allowed without the proper credentials.
So try as I might,
All I received was rejections and denials.

All the earthly riches could not open the gate.
Even a good life would be in vain.
Many unrepentant sinners have met their fate.
They thought heaven could be entered by worldly gain.

Then I heard about Jesus.
My friends told me He paid the price.
He died on an old rugged cross to save us.
He gave the supreme sacrifice.

For you and me He bled.
He died in our place.
Our debt has been paid.
We are saved by grace.

On the cross His blood was spilled.
Jesus gave His life so we could live.
God's salvation plan was revealed.
The plea of sinners is for Him to forgive.

Believe He died,
Sins can be forgiven.
On the cross He was crucified.
I am glad I know He has risen.

"Lord Jesus, forgive me, I pray."
Faith is the key that unlocks the gates of heaven.
Time to depart could be any day.
"Look, the pearly white gates are open!"

# God Opens the Door
## June 5

When God opens a door,
He sends down a blessing.
Not just one, there will be many more.
He gives a sweet Holy Ghost refreshing.

A door opened by man
Could be closed in a hurry.
A change of heart the door will slam.
A door opened by God, no need to worry.

Just go at His command.
Yield to the Holy Spirit,
Take hold of the Savior's hand.
God opens the door, please don't close or ignore it.

It may be hard to understand the reason
Why God would have you to pass through.
The high calling of God, He has a special mission
And sometimes this blessing is just for you.

An open door has many possibilities.
So don't linger behind.
A delay could be lost opportunities.
Follow Him whole heartily with a made up mind.

God is pleased when you obey.
Be a faithful servant.
Respond to His command without delay.
When obedience is observed, victory is eminent.

The door is open.
Don't look back, just walk right on through.
When God looks down from heaven
Will He find a servant, faithful and true,

Or unfaithfull and still standing at the door?
Sadness comes if you are disobedient to His will.
A door closed, fret not, God will open many more.
Despair turned into joy as He has a new plan to reveal.

When God opens the door; never close it.
Help someone along the way.
Walk with the Lord and be led by the Spirit.
Be a faithful servant; take the time to pray.

# The Prayer of Faith
## June 6

Many prayers ascend to the heavenly Father,
He hears voices of praise and devotion.
Begin the day with prayer.
The wheels of faith are set in motion.

On bended knee the people cry.
Worshippers of God are in every state.
Deep spiritual thoughts on angel wings fly;
Angels in white they open heaven's gate.

Before the throne room of mercy
God's people gather around.
In the presence of the Almighty
Guidance for the day is found.

Now, angels carrying a message,
It is a wonderful thought, yes indeed.
But you are taught down through the ages.
Jesus Christ himself is the one who will intercede.

On your behalf He stands
And He submits all of your petitions.
He is a mediator between God and man.
Holy and divine is the intercession.

In the presence of a kind and loving God:
He gives a spiritual touch for the day.
Someone cries for mercy and pleads the blood.
He sends down a blessing without delay.

God is on the throne.
Perhaps you can remember the place
Where you first met His Son?
A life was changed by His marvelous grace!"

All across this land on bended knee
Sincere heartfelt words are spoken.
His heart is receptive to every plea.
He responds immediately to the heartbroken.

The prayer of faith is not seen.
Many longing hearts receive
From God's boundless love; His blessings descend
On those who believe.

# He Calls Me, Friend
## June 7

He calls me, friend.
Joyful words to hear,
Love and mercy ascend.
Jesus is always near.

He is closer than a brother.
I have fellowship with Him.
Each day I am brought closer to my Father.
Grace in the heart, I will rejoice with a new hymn.

Words of praise arise
Because Jesus is my friend.
He's not a make believe or in disguise.
His love is real, no need to pretend.

Call upon Him day or night
I know He is always there.
He greets me in the morning light.
Thou my burdens are heavy to bear.

With Jesus the weight I share.
He carries the heaviest part of the load.
Love for Him is to always care.
He is a friend who gave His own blood.

He always stands by my side.
Grace and mercy to impart,
His commitment is to forever abide
And never to depart.

Fellowship with Him is a wonderful blessing.
Listen very closely,
Jesus refers to me as a friend!
He didn't call me His enemy

Nor did He specifically call my name.
But for sinners of disgrace,
His love and mercy is the same.
We are His friends by God's grace.

He calls me, friend!
Glory to God in the highest.
It's not very hard to apprehend.
Jesus is the Christ!

# Be Of Good Cheer, It Is I
## June 8

"Be of good cheer; it is I" (Matthew 14:27).
It is a special visit indeed.
If you were visited by the prophet Jeremiah,
Don't be surprised if he begins to weep.

Or maybe Abraham,
One of God's faithful children,
God said He would provide a lamb.
Truly Abraham must be your friend.

But wait; there comes Moses.
He led the people out of Egypt.
They crossed the Red Sea.
Perhaps he will read his transcript.

The Disciples of Christ,
They came to be with you.
Surely your life must be blessed
To be visited by the faithful and true!

But listen very closely:
"Be of good cheer; it is I."
The one who gives salvation so freely,
He has promised eternal life.

It is I; be of good cheer.
Jesus Christ himself, He came from glory
To stand by your side; He's always near.
What a wonderful way to end this story.

Jesus will never leave you.
He will go with you all the way.
On the mountain or in the valley, too.
He is with you every day.

Faithful men were chosen by my imagination
To come and visit before you die.
The truth in a real life situation,
Jesus said, "Be of good cheer; it is I."

Disciples, apostles, and prophets, they all came.
But there was only one you wanted to see.
When Jesus spoke you rejoiced in His name.
He came because you believe.

# A Walk with the Lord
## June 9

A walk with the Lord,
At the beginning of the day.
The sun is shining.
His love is revealed in a bright and glorious way.

Radiant beams from above,
No dark clouds in the sky.
The earth is filled with His love.
The Lord of glory walks by.

Take a walk with a friend; Jesus is near.
Go down memory lane.
He will most certainly appear.
He is just waiting to hear His name.

Think about the blessings,
They come down from Heaven's throne.
From a heart rejoicing,
Be thankful for God's Son.

Walk with Jesus all the way.
He will be your best friend
Even if He was turned away.
Fellowship restored at the grasp of His hand.

He will never leave
Or walk away,
He is faithful to forgive.
Jesus is the only way.

Walk by His side.
Don't forget to pray.
The presence of the Lord abides
He will not turn away.

The disciples talked about Him.
They knew Jesus was in their midst.
He came down to bless them.
They were in the presence of Christ.

Walk with the Lord all of your life through.
If you talk with a friend,
Don't be surprised if Jesus is there too.
His love will not waver; He is always forgiving.

# A Daily Walk with the Lord
## June 10

A walk with a friend begins early in the morning.
Surely this is a good way to begin the day.
Jesus appears as we are walking.
God will join with us as we pray.

He listens intently to the words we say.
Sometimes there is a word of encouragement
Or He speaks softly and gently, "let's go this way."
The path of His choice will be sufficient.

Every day is different; no two days are the same.
We often need guidance from heaven.
Direction in life always comes in Jesus' name.
The best path to follow is the one of the forgiven.

This is a good day for a walk with the Lord.
Leave all worldly cares and troubles behind.
There is no need to carry a heavy load.
Just rely on Jesus all the time.

There are many people who love to walk.
A friend meets with them along the way.
It is only natural for them to talk.
They are blessed as Jesus walks with them every day.

A daily walk is a time of refreshing.
Jesus comes down to walk with us.
A soul is revived with a heavenly blessing.
He gives grace for the entire distance.

He will not leave us for a little while
And then come back in a day or two.
Jesus is a friend even in that last long mile.
He will carry us if He has too.

Most of the time a walk is planned.
We know the day, hour, and even the minute.
However, a special visit may be unexplained
And we will be touched by the Holy Spirit.

Jesus is here; He is always on time.
He gives us an encouraging word,
Love God with heart, soul, and mind.
Well, it's time to take a daily walk with the Lord.

# When the Path is Hard to See
## June 11

Directions for the day,
We will find them in the holy pages.
Divine guidance will come when we pray.
The readers delight is the rock of ages.

The pages are worn,
Like footprints in the sand.
The tracks are filled in as the wind is blown.
A faded path is hard to see; keep holding His hand.

The Master of the storm,
The words may fade and footprints vanish.
When He speaks there is a deep spiritual calm.
It is not God's will that any should perish.

Sometimes the word is forgotten.
As the years go by, the memory is not the same.
Jesus said He would go with us to the end.
If our strength begins to fail, remember Jesus' name.

He will prevent a fall.
His promise is to go all the way.
No matter if we are weak and frail,
The days of our youth are not meant to stay.

Days of our lives, so quickly they are gone.
There has never been a day,
Jesus has left us all alone.
He will not start now; let us pray.

"Our kind and gracious heavenly Father,
Help us today to go on.
We need divine strength a little longer.
We are almost home."

Words will fade
And the pathway will grow dim.
But the decision to live for Christ was made.
We made a commitment to follow Him.

On the windblown sands of time,
The pathway of life is hard to see.
Love Him with heart, soul, and mind.
Jesus is still calling: "Follow me!"

# Greater Is He
## June 12

"Greater is he that is in you" (1John 4:4).
Satan is our enemy;
This is most definitely true.
He is always looking for workers to employ.

He will try
To fight with all of his might.
Even until you die,
Satan wants to claim your birthright.

He would steal the certificate of the born again.
He cannot erase the blood of Jesus Christ.
In every believers heart is the blood stain.
This is a permanent seal of the holy and blessed.

Satan is always trying to drag you down.
He will give a large rock if you are in quicksand.
He does not want you to stand on solid ground.
Faith in Christ, on the solid rock you stand.

When Christ lived on earth
The enemy tried his very best
To defeat God's Son, even by death.
Jesus was laid to rest.

Satan thought the battle was won.
The grave was only a temporary place.
God raised from the dead His Son.
And now the world can see the power of His grace.

So when Satan comes against you
With all of his power and might,
You can know that this is true:
Jesus won the victory in the final fight.

"Greater is he"
who conquered death, the grave, and hell.
He abides in you, Jesus Christ of Galilee.
He defeated Satan on Calvary's hill.

Victorious in battle over sin,
A Christian soldier stands.
The final fight to win,
Just keep holing the nail scarred hands.

# The Savior's Path
## June 13

Be careful you are walking the sinner's path.
Broad is the way that leads to destruction.
A perilous journey without faith
Opens the graves of corruption.

Walk by the cemetery,
The days of peace and joy are gone.
Fellowship with God is only a memory.
Soon your name will be engraved in stone.

You would like to walk on by.
Come back at a more convenient season.
Dark shadows cross your path; it's time to die.
No more days are granted, not even one.

The grave is patiently waiting.
No one will be rejected.
Death comes to claim when the heart stops beating.
All will be accepted.

Go back to the place where two paths divide.
The graveyard has not sent any invitations.
The broad path or the narrow, please decide.
Remember death will come without a notification.

Sinners follow a wide path.
All claims to heaven denied.
This will be a time of God's wrath
Unless the blood is applied.

Salvation by grace is the Savior's path.
Narrow is the way that gives a glorious expectation.
This is a journey traveled by faith.
Christians will rise from the grave in the resurrection.

The grave for them is just a temporary place.
Peace and joy the grave cannot claim.
A home in heaven awaits those saved by grace.
The graves will open in Jesus' name.

If the time comes to die,
A cemetery on a hill awaits your arrival
And you will meet Jesus in the sky
Your time with Him will be eternal.

# A Gentle Shower from Above
## June 14

From a clear blue sky, the rain came.
I am aware you may not believe it.
As I called the Lords name,
I felt the sweet, sweet Spirit.

I know the sun was shining.
Not a cloud to be found,
But it was raining.
I was standing on holy ground.

With my hands raised
Toward heavens throne,
From a heart of praise,
I gave honor to God's Son.

He sent the rain,
A gentle shower refreshing,
His mercy to sustain.
I received a deep spiritual blessing.

When I called His name,
I was overshadowed with His love.
The rain came.
I felt the sweet presence of the Lord.

From a dry and thirsty land,
A sincere heart confessing,
To be touched by the Master's hand,
Truly that is a wonderful blessing.

To come into the presence of the Most High,
Rejoice in the love and mercy.
He will send the rain, even in a cloudless sky.
A sinner saved by grace cries glory.

It is beginning to rain.
A gentle shower comes from above.
A sweet Holy Ghost refreshing
Fills each heart with an abundance of love.

Rejoice in the Holy Spirit.
He comes down to bless the sincere.
This is a good day for a visit.
God, Jesus, and the Holy Ghost are here.

# A Personal Visit
## June 15

Now I can't talk long.
I have a very special friend to greet.
But if you would like to come along,
My friend I would like for you to meet.

You are most certainly welcome.
I'm sure you will find
It is a great pleasure to have Him in your home.
He is loving and kind.

He is making a personal visit
To talk over some eternal concerns.
He has quite a list,
But it all has to be confirmed.

I also have my petitions.
He will go over each one.
The approval and final completion
Will be accomplished by God's Son.

The Lord is coming.
I hope you decide;
With all of His wonderful blessings,
Please invite Him to come inside.

Here He comes now!
Oh, the glory of His presence,
The love of God to know.
In this holy place, God is present.

Upon this sacred land,
Jesus brings a special blessing
See the nail print in His hands?
They are the marks of pain and suffering.

Jesus Christ, my Lord and Savior,
He is the King of Kings.
Please open the hearts door.
The gift of forgiveness He brings.

He has come into this place.
He is a very special friend to greet.
To offer an abundance of grace,
My friend I want you to meet.

# Rejoice in the Holy Spirit
## June 16

Jesus came by today.
I felt a sweet, sweet spirit.
God blessed me in His own way.
A gentle touch from heaven, I could feel it.

He met me in prayer.
When I opened the window of my heart,
He was there.
Grace was His to impart.

Just one touch of His hand
My soul was revived in spirit.
Fellowship with Him was grand.
I am so glad He came by for a visit.

A day spent with Him is divine.
We have a special meeting place.
He is welcome any time.
I thank Him for His grace.

Jesus came down to be with me.
He left the throne room above.
Come into my heart was my plea.
Now I know of His great love.

The window of my heart was open.
The Savior, I could see.
I know my sins are forgiven.
Thank you Jesus for setting me free.

Many years ago with many sins to bear,
As a sinner, I walked down the aisle.
At the altar, I met Jesus there.
He stayed with me for a while.

Peace was made with God that day.
I really started living.
When I knelt to pray,
God recorded my name in heaven.

Now I rejoice every day in the Spirit.
Thankful for all the blessings,
I look forward to each visit.
Well it is time for another meeting.

# He Walked Among Us
## June 17

I talked with a friend today.
"Did not our hearts burn within?"(Luke 24:32).
The Lord met us along the way.
My friend and I talked about heaven.

He mentioned his family.
A couple members had died.
He wanted to see them in eternity.
We also spoke of our Lord who was crucified.

We both agreed
We wanted to see Jesus.
In our hearts we knew who set us free.
Today He came down to walk among us.

He gave us a deep longing,
Our loved ones to be with them.
Soon we would be leaving,
For now we have sweet fellowship with Him.

Oh, what a blessing
To be in the presence of God.
The scriptures were open.
Our hearts were receptive to the Word.

Jesus is in the midst.
Where two or three or gathered together,
Souls are blessed.
He gives us the hope of living forever.

To know that He is coming again,
The trumpet will sound.
Let the family reunion begin.
Saints will be heavenward bound.

"In a moment,
In the twinkling of an eye,"(1 Cor. 15:52),
There will be redeployment
When the Lord comes in the sky.

Until He comes,
Whatever the day or hour,
Watch and pray; we are going home.
Saints of God will rise by the resurrection power.

# Touch the Lord
## June 18

Touch the Lord.
A blessing is on the way.
Be receptive to the Word.
A miracle may come today.

Reach out and touch the hem
Wait patiently for the blessing.
All miracles come from Him.
Faith claims the healing.

'Call unto me, and I will answer you."
Whatever God said,
He has the power to do.
A sick man rises from his bed.

God receives the glory.
Just a touch of the Master's hand,
The deaf hear, and the blind see.
The lame can walk at his command.

Reach out and touch the Lord today.
With many requests to plead,
Take the time to pray.
To the heavenly Father, He will intercede.

A spiritual blessing is on the way
A miracle is in the making.
The answer to prayer comes without delay.
There is no hesitation in His giving.

Touch the Lord now, a blessing He will impart.
A gentle spirit comes down.
He gives out of the abundance of His heart.
Grace and mercy always abound.

Take the time to pray,
God will heal.
A special blessing is coming your way.
The power of God and the glory He will reveal.

Reach out and touch the hem.
Jesus is walking by.
A touch from heaven, thank Him!
The prayer of faith God will not deny.

# Our Heavenly Father
## June 19

The morning hour has come.
This is a day of sweet communion.
A special meeting place is the home.
God will listen to the prayer petition.

A blessing He will bestow.
No one noticed at first,
But God was opening the window.
He was pleased at the mention of Christ.

Fellowship with God has begun.
Those in is His family call Him Father.
Intercession is made by His Son.
The love grows stronger at the family altar.

He gathers the family together
And holds them with a loving embrace.
His heart is receptive to every prayer.
Thank Him now for His grace.

Our heavenly Father,
The words echo throughout the land.
The blessing is to be in His favor
And touched by His hand.

Let the emotions of the heart flow freely.
Worship Him with a heart of praise.
He will bless abundantly.
Worship Him with holy hands to raise.

Give Him praise, glory, and honor,
All of heaven will come down.
Rejoice, Jesus is the Savior.
Sins are forgiven; the grace of God does abound.

Pray in the spirit.
God is listening.
Open the door for a divine visit.
Soon the gates of heaven will open.

God is opening the window.
He hears and answers prayer.
With the head bowed low,
Let us pray; "Our heavenly Father."

# Walking With the King
## June 20

I'm walking with the King,
The highway to glory,
Heaven is waiting.
There is more to this wonderful story.

Yes, He walks with me.
All along life's way,
Everyday His love and mercy
Unite together to create a glorious day.

The sun is always shining,
Even in the worst storm,
Many wonderful blessings
As Jesus leads me to my new home.

Oh, let me tell you more.
As I walk the King's highway
In the presence of the Lord,
Someday I will be called away.

I know it won't be long.
Just a few more miles
To see the lights of home.
I can wait a little while.

Maybe around the next bend
Or across the crystal sea,
The angels of God descend.
I know they are coming for me.

I do not know the day or hour
When Jesus is coming.
I will leave this earth by resurrection power.
With the Savior I am walking.

Blessed peace is mine
As Jesus walks by my side.
It is only a matter of time.
The gate to the kingdom will open wide.

I'm walking with the King.
But, for this wonderful story,
This is not the end.
Soon I will be at home in glory.

# Rescue from the Flames
## June 21

It is that time of year
To gather all the crops in.
Get out the harness gear.
Place the corn in the bin.

Two young mules to train,
Never before worked together,
Side by side to reap the sugarcane,
There is wheat in the field to gather.

The work is finally done.
All the hay is in the barn.
It's time to go home.
A nights rest is needed at the farm.

But during the night,
When all seems to be peaceful and quiet,
Disaster strikes!
A spark then a flame ignites in the morning light.

The barn is on fire.
Two mules on the inside,
Smoke fills the air.
The door swings wide.

The animals will die
If they stay in the barn.
The farmer covers their eyes
And leads them out without harm.

The neighbors gather around.
The fire is brought under control.
All the animals safe and sound,
Safe on the outside is a young foal.

Now these are just imaginary thoughts.
A rescue from the flames,
Of a fire that was severely fought,
But what if a fire really came?

Jesus came to save us from the flames.
He will deliver from the torment.
Salvation to claim,
To escape the fire, we must repent.

# Come and Dine
## June 22

After that Jesus had risen,
He appeared to His disciples the third time.
A special invitation for the chosen:
"Come and dine" (John 21:12).

Jesus stands on the shore.
The disciples went fishing.
Just as before,
An empty net they were dragging.

They worked all night,
Nothing to show for their labor.
But Jesus was in sight.
Soon they would have breakfast with the Savior.

No fish were caught, not even one.
But a stranger on land,
A visit by God's Son,
The disciples obeyed His command.

"Cast the net on the right side" (John 21:6).
Before Jesus spoke, no fish on board,
All night they tried.
Soon one hundred and fifty-three fish lay on the floor.

Early in the morning
The boat was full.
A vessel overflowing,
Now there were too many fish to pull.

Fish in abundance,
Blessings untold.
Blessed assurance,
Jesus is Lord.

The Lord had prepared a fire;
He was waiting on shore.
His disciples would soon be there.
Faith in Him would be restored.

When you wake up in the morning,
The Lord has a wonderful invitation.
"Come and dine."
Experience the joy of salvation.

# Come Unto Me
## June 23

The words Jesus spoke,
Written with many infallible pages.
They are filled with hope
For the eternal ages.

"Come unto me" (Matthew 11:28).
When a prisoner of sin,
The captive is set free.
Let a new life begin.

"Come unto me."
When the heart is heavy laden,
The Lord responds to each plea.
Let Him carry life's burden.

"Come unto me."
When in the valley of despair,
The hope of heaven is with Him to be.
Saints will meet Him in the air.

"Come unto me."
When upon the mountain of grief,
Just to know the Lord is with thee.
He faithfully honors the Christian's belief.

"Come unto me."
When the path of life is too steep,
Victory is promised to those who believe.
He has the power to keep.

"Come unto me."
When in the battle of life,
He will conquer the enemy.
Let Him remove all strife.

"Come unto me."
When the world passes by,
He will give love and mercy.
Peace with God is for Him to abide.

"Come unto me."
When the Holy Spirit is drawing,
He loves to hear the words: "I am sorry."
Grace is freely given.

# Come and Go with Me
## June 24

Come and go with me
Through the storms of life.
Let us follow the man of Galilee.
He will shelter us from all harm and strife.

When the rain clouds hover,
Lightning flashes in the sky.
Dark clouds cover.
Peace with God abides.

Troubles on every side,
Many friends have forsaken.
But the Lord, He abides.
A strong hand is not mistaken.

He said He would never leave,
That He would go with us all the way.
If a storm we face, only believe!
Deliverance may come today.

Walk with me through the storm,
Eternal life to claim,
A life He will transform.
There is peace in Jesus' name.

Come and go with me.
Let us walk with the Savior,
The kingdom of God to see.
Jesus will never leave, not ever.

The Lord bids us to come.
A few more weary days, and then
We will see the lights of home.
Enter into the glories of heaven.

Lay the old cross down.
The storm is past.
The crown of righteousness is won.
We are home at last.

Come and go with me
To a sweet dwelling place bright and fair,
In the kingdom of heaven, we will forever be.
Oh what rejoicing when we meet Jesus in the air.

# Trust in the Lord
## June 25

My most valuable possession
I would not keep in a bank vault
Or on the mountains of Mount Zion,
Nor would I go to the president to consult.

I don't know if he would reply
And send out the national guard,
But the value is way too high
Even in Fort Knox to be stored.

I carry it with me every day.
It is kept safe and secure.
Many people I pass along the way.
They know the value of a soul; it must endure.

My God is able to keep
That which I have committed to Him.
His will for my life is mine to seek
And my desire is to praise with a new hymn.

Trust in the Lord.
He has a strong grip to hold.
Inspiration comes from His Word.
Faith in Him is better than silver or gold.

My most prized possession—
Yes, that is my soul.
I came to Jesus with my confession,
And now salvation I know.

So my most valuable treasure—
It is the heart of my love.
God is able to keep it I'm sure!
Let His love come down from above.

Trust in the Lord,
I will follow Jesus all the way.
Victory will come on the narrow road.
His grace is sufficient every day.

Hold fast, obey His commands.
If in doubt for a moment,
Behold the nail scarred hands.
Undefeated in battle, He arose triumphant.

# Follow Jesus
## June 26

Where He leads I will follow.
If it's up the mountain side
Or in the valley low,
Jesus is my guide.

He watches over me,
Even in the morning light.
I know He will lead.
He is with me in the darkest night.

He knows the way.
It's always onward!
He encourages me to watch and pray.
Jesus is my Shepherd.

Sometimes the path is dark and drear
And I feel alone.
Directions from God begin to appear.
He is pleased when I follow His Son.

If I turn and run,
Disobedient to the Word,
Unfaithful to God's Son,
I will miss heaven's reward.

Jesus is the only way.
There is no salvation in any other.
His command is to watch and pray
And to love one another.

Sometimes I stumble and fall,
But Jesus is always there.
I remember the three nails
And the cross He had to bear,

The crown of thorns He wore,
A grave that was conquered,
The stone that was rolled from the door.
From the dead He was resurrected.

Follow Jesus, Faithful all the way.
If the way of life is forsaken,
There may not be enough time to find a stray.
Be steadfast, unmovable, Heaven's gate will open.

# The Trinity as One
## June 27

A visitor from heaven came for a visit.
Jesus came by today,
Also God the Father and the Holy Spirit.
Truly it was a blessing for them to stay.

Jesus drew near
When He heard His name in prayer.
He did not hesitate to appear.
He will come no matter the day or hour.

Early in the morning,
With holy hands to raise,
Come before Him rejoicing,
A joyful heart will praise.

He will come in the late hours of the night.
When the door of the heart is open,
A visit from heaven is His delight.
His merciful kindness is everlasting.

There is a sweet, sweet Spirit in this place.
The gentleness is from God above
And there is an abundance of grace.
Jesus blesses this encounter with love.

One touch of the nail scarred hand
Will bring tears to the eyes.
He gives strength to stand.
A soul triumphant will arise.

As a gentle wind blowing,
The Holy Spirit refreshes the inner man.
The work of God is restoring
A life yielded to His command.

Jesus is coming without delay.
Please make Him welcome.
He may want to come back another day
Soon He will open the gate to the kingdom.

The trinity as one,
He came by for a visit.
God came with His Son.
Fellowship was complete with the Holy Spirit.

# Come On In
## June 28

The overland express—
No ticket required.
Not even a home address,
But entrance is acquired.

According to our hearts desire
To enter heavens pearly gates,
To meet the Lord in the air,
Sins we must forsake.

In order to go to heaven,
To have fellowship with God,
All sins can be forgiven.
Oh, how precious is the blood.

Admission will be granted.
If Christ has been accepted;
The huge wall of sin dismantled,
The ways of the world rejected.

Now some people may try to sneak in
Or climb up some other way.
They keep holding on to sin.
From Christ they walk away.

Without Jesus in the heart,
There will be a rejection.
The unbelievers will depart.
The faithful and true will have a reception.

Jesus gave the invitation.
The call today is the same, "Come!"
Follow Him without reservation.
Soon it will be time to go home.

He died for our sins,
The just for the unjust.
The Lord is coming again.
He will honor our faith and trust.

Heaven is waiting, but one thing is required.
Believe that Jesus died and arose again.
The old certificate of sin is expired.
The gate of heaven is open; come on in!

# The Lord Be with You
## June 29

Greetings, my friend,
With joy and peace—
What a wonderful way to begin.
Start each day with grace.

Joy for the morning
All along life's way,
A happy heart will sing.
A joyful spirit is the sunshine of the day.

Sing a beautiful new hymn.
With words of love to express,
Give praise and worship Him.
Be thankful your life is blessed.

He gives a peace that will remain
In the horrific storm
Or in the torrents of rain.
Peace will come.

Peace, grace, and love,
Truly, it is a good beginning
To be touched by the hand above.
His love and kindness is unending.

The Lord be with you;
This is my prayer.
Keep the faith as you pass through.
All the places you go, Jesus will be there.

As you travel across this land,
With a heavy cross to carry,
Keep holding His hand.
When you are with the man of Calvary

You are never alone.
Where two are bound together,
One is weak; the other is strong.
He is a friend who is closer than a brother.

The Lord be with you.
Begin each day with peace.
He will see you through.
A cross held high will end the day with grace.

# Bind Us Together
## June 30

I once saw an illustration.
Eleven sticks were tightly bound.
Now this may represent the church congregation.
Unity and strength could be found.

Pick up one of the sticks.
Hold it in your hand.
See how easily it breaks.
So is the strength of man.

It is very weak and frail
If there is only one,
But let me go into more detail.
There is strength in God's Son.

Eleven disciples were joined.
Bound together by God's love,
A new strength they found
When they sought the Lord above.

When the congregation is bound
In love and in unity,
There is power and strength all around.
Bound together there is hope of eternity.

One disciple could not stand.
The story I have to tell.
He withdrew from the Master's hand
And to his death he fell.

The disciple who walked away
Was very frail and weak.
He failed to pray,
No power to defeat.

If we try to stand alone
Without the cords of unity,
Without God's Son,
No hope of eternity.

Bind us together.
A strong and mighty cord
In unity and strength forever,
Together we will meet the Lord.

# A Divine Sacrifice
## July 1

Jesus paid the price,
The cost of our salvation.
By a divine sacrifice
He resisted all temptations.

The nails were driven into His hands.
For you and me He died.
I know it is hard to understand
Why the Son of God was crucified.

His precious blood was spilled.
For our sins the debt was paid.
He was buried and the grave sealed.
To rise from the dead, souls would be saved.

Our sins could not be forgiven
Without the shedding of blood.
We cannot go to heaven
Unless the blood is applied; Jesus is our Lord.

A lamb or a calve is not sufficient
To save our souls.
Only the blood of Christ is efficient.
The love of God we will know.

A divine sacrifice,
An offering to the Most-High God,
The blood of Jesus would suffice.
Only He could save the sinners of the world.

If the Son of God set us free,
Then we are free indeed!
Jesus died that He might save you and me.
Forgive them was His hearts plea.

We are bought with a price.
God's Son, oh, but that's too much to give.
Give a lamb for a sacrifice,
Not a man's life.

A divine sacrifice He gave for us.
Jesus on a cross, His life He would give.
Holy, pure, without blemish, oh, so precious,
He died so we could live.

# Final Review
## July 2

A life in review,
Many chapters in the book,
Let us examine just a few.
Briefly, a quick look!

Each page is filled with kindness,
Love and mercy, too.
The past reveals a heart of tenderness.
Good deeds shared, more than a few.

Many wonderful things
Happened along the way.
Lives touched by your caring
And hearts filled with thankfulness every day.

Truly your life has been blessed.
A generous heart is always giving.
Yes, the book is full of good deeds expressed.
Many times forgiveness was given.

Your life seems to be so full,
The pages of life God has read.
He has read them all.
He didn't miss a single word.

Now your life is in review.
God is looking down from heaven.
He knows all about you.
Something seems to be missing.

He reviews the pages again.
The mention of His Son,
Forgiveness of sin,
Days of worship and praise, He found none.

Truly this will be a tragic end.
If the blood is not applied,
The gate to heaven will not open.
There is hope in the crucified.

Suppose a page could be rewritten.
The mention of God's Son in daily living,
By faith in Jesus, sins are forgiven.
Final review: God is pleased with the ending.

# Only by Permission
## July 3

Enjoy the comforts of home,
Sit next to the fire,
The mat in front of the door says welcome.
Yet the door is locked; no one can enter there.

The sign is a friendly gesture.
It is a nice greeting.
Friends and family love to visit, I'm sure!
But they have to wait outside until I let them in.

They will only come in with permission.
If the door remains locked, they will graciously leave.
To turn them away I must have a really good reason.
A welcome sign is a good way to deceive.

Now let's just suppose a good friend of mine,
He comes by your house today.
Patiently He waits; there isn't much time.
It is possible He may come back another day.

The sun sets a little early tonight
And you fail to rise with the morning sun.
A family member opens the shades of light.
It is too late for Jesus to return.

Let's briefly review this story again.
A welcome mat on the floor,
Friends and family are invited in.
Sometimes they leave because of a bolted door.

My friend came by for a visit yesterday.
Later, sadness and sorrow occupied the place.
Mourning and crying was on the schedule for today.
The hope of the family was to sing amazing grace.

Allow me to introduce my friend.
The door of the heart He is knocking.
Please invite Him in!
There is no promise of His returning.

If Jesus comes by today,
Remember He only comes in by admission
That you are a sinner; He will come in when you pray.
Open the door: Jesus only comes in by permission.

# God Bless America
## July 4

One thing about a poem,
We can tell a wonderful story
About our heavenly home
Or the American flag we call Old Glory.

Look at the flag,
Tell me what you see.
Maybe there are thoughts about your dad.
He is fighting for you and me.

In a faraway land,
The battle rages on.
Soldiers fight on the desert sand.
Someday they will come home.

Oh, America, home of the brave,
We plead for thee.
So many lives to save,
Bring our soldiers home is our plea.

If a battle is worth fighting
To set the captive free,
Many soldiers are dying.
The American flag is flying for thee.

Now I don't want to end this story.
It is good to talk about our freedom.
But I need to tell you of God's glory.
The blessed hope is to enter the kingdom.

If a battle is worth fighting
For your sins and mine,
Jesus is on the cross dying.
His love is for all mankind.

There is a pardon for those who believe.
Heaven awaits our arrival.
This freedom is not a temporary reprieve.
Life in Christ is for the eternal.

God bless America, thank Him for our freedom.
Let the flag fly for His glory.
Our desire is to make it home,
Faithful to God and loyal to country.

# What manner of man is this?
## July 5

He gave us mercy as a token
Of his great love.
His heart was broken.
God the Father looks down from above.

Jesus had compassion
For the lost of this world.
He suffered at the cross of humiliation
So He could bring us back to God.

The suffering was unbearable,
Yet he stayed on the cross.
He endured the unimaginable.
The price of redemption—see how much it costs!

He wore a crown
That only love could endure.
A woven wreath of thorns,
They pierced the flesh of the holy and pure.

He felt the shame
From a loving heart,
No one to blame,
Only forgiveness He would impart.

On a cross He hung, soon to be a lifeless form.
He felt the pain as they drove the nails.
His back was beaten; His flesh was torn.
Only by love and grace could He prevail.

"What manner of man is this?"(Matthew 8:27).
Behold the Son of God,
We have just met the Christ,
And we see the power of the blood.

From His wounded side,
A soul-cleansing flood,
Jesus was crucified.
The wrath of man He withstood.

He arose from the grave.
Let us worship and love Him.
Even in pain and suffering, He could say,
"Father, forgive them"(Luke 23:34).

# Who is this man?
## July 6

The gloom of the sepulcher,
Dark clouds cover the sky.
A man is placed on a wooden structure.
Today He will die.

Well, who is this man?
He is the good Shepherd.
Sheep are kept safe by the staff in His hand.
He watches over the herd.

He is the Bridegroom
And He patiently waits for His bride.
He is coming soon.
The gate to heaven will open wide.

He is like a thief
That comes without warning.
He never stole anything in His life.
When He returns, His appearing will be alarming.

He was called a king,
But they wanted to kill Him with stones.
Death on the cross was by crucifying.
His crown was made of sharp thorns.

Would you like to know more?
Well, He was dead.
Now He lives forevermore.
On earth He had no place to lay His head.

He was called the Word.
So, who is this man?
Why, He is the Son of God,
Resurrected by Gods almighty hand.

He is a man with a very big heart.
Jesus is the Christ.
He gives of His love so freely to impart.
All who believe are blessed.

This man of Galilee,
He is my Lord and Savior.
By His merciful kindness I am free.
With Him I will live forever.

# Make the Call
## July 7

Seek and you will find
Peace in the heart,
Sins must be left behind.
A blessing God will impart.

God is not so far away,
That He cannot hear the pleas.
Today is a good time to pray.
It doesn't hurt to say please.

He is not on a vacation.
Call upon Him today.
He will come without hesitation.
There is an urgency to pray.

Please be aware of the time.
Death may come before nightfall.
Get on the prayer line.
He is not too busy to answer the call.

He is waiting.
This time with Him will be personal.
He may even open the gates of heaven.
The prayer of faith leads to the eternal.

Jesus will make intercession.
The cries for mercy will not be denied.
He responds quickly to a confession.
God is receptive to the blood applied.

Make the call.
It is not too late.
Make a commitment to give Him all.
A delay could be a terrible mistake.

Jesus is on the main line.
The search for God will end.
Love Him with heart, soul and mind.
Ask Jesus to forgive all of your sins.

God and man joined together by this connection.
Sins are forgiven.
Hope of the believers is the resurrection.
The gate to the kingdom is open.

# Holiness is the Only Way
## July 8

He was buried in a borrowed grave.
No intentions to stay.
He was resurrected with power to save.
Jesus arose the third day.

He ascended to heaven.
No one knows the day or hour
He will descend.
He is coming back in great power.

Jesus forgives sin.
Just come to Him believing.
The Holy Spirit will descend.
This is really a good time for rejoicing.

This is why He came—
Salvation to impart,
Just believe in His name.
He will honor the cry of a repentant heart.

Sin is a burden
That is really heavy to bear.
In heaven a corruptible life is forbidden,
A sanctified life begins here.

Grow by grace in God's favor.
Sins are washed away.
Walk daily with the Savior.
Holiness is the only way.

Stand before the gate in a robe of white
Sanctified by the blood of the lamb.
God welcomes the pure in heart, it is His delight.
Words of praise ascend to the great "I Am."

Angels gather around.
The book of life is open.
Oh, what rejoicing when your name is found.
Enter into the glories of heaven.

Walk the streets of pure gold.
Sit down with the Master.
Talk with the prophets and disciples of old.
Worship and give praise to God the Father.

# The Fire Escape
## July 9

The building is on fire.
It started from an electrical short.
Sparks flew from a bare wire.
The fire spread through the airport.

The smoke could be seen for miles.
We could hear the sound of the sirens.
A parent tries to save a child.
The firemen would soon be on the scene.

Men, women, and children are trapped inside.
The flames reach higher.
Residents of the community have gathered outside.
They have come to help fight the fire.

A way of escape has been found.
The people climb down the fire escape.
Soon they are safe on solid ground.
They have only minor scrapes.

But some of the individuals go back into the fire.
Their life may be taken.
A short life on earth will expire.
The way of safety and peace is forsaken.

Now this story is not true.
But in reality we can escape the fire.
We need to know what to do.
First of all, we need to go to God in prayer.

"Except ye repent,
Ye shall all likewise perish"(Luke 13:3, 5).
Believe in Jesus, whom God has sent.
He will give a crown of life to cherish.

If we turn from our sins,
Salvation is in Jesus' name.
If we go back in,
How can we escape the flames?

There is only one way, my friend.
Avoid the flames of perdition.
Take hold of the nail scared hand.
The way of escape is by salvation.

# Pardon Me
## July 10

Pardon me!
I am sorry for all the things
I committed against thee.
Forgive me for my transgressions and sins.

All the times I walked away,
No honor to give,
No time to pray,
A dishonorable life is the way I lived.

I am truly sorry for my sins.
The ways of the world,
I invited them to come in.
Hear my hearts plea, oh Lord!

Have mercy on my soul.
Let the blood be applied.
My heart is deeply sorrowful
For the many times Christ was denied.

For my faith to live again,
Peace and joy to abide,
Please, Lord, forgive me of my sins.
My transgressions are like a river, deep and wide.

The Lord will never forsake
A heart that is sincere.
He will transform and remake.
A pleading heart He will hear.

Pardon me for all the wrong,
The shame, and the disgrace,
I have been away too long.
Will you show mercy and give me grace?

The Savior's reply:
"I forgive."
With His blood applied,
I have a new life to live.

The Lord is attentive to the heart's cry.
Yes, He hears the cries for mercy.
A repentant heart He will not deny.
Lord, I am a sinner; please pardon me!

# Saved from Sins
## July 11

A strong and mighty current,
It is a devastating flow.
Souls will perish unless they repent
And the God of heaven they know.

In sins boundless ocean,
Sinners enjoy the pleasures of the day,
No remorse or sorrow for any sin.
Every day they go deeper into the sea of dismay.

No concern for tomorrow,
Enjoyment for the day is unrighteous living.
Soon there will be a grave of sorrow.
The waves of sin are unforgiving.

Many souls are perishing,
Unaware of their perilous journey.
The effects of sin are quite alarming.
Peace won't come until they say, "I'm sorry!"

God is looking down from above.
He would help in a moment's notice.
A sinner is unaware of His love.
Without God a life is void of peace.

Everyday just a normal routine,
Live anyway you want to.
The cares of the world are degrading.
Sin has a captive hold on you.

Jesus came to save.
All sins can be forgiven, yes, all of them.
His life He gave.
But you must believe on Him.

Jesus wants to be your Savior.
Please don't pass Him by another day.
The blessing is God's favor.
Salvation comes when you pray.

The current of sin is strong.
A few words of a repentant heart,
The violent waves of sin are gone.
Peace comes to stay; He will never depart.

# At an Old Time Altar
## July 12

When darkness turned to day
Many years ago,
I met the Lord along the way.
The pathway of life He came to show.

At an old-time altar,
On my knees I knelt.
In the presence of God the Father,
The sweet Holy Spirit I felt.

I asked Jesus to forgive me.
I don't remember all the words.
But I could see Jesus on the cross of Calvary.
They crucified my Lord.

That day the Lord forgave.
I know He was persistent.
My soul He came to save.
But, at times, I was resistant.

So many times to walk away,
He would never let me go too far.
He was drawing me in His own gentle way.
Each day I was a little closer to the altar.

That day I knelt to pray,
The blood of Jesus was applied.
In my heart He came to stay.
I met the one who was crucified.

From the altar I arose.
Alive from the dead,
My sins have been disposed.
For me His blood was shed.

The light shines brighter still.
The Lord has never left me,
And I know He never will.
Each day I thank Him for His mercy.

At an old time altar,
I remember the place
I talked with God the Father.
He saved me by His grace.

# Blind, but Now I See
## July 13

A touch of the Master's hand,
Many miracles to perform,
The healing of a blind man,
His life would be transformed.

He could not see.
His life was in total darkness.
But he met the man from Galilee.
The Lord would bless.

It is a blessed day
When Jesus walks by.
He hears us when we pray.
The Lord touched the blind man's eyes.

It is true!
His eyes were open.
The beauty of the world came into view.
God's creation is a wonderful thing to discern.

A miracle indeed,
From the darkness to the light,
The blind man could plainly see.
Jesus blessed him with the gift of sight.

He received his healing.
All things he could see clearly,
Most of all the love of God revealing.
Now he could see spiritually.

From the dark path of sin,
He no longer has to walk in the darkness.
The light from heaven shines in.
The way before him is the path of righteousness.

Let me tell you, my friend,
Physically you see;
Spiritually blind.
A touch of the Master's hand is what you need.

Just like the blind man,
A miracle for all of us,
A touch of the Masters hand,
I'm sure we will see Jesus.

# The Stain of Sin
## July 14

The wood receives the stain;
It covers the surface.
It penetrates deep into the grain.
The next step is a final coat of glaze.

The project has a beautiful shine.
Place it on display
And admire the natural design.
The stain has a few imperfections, to your dismay.

The woodcraft has to be refinished.
Take it back to the shop
And try to take off the old finish.
You must completely restore the top.

The glaze is removed first.
Sandpaper will take away the stain.
But the stain—that is the worst,
For the wood, it has many veins.

When the labor is finished; the stain is gone.
The new surface is bright and clean.
All of the hard work is finally done,
Even thou the wood had deep stains within.

A stain can be removed with paper and sand.
But to remove it from the heart,
It takes a touch from a divine hand.
Only God can clean each part.

Though the heart, it is blocked with sin.
The blood of Jesus Christ is the only way
To remove and cleanse the stain.
Impurities of an old life will vanish when you pray.

"Thou your sins be as scarlet,
They shall be as white as snow" (Isaiah 1:18).
Invite Jesus to come into your heart.
The stain of sin has to go.

Let Christ take away the old,
The deep stains from within.
The love of God will unfold
When you invite Jesus in.

# Clay Pits of Sin
## July 15

Bottles can be found
In the mud, the mire, and the grime.
Sometimes we have to look all around.
A treasure on a hill is worth the climb.

A collector will search all day.
Once a bottle has been discovered,
He begins the excavating process without delay.
The glass is gradually uncovered.

The laborer works with great care.
He is very careful with his digging.
The hired servant tries to save the glassware.
Many bottles uncovered, only one is worth keeping.

The bottle seems to be worthless.
If I found it, I would just cast it away.
A collector knows its value is priceless.
To reveal its worth, just use a little water spray.

The bottle will be cleaned.
The mud and dirt removed.
They may use chlorine.
Whatever they use, it has to be approved.

The owner will not discard
Or get rid of any of his precious gems.
If need be, he will post an armed guard.
He will secure and protect all of them.

Many collectables are displayed in an exhibit,
From the mud and grime to a more respectable place.
God takes a sinner from where He found it,
From the miry clay to the rock of ages by grace.

God saved us from the miry clay,
Yes, the horrible pits of sin,
The day we knelt to pray.
Jesus precious blood cleansed us within.

Ours sins are washed away.
The dirt, the filth, and all of the pollution,
God watches over us every day.
A soul saved is His prized possession.

# Have Not Seen but Believe
## July 16

"Blessed are they that have not seen,
And yet have believed"(John 20:29).
Those who believe have pardon for their sins,
Salvation is for all who have received.

We never saw Jesus in person,
And we never saw Him heal the blind.
The fact remains He is God's Son.
There is no reason for us to pretend.

The world would keep Him in the grave.
Faith greets Him at the door of the heart.
He is always welcome every day.
If the door of faith is locked, He will depart.

He has set us free.
When we were burdened down with sin,
Although His face we could not see,
He did not hesitate to come in.

Now some people saw the miracles.
They saw Him open blinded eyes.
But their faith was like wooden nickels.
They couldn't buy anything if they tried.

But the Bible says, "Blessed are they
That have not seen, and yet have believed" (John 20:29).
In the realm of faith, we can see;
We don't have to be deceived.

Jesus is who He claims to be.
"Art thou the Christ, Jesus said, I am."(Mark 14:61, KJV).
Faith in Him, He will set us free.
Believe on His name.

Now our faith is far better than gold.
This precious metal can be worn on the wrist.
It can even be sold.
But life is empty without faith in Christ.

Have not seen the Christ,
The Holy Spirit brings conviction.
Jesus is not in the grave with the deceased.
He has risen! Our belief is in the resurrection.

# Forgiveness
## July 17

Forgiveness is the union
Between the heart and the soul.
Pray to God for that reunion.
Peace with God is so wonderful.

If you cannot forgive your brother,
Whom you have seen,
How can you go to your heavenly Father
And expect your heart to be clean?

Go to God in prayer,
He wants to forgive.
The throne room of mercy, He is there.
A special blessing He will give.

It's one thing to ask forgiveness for your sins,
But it's quite another
When caring a burden for a friend;
God is gracious to help each other.

Remember the Christ of Calvary.
Those who crucified Him, He forgave.
No one was excluded from His mercy.
His loving kindness is for all who want to be saved.

From a heart of love,
He prayed to God the Father.
"Forgive them; for they know not what they do" (Luke23:34).
The blessing is to forgive one another.

Forgiveness in the heart,
It is the door to the soul.
Kindness is a good thing to impart.
Souls bound together by love are peaceful.

Peace and joy abide when you forgive.
Remember the death of Jesus.
He died for all, the blessing of life to give.
A forgiving heart is very precious.

Jesus forgave; what about you?
Open up the door of peace.
A sorrowful heart and forgiveness pass through.
Grace always abounds when the burden is released.

# My Confession
## July 18

I am a Christian.
Jesus Christ is my Lord.
My sins have been forgiven;
He guides by His Word.

A born again believer,
The title belongs to me.
Jesus is my Savior.
Every day I am thankful for His mercy.

I was a sinner in disgrace.
At the cross of repentance,
God saved me by His grace.
He granted me my independence.

I am washed in the blood.
A multitude of sins I knew.
His love covered me like a flood.
Now my life is brand new.

The way of the transgressor is hard.
I invited Jesus to come in.
To Him I surrendered my heart.
He forgave me of my sin.

I am a child of the King.
Adopted into the family,
My soul has been redeemed.
I am on my way to glory.

I am an heir.
The inheritance is mine.
Some day to meet Jesus in the air,
I will walk the streets of glory divine.

I am a beneficiary of His love.
His loving arms embrace.
I will meet the Lord above.
One day soon I will look upon His face.

I am filled with the Holy Spirit.
I have a new sanctified life.
Please, Lord, help me to live it.
Deliver me from all trouble and strife.

# The Path Less Traveled
## July 19

A road well-traveled,
Probably not the best choice.
This is the one you selected.
It's not too late to change course.

Where does your path lead?
Many travelers have walked the path of pleasure.
Warning signs were not read.
Live as you please can be a deceitful lure.

No reward at the end,
Live and die, where is the gain?
A grave yard on a hill, my friend,
Even there you will not remain.

Follow the path of corruption,
Yield your life freely to sin.
Hell will be the place of your deception.
No pearly gates to enter in.

So if you live as you please,
You will have your earthly reward.
At the end of your journey, no peace.
Don't you think it's time to accept the Lord?

The pathway of life is clear.
Repent of your sins!
You will find Jesus is near.
Jesus on the cross is where a new life begins.

If you choose the pathway that is less traveled,
You will go to a wonderful place.
The glories of the Lord will be revealed.
Pearly gates will open for those saved by grace.

Broad road of sin, despair and torment,
Narrow way for life everlasting,
But only if you repent,
Then you can go to heaven.

The choice is yours my friend.
Which path will you follow?
Your days on earth are coming to an end.
You are not promised tomorrow.

# It Is Your Choice
## July 20

A sinner's life and a Christian's,
Compare the two.
Let go of all resistance.
You will see what is in view.

Let me tell you about the two sides.
The good and the bad,
It is your choice; you decide.
Which one you would like to have.

"Eat, drink, and be merry" (Luke 12:19).
That's the one you should dread.
If you have to get up early,
You can hardly get out of the bed.

Sing, pray, rejoice,
When you get up early in the morning,
Certainly, this is a good choice.
At the end of the day, you'll still be singing.

Whose side are you on
When the day is over
And you have to go to the great beyond
When it is time to cross the river?

If you choose the merry-go-round of sin,
A decision for Christ, you decide to wait.
The sins of your heart are locked in;
There is no key for heaven's gate.

Entrance to heaven will be denied.
A sinful life is your pleasure.
You chose to live for self instead of the crucified.
In heaven you will not have any treasure.

If you choose the salvation plan,
Accept Jesus Christ as Lord and Savior.
Take hold of the nail scared hand.
God will open heaven's door.

A sinner or a Christian in deaths dark hour,
The decision is up to you.
You had better hurry; Jesus is coming in great power.
Only a little time left, what are you going to do?

# Just a Beggar
## July 21

Just a beggar
Looking for some bread
From heaven's cupboard.
My soul needs to be fed.

I sit down at the table
Just in time for prayer.
Many promises in the Bible,
The Lord always meets me there.

For a poor, hungry man,
He fills up the platter.
A little bread from the Master's hand,
He mixes up the batter.

The bread is fresh.
With many wonderful ingredients,
He brings forth the very best.
He just wants me to repent.

I have a deep-down longing.
A spiritual hunger to imply.
Bread from heaven,
It is the only thing that will satisfy.

The bread of life to rise,
The cup of mercy to fill,
With holy hands to raise,
There must be a complete surrender to His will.

The cup of salvation overflows.
The bread has been leavened.
A wonderful blessing to bestow,
It comes from the throne room of heaven.

A deep longing for Christ
The vessel of life will be filled.
The command is to love God first.
Blessings come to those obedient to His will.

Just a beggar
At the table of the Lord,
He always meets me there.
He supplies a fresh refilling of the Word.

# All Have Sinned
## July 22

He that hath not sinned
Cast the first stone.
Jesus spoke to the men.
They left the woman alone.

It is a blessed day
When a person turns from sin
And walks away.
A new life begins.

Come with me to a place
In the imagination field.
All of the human race
Needs to visit the crucifixion hill.

Jesus is being crucified
For the sins of mankind.
Soon He would die.
It's only a matter of time.

Jesus died for all.
Sinners in disgrace,
He answered heaven's call.
He died in our place.

If anyone here has not sinned,
Then walk away.
Leave the crucifixion scene.
I believe we have to stay!

For sinners, Jesus died.
Yes, that includes you and me.
When His blood is applied,
A repentant heart receives mercy.

All have sinned.
One man died for all.
Oh, how great the love, His arms extend.
Jesus was obedient to do God's will.

On the cross our sins to bear,
I cannot even imagine
The extreme anguish He felt there.
Only with love could He endure the suffering.

# In the Garden of Sin
## July 23

In the garden of sin
Planted many years ago,
A sinner was a long ways from heaven.
Each day there were sinful deeds to sow.

See how the garden grows.
The field is full.
Corruption fills each row.
So are the weeds of sin in the soul.

In the winter
The harvest field grows cold.
In the eyes of a sinner
There is much to be told.

The crop for today,
Gather it in the barn.
Soon it will decay.
But tomorrow there is no concern.

When the harvest is in,
And all the work is done,
At the end of the day what happens then?
It's time to go home.

Your eternal resting place,
But from a garden of sin,
It may be a time of disgrace.
Certainly it will be a place of torment.

In the garden of sin,
The seed of faith is found.
Where a new life begins,
The grace of God abounds.

Soon the garden is full,
Overflowing with His love,
Goodness and mercy in the soul.
Sweet showers come from above.

When your work on earth is done,
At the end of the day what happens then?
It's time to go home.
A place we call heaven.

# One Lost Lamb
## July 24

Astray from the fold,
One little lamb
Out in the cold.
The shepherd calls it by name.

The lamb does not come.
The shepherd leaves the ninety-nine.
Hopefully, he can bring the little lamb home.
It may be caught in the vines.

The good shepherd will search;
He walks the dark hills.
His eyes intently scan the earth.
The cold, wet air he can feel.

The small lamb is defenseless
For a hungry bear or lion.
But the shepherd, his search is endless.
He will not leave the lamb all alone.

Finally the search is over.
The lamb was found next to the cliff.
The shepherd places it upon his shoulder,
Safe and secure, what a relief!

Now the poem I just told,
It foreshadows this story.
Christ is the shepherd of the fold.
He is the Lord of glory.

We are as the sheep of His pasture.
He knows each one by name.
Sometimes there is a departure;
One lamb will leave and the others remain.

A shepherd will search for a lamb gone astray.
A single lamb left the fold.
The Lord will look for the stray.
He will be satisfied when the lamb He holds.

One lost lamb,
The good Shepherd is calling.
Can you hear your name?
Come home; heaven is waiting.

# Empty Seats
## July 25

Get on the glory train.
Ride the eternal express.
We are going to see the King,
But first we must confess

That Jesus Christ is Lord.
For our sins He died.
For the sins of the world
He was crucified.

We must believe
He died and arose again.
Grace is the gift we receive.
Faith in any other is vain.

If the blood has not been applied
To the heart of a sinner,
Entrance to heaven will be denied.
"Depart from me" final words for the pretender.

Not everyone that saith, "Lord, Lord,
Shall enter into the Kingdom of Heaven" (Matthew 7:21).
According to His holy Word,
To enter in we must be forgiven.

The eternal departing station,
God requires us to repent and believe
In the death, the burial, and the resurrection.
Soon a crown of life we will receive.

Long ago empty seats on the glory train,
Salvation was rejected.
But now eternal life is ours to gain.
Jesus Christ is accepted.

Eternal life is ours to claim.
Soon we will depart.
Our seat is reserved in Jesus' name.
Love God with mind, soul, and heart.

The train is about to leave.
No one knows the day or hour.
The gates of heaven will open if we believe
And we will depart this earth with resurrection power.

# The Path of Sin
## July 26

The old path of sin,
Where does it lead?
Tell me before it ends!
There are many footprints indeed.

The grass is laid low.
Many travelers are deceived.
But I want to know—
Where does it lead?

The end of the path,
Is there a bright shining rainbow?
Or maybe God's wrath!
Certainly I would like to know.

Now this old path:
Pleasures of sin abound.
Many sinful lives were lead to their death.
God's grace was not found.

Everyone will die.
We already know,
But if Christ is denied,
Eternal punishment is below.

So don't walk the path of sin.
It is not too late to repent.
Make sure Jesus abides within.
A life in Him is peaceful and content.

Where does the path end?
The final breath is death.
If we are on the path of sin,
We are walking the devil's path.

Turn from this pathway;
It is the path of corruption.
Now is the time to pray.
Jesus will save without hesitation.

Take hold of His hand.
Walk the straight and narrow path.
Cross over into heavens promised land.
We can escape God's wrath.

# Sin Was the King
## July 27

Sin was the king.
He sat upon the throne,
Bear with me as I like to imagine.
Sin and Satan become as one.

He was a wicked tyrant.
I obeyed his commands.
I yielded to him as a servant
And gave my life daily to his demands.

Sin has many followers.
I was one of them.
No concern about tomorrow,
My soul was condemned.

The king pretended to be my friend.
He offered me wages
And smiled with a big grin.
Satan wanted me to be with him in the eternal ages.

I heard of a man named Jesus.
A crown of thorns He wore.
He died to save us.
An old rugged cross He bore.

Down at the altar, the sinful king was dethroned.
Jesus saved me from my sins!
He gave me a new home.
I no longer follow the tyrant king.

A new king sits upon the throne.
He is the Lord of lords and the King of kings.
One day I'm going to that heavenly home
I will worship God reverently as the angel choir sings.

Where sin did abound
When my soul was condemned,
The Grace of God I found.
Jesus set me free when I believed on Him.

Sin was the king.
He sat upon the throne,
Now to Christ I cling.
In the throne room of my heart is God's Son.

# A Wasted Life
## July 28

The harvest is ripe.
The labors are few.
Work while there is light.
The Lord has a work for us to do.

A wasted life can bring ruin
To a harvestless soul.
No time to pray, very little spiritual rain.
The garden will cease to grow.

The earth becomes dry,
No fruit to bear.
A cloudless sky,
There is no moisture in the air.

The crop slowly withers away.
Oh, for the joy of a spring shower,
That it would come without delay.
A refreshing rain is needed in this day and hour.

To revive and restore,
God will send a spiritual rain from above.
Rain from heaven: the soul can always use more
Rain from the fountain of His love.

When the rain comes down,
The crop begins to grow.
Goodness and mercy abound
When we plant a new row.

Confess our sins.
Let the tears of joy flow.
A spiritual refreshing,
The love of God we will know.

A life that was once wasted,
Come and see the harvest field.
When sins are confessed,
Look at the garden now: an abundant yield.

The harvest is ripe.
Go and gather in the grain.
Work from morning till night.
There is an abundance of rain.

# A Blind Beggar
## July 29

A beggar sat by the wayside.
He was hungry and cold.
Many people passed by.
Through my imagination, this story is told.

Now, this young man,
He could not see.
He held a cup with trembling hands.
The multitude heard his plea.

An old coat he wore.
The lining was thin, bare.
His clothes were ragged and tore.
He sat in the bitter cold air.

He held an empty tin cup.
I can hear him begging.
He held the cup up.
He heard no coins a-jingling.

In the late evening,
He sat there all alone.
Truly he was freezing.
No place to call his home.

Today, Jesus is walking by.
Oh, it is a blessed day
When Jesus stands by our side,
When He comes to help us along life's way.

The beggar was blind,
But now he can see.
A touch of the Master's hand,
The Lord set his spirit free.

A blind man begging,
A soul in need of some bread,
He received a greater blessing.
His eyes were opened instead.

From darkness to light,
A miracle was his to see.
The blessing was his sight.
All things are possible, only believe.

# Sin Opens the Gate
## July 30

A lie is a cover,
A little bit of dirt.
When it is uncovered,
There is a whole lot of hurt.

With the lies of sin,
Many weeds may grow.
In a nice beautiful garden,
Gradually it will destroy each row.

It is such a small lie.
Day by day
The flowers begin to die.
Be careful what you say.

A lie will haunt you
All the way to the grave,
Even if the skies are blue
And the clouds are a hazy gray.

A lie will follow.
Sometimes it opens the door
To be found lurking in the shadows.
Only one lie can make many more.

If a lie is covered
In the deep furrows of the earth,
The lie can be uncovered.
Words rightly spoken can reveal the truth.

The way of sin,
It is the devil's path.
Follow it to the end;
You will have to deal with God's wrath.

If the Son of God set you free,
All of your sins are forgiven.
Then you are free indeed.
There is a blessed hope of heaven.

Sin opens the gate
To eternal separation
Truth opens the heart;
It gives a wonderful salvation.

# Let Us Reason Together
## July 31

"Come now, and let us reason together" (Isaiah 1:18).
At the crossroads, which way to take?
The broad road or the straight, one or the other?
I know it is an important decision to make.

If we choose the right one,
We can live with it.
But if it is the wrong,
There could be a whole lot of heat.

Well, let's take a look at the broad path
Many people have decided to follow.
The final result is God's wrath.
The consequences of sin lead to sorrow.

Death, pain, and eternal separation
From a holy, righteous God,
The broad road is one of destruction.
This is the wrong road.

Broad is the way, and wide is the gate.
Many are knocking on the door.
It looks like it is too late!
The dark shadows have already crossed the floor.

Since we are at the crossroads,
There is still a little time.
If we reason together with the Lord,
The right path we will find.

We looked at the broad path of sin.
Now look the other way; we have Jesus to follow.
He will show us the way to heaven.
The path of life is straight and narrow.

He offers guidance from His Word.
The straight-way leads to eternity.
Walk the path with the Lord.
He opens the gate of glory.

Reason together, change of heart and mind,
The path of sin and righteousness divide.
Only one leads to heaven divine.
The time is now to decide.

# Left Town, No Regrets
## August 1

There is a special place,
Sinners gather around.
At the cross souls are saved by grace.
It is time to leave the old town.

Many years has gone.
Remember the days of corruption.
The love of God was not known.
My life was void of salvation.

The ways of the world held fast.
Unrighteousness was a daily routine.
No way to escape the sins of the past.
My heart was not clean.

Condemned to stay,
No hope of leaving
The old town of dismay,
But I was set free by believing.

I left town with no regrets.
Not looking back or planning to return.
Jesus paid my debt.
Freedom came when I made the right turn.

He gave all He could give.
The ransom has been paid in full,
His life, so I could live.
His death for my freedom was extremely painful.

On my knees in prayer,
God heard the pleas of my heart.
He saw that my burden was heavy to bear.
Sins were forgiven with grace to impart.

If sin gives a special invitation,
Good times and pleasure forevermore,
Remember the crucifixion,
The pain and suffering He bore.

Think about the old town
Where a sinner left a life of disgrace,
A new life in Christ was found.
Give thanks to God every day for His grace.

# One Word Assignment
## August 2

We have a very important assignment.
I hope you like to write.
Please don't worry it will only take a moment.
The placement of one word, but it has to be just right.

The word is: Jesus.
The place you choose; well that's up to you.
Your decision will affect all of us.
A mistake will be very costly too.

Now, I will give you a small hint.
Paper is a good material to write on.
Soon the print will fade and you will wonder where it went.
The word was fresh to begin with, now it is gone.

I hope that was enough to get you started.
The word Jesus must have a lasting impression.
Bring your work back to me when it is finished.
The class will know the results of your confession.

It is only one word!
How hard can it be?
Maybe a radio or TV the name will be heard.
The word fades quickly just like the printed page you see.

Well, class has resumed.
I want to see how well you have done.
Let's see some of the places you have named.
The class will decide if it is right or wrong.

This looks like a good place.
Write the name in the sky.
The word quickly turns into a cloudy haze.
Nothing is left to see when jets pass by.

Here is another good thought, I'm sure you will agree.
Write it on the sand.
Well, not much hope there for you or me.
The water from the sea rushes across the land.

There is only one place for a lasting impression.
Write it on the tables of the heart.
Well class, what is your decision?
We agree; Jesus will never depart.

# Jesus Is the Christ
## August 3

Who is this man they call Jesus?
Well, He is the one who took our place.
He died on a cross to save us.
Those who love Him sing amazing grace.

On a cross to hang,
He gave His life to set us free.
He endured the pain.
Salvation is for you and me.

Jesus Christ was crucified
For your sins and mine.
On an old cross He died.
He loved us with heart, soul, and mind.

Oh, how great the love
To stay on the cross at Calvary's hill.
He could have called angels from above.
But that was not God's will.

He hung on a cross
And was placed in a grave.
His love for mankind, see what it cost.
He gave His life, our souls to save.

Who is this man
Whose precious blood was given?
The nails were driven into His hands.
He died so our sins could be forgiven.

No greater love has any man than this.
His life to give,
Heartfelt emotions to express,
The passion of His heart is to forgive.

Now we can sing the old hymn:
"Amazing grace that saved a wretch like me."
Our sins are forgiven because we know Him.
Life eternal is promised; salvation is free.

Jesus is the Christ,
He is the beloved of the Father.
All of humanity is blessed.
He is Master, Lord, and Savior.

# The Lord Is My Salvation
## August 4

The Lord is my light
And He is my salvation.
The souls delight;
It is a wonderful transformation.

From the darkness of sins
To the light of His glory,
The light of His love forever shines.
It shows the way to eternity.

Radiant beams from above
Shine upon me,
Fill my heart with love,
Bless my soul with compassion and mercy.

A glorious light to reveal
The straight and narrow way,
To live according to your will,
Yes, my desire is to follow every day.

From the path of corruption,
My sins He forgave.
Oh, for the joy of salvation,
My God can save.

To as many as the Lord calls,
Whosoever will, let him come unto me.
A message for one and all:
Jesus can set us free.

He is able to save to the uttermost.
A light shines in sins dark valley.
He came to save the lost.
He offers mercy for you and me.

A light for the day
From the pathway of sin,
Turn and walk away.
Eternal life we will win.

Arise, my friend!
The light from heaven shines.
Let the words of praise extend.
The Lord is my salvation.

# Grace Abounds
## August 5

Called to be a servant,
Delivered from a life of sin,
God is pleased with the obedient.
He blesses those who endure to the end.

His holy hand is upon them
As they walk with Jesus every day.
God's love abounds as they follow Him.
No grace is withheld as they pray.

Those with a repentant heart
He has called for service.
The faithful and true will not depart.
They are committed to live for Jesus.

Holiness is the way.
This is God's standard of living.
He is honored when sins are turned away.
A special blessing is promised for the believing.

Love God is the command.
Be steadfast, unmovable, always abounding.
Keep holding the nail scared hand.
He blesses those who are forgiving.

Show a little kindness,
Help someone along the way.
It is His good pleasure to give peace
That no one can take away.

Serve Him with a made up mind.
Never turn and run.
Be patient, it is only a matter of time.
This earthly race will be won.

God called many servants.
Those who are faithful and true,
He will reward the triumphant
As gates of heaven they pass through.

A crown of righteousness will be given.
Let no man take thy crown.
Keep on living.
Once there was sin, but grace abounds.

# Thou Shalt Not
## August 6

I am sure you would agree
If you ever wrote on a stone,
Many years for the world to see,
The stone is very hard to write on.

To make a lasting impression,
The words must be cut very deep,
More than just a slight incision.
God gave us an important message to keep.

I know you have heard.
The story of the Ten Commandments.
The Lord wrote down each word.
Yes, the message was heaven-sent.

Moses delivered the message.
The word has gone forth.
It expands the eternal ages.
This law is for every person on earth.

I know men have tried to destroy,
To stop the inspirational word.
Let me tell you the real story.
God demands obedience throughout the world.

Yes, the law may be taken down.
From the court room hall
Or wherever it can be found,
Even from the library wall.

Let me tell you, my friend,
It is the commandment of the Lord,
A word from heaven.
It will be heard.

The stone may be broken.
Many pieces broke apart.
But the Lord has written
An eternal message; it is on the heart.

Now this is just a thought.
It concerns this document.
Thou shalt not
Be disrespectful to the commandments.

# The Miry Clay
## August 7

In the miry clay,
I was slowly sinking out of sight.
Oh, that someone would come by today,
Save me before the darkness of the night.

The clay is all around.
It seems as though there is no escape.
The hope of standing on solid ground,
I want to be set free from this death trap.

Time is running out.
If only someone would come by,
This may be my final hour.
Please, come and rescue me, lest I die.

The presence of death, I can feel it in the air.
I sink deeper into the clay.
No escape from this eternal snare.
My only hope is to pray.

Lo and behold,
A hand reaching down for me,
It's the hand of the Lord.
From the miry clay, He set me free.

Salvation of my soul,
He saved me from the depths of sin.
Heaven is my goal.
Just a few more days, I will enter in.

Upon the solid ground I stand,
On the rock of ages.
With my hand in His hand,
Saved by God's grace.

The miry clay was dragging me down.
Deeper and deeper into a life of sin,
Jesus lifted me up; now, I'm heaven bound.
Thank God I'm born again.

I'm so glad the Lord lifted me.
I was sinking in despair.
Now because of His mercy,
I will meet the Lord in the air.

# The Verdict
## August 8

A trial is about to begin.
The jury has been selected.
The lawyer prepares to defend.
The defendant will be the one affected.

So let us begin the trial.
The solemn oath is given.
All proceedings may take a while.
The final verdict will be in the end.

Will the defendant please rise!
Do you affirm to tell the whole truth?
Now we don't want any lies.
Remember, you are under oath.

How do you plead?
"Well, your Honor,
I don't tend to mislead.
The court I will not dishonor.

I know there are many crimes.
Offences I did commit.
So many you cannot count them in a lifetime.
I confess; I did it!

But my plea is not guilty!"
Oh, but you just now confessed.
Your Honor, give me liberty.
My sins have all been addressed.

"If any man sin,
We have an advocate with the Father,
Jesus Christ the righteous," He abides within (1John 2:1).
I confessed my sins at the altar.

"Has the jury reached a verdict?
For death or liberty,"
"Yes, Your Honor, we cannot convict.
We find the defendant not guilty!"

The trial of a faithful life ends.
Jesus is on the throne.
A believer confessed; sins were forgiven.
The Judge grants a full pardon.

# The Pathway of Life
## August 9

Along the pathway of life,
I was walking one day.
In the midst of trouble and strife,
Jesus met me along the way.

A weight I was carrying.
It was heavy and hard to bear.
The burden of my soul was heavy laden.
On the pathway of life, I met Jesus there.

He lifted the burden.
No longer am I worrying.
He forgave me of my sins.
Now my heart is rejoicing.

I continue my heavenly journey.
The heavy weight has been replaced.
I'm on my way to eternity,
Saved by God's amazing grace.

The weight of sin is gone.
Peace and joy remain.
The gate to heaven is just beyond.
Faith in Christ is not in vain.

So walk with the Lord.
Carry the cross daily.
Read and obey His Word.
He is preparing a home in Glory.

Jesus is walking with me,
My burden to bear.
He has set my spirit free.
One day I hope to meet Him in the air.

Let me tell you, my friend,
When Jesus meets you along the way,
He wants you to go to heaven,
A new life to receive; don't turn Him away.

Jesus said, "Follow me,"
The Savior is calling.
The pathway of life is plain to see.
It is not too late to start walking.

# To Follow a Sinful Path
## August 10

A sinful path is followed.
Unrighteousness is the game.
Every day is borrowed.
Many lives are filled with shame.

To follow a sinful path,
This is the one of corruption.
No fellowship with God in death,
A life is void of salvation.

The pleasures of the world
Lead down a path of sorrow.
But the ways of the Lord
Will have to wait until tomorrow.

Death is never willing to wait.
There are so many sinful things to do.
The path of life, many will meet their fate.
The gate to heaven, they will not pass through.

Listen, my friend!
Let me give you a fair warning.
Sinful pleasures they will come to an end.
A penalty for sin will be alarming.

Live ungodly today!
Don't worry about tomorrow,
Just follow the corruption way.
Soon you'll be in a grave of sorrow.

There is no joy in the grave.
All the pleasure days are gone.
Jesus gave His life to save,
But you waited too long.

You may have a second chance
If the door of life is still open.
Call upon God for deliverance.
He will write your name with the forgiven.

Pleasures of sin for a season,
Life ends when you stop breathing.
Faith in God's Son,
Now is a good time to start living.

# Apples of Sin
## August 11

Apples of sin,
It's just a tiny spot.
One bad apple a basket of fruit will ruin.
The decay spreads through the entire lot.

Just a small brown stain
On a bright red apple,
It can hardly be seen.
Time passes; the fruit is not fit for the table.

A basket full of food,
You have to throw it away.
It is no longer any good.
Don't waste any time; get rid of it today.

This waste could have been prevented.
It was a matter of separating the bad from the pure.
The bad apple should have been removed.
It would have stopped the spoil, I'm sure.

The apples of sin:
Remove the first sign of decay.
Before the corruption spreads to the end,
Don't wait till the end of the day.

Get rid of the bad,
Or the soul will perish.
The blessings of God you could have had.
Perhaps there is one little sin you like to cherish.

I know it is just a small thing,
The sin you would like to keep.
Beware; corruption may set in.
The harvest of blessings will be a poor crop to reap.

It is better to remove one sin
From a basket that is full
Of all the blessings, eternal life to win,
Than to be cast into hell.

A basket of spiritual blessings
Washed and pure,
No apples of sin,
Holiness unto the Lord, I'm sure.

# The Anchor of the Soul
## August 12

He is the anchor of the soul.
With merciful kindness He will reveal.
No drifting from His strong hold,
But steadfast, unmovable is God's will.

No returning to the old ways of sin.
The sinful pleasure days are gone.
There is no good reason to return again.
The hope of eternity is in God's Son.

Heaven awaits, keep holding on
Or the joy of the Lord will vanish.
In the sea of life all alone,
But God is not willing that any should perish.

Salvation to impart,
His hand is extended to the believing.
He is listening to the pleas of the heart.
A soul will be saved by His forgiving.

Drifting away, but not for long
The Savior came to save.
He will forgive all the wrong.
His promise is to stay.

Once again in His loving care,
A drifting sinner was found.
Forgiveness was the answer to prayer.
God's grace and mercy always abound.

Jesus has a very strong grip.
He is able to save the perishing,
Oh how great the love for those who tend to slip
And retreat back to sin.

The anchor holds in the deep.
No waves too strong
That His grace cannot keep.
His love is an everlasting bond.

Keep holding on.
God is faithful and just to forgive.
Be patient, it won't be long.
Heaven will be a wonderful place to live.

# A New Image
## August 13

Paint a picture on a canvas of white.
Many colors are used in this painting.
But it is really a reflection of life.
The image is still developing.

A beautiful landscape scene,
How about a self-portrait?
The canvas is ready; let's begin.
Place the colors on the palette.

First the old picture is painted over.
I like to use a pearl white.
It takes many layers to recover.
I want to hide the darkness of the night.

Well, I've changed my mind.
A self-portrait just won't do.
A new image to define,
The sky is still a heavenly blue.

In the picture of life, the image begins to fade.
The marks of sin disappear.
An unrighteous life is a vanishing shade.
A new character begins to appear.

Old sins are gone.
There is not a trace.
A new image is shown.
This picture reveals one of grace.

There is much work to be done.
A transformed life takes time.
It is best to continue on.
Peaceful thoughts are on the mind.

Remember the day,
Sins were forgiven.
The altar was a good place to pray.
God opened the windows of heaven.

The heart is still rejoicing.
A life in Christ began that day.
The image is developing
And sins are so graciously taken away.

# Paid in Full
## August 14

He paid the debt in full,
A huge price to pay.
No way to repay; He paid it all
Payment for sin was made.

The price was high
But on the cross He stayed on.
The price of freedom was for Him to die.
The cross held a lifeless form; behold God's Son.

A sacrifice of Jesus' life for freedom,
Paid for with His precious blood.
His love was not random.
No person on earth was left unloved.

He suffered and He bled.
The punishment was meant for us.
But He took our place instead.
The voice of praise is heard, "thank you, Jesus."

On the cross He felt the excruciating pain.
His death was for the unholy,
For mankind He was slain.
He paid the debt at Calvary.

The Holy One of God,
He took our place.
He died for the sins of the world
So we could be saved by God's grace.

The price for sin
Was a high price to pay.
Open the heart and invite Him in.
Now is a good time to pray.

Consider the price.
His life's blood was spilled at the crucifixion.
He gave the supreme sacrifice,
His life for our salvation.

Our debt is paid in full.
Go thy way and sin no more.
Rejoice and be thankful.
For the believers, God will open heaven's door.

# Life Is Worth Restoring
## August 15

Put on a fresh coat of paint.
Make sure you scrape away the old.
The house will be protected from the rain,
From the snow, ice, and the bitter cold.

The paint should be stirred,
All the chemicals mixed together.
A new coat each and every year,
It will protect the house a lot better.

Now the soul is different to restore.
It still takes time,
Days, weeks, or even more.
The inspiring thoughts come from the mind.

The restoring process begins with the heart.
Start each day with prayer.
A special blessing God will impart.
The burden of life He will bear.

Sins definitely have to go.
There is no glory in them.
Be patient as the work may be slow.
In time all praise and honor will be to Him.

The impurities of the heart cannot remain.
This is a labor of love
That can only be performed in Jesus' name.
This blessing is directly from God above.

Now for the sins of scarlet,
This deep cleaning requires the blood
And a special touch by the Holy Spirit.
Salvation by grace is the work of God.

A daily walk with Christ is neglected.
Fellowship with God is missing.
To drift back into the ways of world is expected.
Gone back into sin, but a life is still worth restoring.

The value is too high to leave in sin.
Now is a good time to restore.
God's love is the same as it always has been
And He wants to bless even more.

# I Know What I Need
## August 16

Anoint me, Lord.
Hear me when I pray.
Give me courage to speak thy Word.
Help me to live for you each day.

When I am weak,
I need the anointing.
The enemy of my soul to defeat,
Yes, I need a Holy Ghost refreshing.

Fill my heart with the joy of the resurrection.
I know that is what I need.
Give me the power to resist temptation.
The blood of Jesus Christ, I plead!

One touch of the Master's hand,
It will give me strength for the hour.
On the battlefield of life, I will stand.
Deliverance will come by His mighty power.

Let the anointing descend.
Victory is mine.
Help me conquer sin.
Be faithful to you all the time.

Lord, fill me with the Spirit.
A touch from heaven divine,
I know that I really need it.
Please, help me keep my life in line.

Anoint me, Lord.
With the oil of peace.
Give me guidance from thy Word.
A thankful heart is open for your loving grace.

Anoint me today
To hold up my cross,
To live the Christian way.
There are many sinners that are lost.

The Gospel to proclaim,
I know that I need to tell it.
That I may go forth in Jesus' name.
Lord, I need the Holy Spirit.

# Turn from Sin
## August 17

Turn from sin
To walk a new path.
Rejoice in the blessings.
Repent, escape God's wrath.

Turn from a life of corruption.
Follow the straight and narrow way.
Bless the Lord for salvation.
Take the time to pray.

Walk with the Lord.
Answer heaven's call,
Be obedient to the Word.
Surrender your heart to His will.

Leave the old sins in the past.
Look to the future.
Believe on the Lord Jesus Christ.
Be ready to meet the Lord in the Rapture.

Keep the faith.
Never turn and run.
Be faithful to the last breath.
From your sins make sure you turn!

Stay away from sin.
It will most certainly
Corrupt the minds of men.
Seek after God reverently!

Carry the cross.
Endure to the end.
Be concerned for the lost.
The hand of mercy you must extend.

Love God with heart, soul, and mind.
Love Him fervently.
Yes, have compassion all the time.
The Lord is coming back; wait patiently!

Turn from sin!
Go and sin no more.
Continue in the faith, my friend.
Soon you will stand at heaven's door.

# The Wolves of Sin
## August 18

Sheep in the field
The wolves attack.
A young lamb is killed.
The wild animals will be back.

The shepherd gathers the sheep.
He places them inside the fence.
One little lamb he failed to keep.
Oh, to build a stronger defense.

The shepherd asleep at night,
Once again the gate is left open.
The sheep wander out of sight.
In the deep darkness the wolves descend.

By the shepherd's neglect,
He lost several small lambs.
He bowed his head with deep regret
And called for the rest of the rams.

A vow he made.
No more lambs to lose.
He would build a strong barricade,
And a wooden gate he would close.

Well, many years have passed.
I am happy to say
In this imaginary story his commitment held fast.
This shepherd kept the lambs safe.

But listen, my friend,
Make sure you close the gate.
To stop the wolves of sin,
Watch and pray before it's too late!

If the gate of salvation you neglect,
The wolves will enter in.
Bow your head in deep regret.
A careless life is an open door to sin.

Seek God reverently.
Keep the gate closed; watch and pray.
Yes, the need is to pray fervently.
Friends and loved ones will be safe another day.

# The Thorns of Sin
## August 19

One day I saw a bird's nest.
It was in a most unlikely place.
Each of the baby birds had a bright yellow breast,
In a rosebush—what an unusual birthplace!

There were thorns all around,
Too sharp to touch,
But the little birds were safe and sound.
The mother brought them lunch.

She landed in the midst of the briars.
The tiny birds opened their mouths.
The worms dangled in the air.
The mother bird from the nest would fly back out.

I thought to myself,
What a terrible place to be born.
Suppose the baby birds fell
Into the rosebush that has many thorns.

But one day I saw
The little birds were gone.
The yard I started to mow.
I heard a golden finch sing a new song.

Think about our birthplace.
Born into a world of sin,
Certainly it is an unusual place
Where a new life is to begin.

We are born into a world of corruption.
The briars of sin are all around.
We encounter sharp thorns of devastation.
Peace with God abounds.

Jesus Christ is our Lord.
He brings peace in the midst of trial.
There is a gentle resting place in the Word.
His love and mercy are undefiled.

Resting in Jesus,
Safe from the thorns of sin,
He came to deliver us.
Our sins are forgiven.

# The Wrestling Match
## August 20

Let the wrestling match begin.
The enemy will try to destroy the soul.
He does everything in his power to win.
His desire is to dominate and rule.

If his endeavor fails, he will try again!
A different plan to use,
On the mat he will try to pin.
His opponent he wants to bruise.

This enemy is not flesh and blood.
If you really want to win,
Determine in your mind to love God.
In your heart, let Christ abide within.

There is a wonderful victory.
The wrestling match can be won,
God will get the glory
But there has to be faith in His Son.

Even though you are weak!
No match for such a powerful foe.
The battle rages all week.
Victory is promised by the God you know.

Call upon God.
Greater is He that is in you,
Than he that is in the world.
Fight to win; this battle can be won, too.

You are so weak,
But He is very strong.
This is no time for defeat.
Prepare to sing the victory song.

Suppose you are knocked down.
God has all power and might.
Get up! His grace will always abound.
He will hold up your hand in the final fight.

Victorious over sin,
A crown of life is won.
The faithful will be rewarded in the end
And all will rejoice in God's Son.

# In the Line of Duty
## August 21

A policeman went to work
Early this morning
At the community park,
He was walking.

His job was to protect,
Ensure safety for the residents,
Any kind of danger to detect,
Crimes he would try to prevent.

But on this tragic day,
His life would come to an end.
Family members come to pray.
His life was to defend.

They give honor to his name.
He was a blessing to the community.
A life has ended, and a soul has been reclaimed.
The rest of his days he will spend in eternity.

I know he will be missed.
But I like to think
Up in heaven with Christ
A new contract signed with heavenly ink,

A new position has just been filled.
A policeman trades his badge
To walk the eternal hills.
Let us look at the holy pages.

His new position in Glory,
But back to earth to send,
The moral of this story:
A guardian angel will defend.

Sometimes life comes to an end.
There are many heartfelt emotions.
But a new life will begin.
God has a divine promotion.

A policeman fell.
In the line of duty,
God sent a new guardian angel.
He has a new badge to carry.

# The Right Road
## August 22

We are going to a city,
Far beyond the sky.
We are on the highway to glory.
Our arrival will be quick as a blink of an eye.

The Bible is the road map given.
In the holy pages there are special instructions.
Our journey begins at the cross with the forgiven.
Heaven will be our home; God gives us divine directions.

On this journey with the Lord,
I heard of a tragic accident.
A bus with many passengers wrecked on the road.
This was a fatal moment.

The right road they failed to take.
One wrong turn,
It was a costly mistake.
Everyone would not return.

A tragedy on the highway,
The heart was filled with sorrow.
On that horrible day,
There would be no tomorrow.

Let's go back to our spiritual journey.
We will probably have to go on the sinner's road
At least until we come to the crossroads of eternity.
This is where they crucified Christ our Lord.

This is where faith makes a right turn.
Sins are forgiven as Christ is accepted into the heart.
Salvation is promised to all who believe in God's Son.
Jesus will go with us; I believe this is the best part.

What if you choose to stay on the sinner's road?
We have already read about a fatal accident.
Will there be a terrible tragedy if you reject the Lord?
It is not too late to repent.

We are going to a city,
The builder and maker is God.
Just believe on the Lord of glory.
Turn right and go straight, this will be the right road.

# Safe on the Inside
## August 23

The sky is a hazy gray.
Frozen icicles hang.
Truly this is a picture of a dismal day.
There is sleet and freezing rain.

On the tree limbs
A sparkling glow.
Down below, a few small lambs,
They play in the wind-blown snow.

The sleet keeps falling.
As I look out the window,
Ice on the tree branches cling,
Their mighty arms held low.

It is a cold winter day.
I'm glad I am on the inside,
Out of harm's way.
Peace and safety abide.

I am sure you will agree.
The beautiful white snow,
Ice-covered trees,
It is a wonderful show.

Now on the inside,
I would like to remain.
If I venture outside,
The picture is not the same.

It is really good to have a shelter
And stand next to the fire.
It is better than being in the cold weather.
A house warm and friendly, I had rather be there.

An inner peace to know,
Safe and secure on the inside,
Radiant beams of His love aglow,
The Spirit of the Lord abides.

I'm safe on the inside with peace and grace.
Sheltered in the arms above,
His loving arms embrace.
Each waiting heart is filled with His love.

# Instant Replay
## August 24

My life is in review.
The past and the present,
The old and the new,
Let me tell you how my life was spent.

Before I met Christ, this is a good place to start.
Kindness was shown along the way.
Help others was the intent of my heart.
I am sorry to say, no time to pray.

Church I did attend.
I would usually stay awhile.
The preacher spoke of sin.
The repentant walked down the aisle.

Way back then in the presence of God to stand.
Just a moment of instant replay,
The pages of life to scan,
But listen to what He has to say.

"I know you not"(Luke 13:27).
Jesus blood was never applied,
No cleansing from a sinful heart.
The kingdom of God is denied.

Depart from me
Into everlasting fire.
It's not enough to do good deeds
If living for Jesus is not the heart's desire.

At the end of the journey,
No matter how much good,
I would have missed eternity
Without His precious blood.

I am happy to say
Jesus is my Lord and Savior.
One day the Lord heard me pray.
Now I'm living in God's favor.

The blessed hope is mine.
Instant replay of the days gone by,
A sinner's life and God's grace combine.
The blood is applied.

# To Be Saved
## August 25

"What must I do to be saved?" (Acts 16:30).
Down thru the ages,
This question has been asked.
The answer is in the holy pages.

God has a divine plan.
On a cross Jesus died.
For the salvation of man,
For our sins He was crucified.

When sins are confessed,
The Lord will forgive.
A soul is blessed
With a new life to live.

There may not be enough time
To search the Bible through,
But just one thought for the mind:
Is forgiveness for sins overdue?

Well, life ends when we stop breathing.
After that it will be too late.
Now is the accepted time for believing.
A delay could be a fatal mistake.

On a cross made of wood,
Jesus hung between earth and heaven.
He gave His precious blood.
With faith in Him, sins are forgiven.

"Believe on the Lord Jesus Christ" (Acts 16:31).
If we confess our sins,
He is faithful and just
To forgive us and to cleanse us; a new life begins.

He will forgive all unrighteousness.
The Bible tells us to repent.
The Lord offers forgiveness.
For this purpose He was sent.

"What must I do to be saved?"
"Believe on the Lord Jesus Christ."
Forgiveness will not be delayed.
Those who receive Him are blessed.

# When I Am Weak
## August 26

A piece of metal will soon break,
A crack in the seam, just a thin line.
Unless special precautions we take,
Its strength will gradually decline.

No power to hold,
When once it was strong,
Too weak to carry a heavy load,
Its endurance will not last long.

We all know
The strength is in the frame.
Its weakness is beginning to show.
There's not much time.

The metal to break,
Unless the crack we weld,
A new seam to make,
The torch is held.

With a steady hand,
The hot welding rods flow.
Now the building can stand.
A strong frame can carry a heavy load.

Think about these words.
"When I am weak, then am I strong"(2 Cor. 12:10).
In our relationship with the Lord,
Our endurance will not last long.

If in the frame a crack appears,
With a good strong weld
The weak line will disappear.
In God's mighty hand, the torch is held.

The love of God will endure.
A good strong frame
I'm very sure!
The building will stand in Jesus' name.

A frame that will stand
When a life is in repair.
One touch of God's almighty hand,
A restored Christian will meet the Lord in the air.

# The Old Sinful Way
## August 27

To travel into the past,
This trip requires a lot of imagination.
Walk the street of the outcast,
Enter into the towns of corruption.

Turn aside from the Christian pathway.
Follow the sinner's path of spiritual darkness.
Sink deeper into sins of the miry clay.
This is the path of the faithless.

Are you sure you want to go?
There is still a little time.
I just want you to know
It's not too late to change your mind.

I know it is a long distance.
To get there faster, try this detour:
Go across the field of unrighteousness.
Leave the path that is safe and secure.

Walk down sins highway.
Enter into the town of transgressions.
The thorns of iniquity are along the way.
The sinful path leads to a deep depression.

The back road is a little scary,
Try carrying the weight of sin.
This extra burden will be heavy to carry.
The town invites the sin bearers to come in.

A sinful traveler is always welcome.
As memory fades, the past is left behind.
Thoughts of heaven return for a journey home.
Take up the cross and follow Jesus all the time.

I'm glad I used my imagination.
The past has too many dangers for me.
I'd rather walk the path of a new destination.
The path of life is love and mercy.

Remember the old sinful way.
Sin marks the place.
Don't turn back, come what may!
Be faithful; keep singing "Amazing Grace."

# Christ's Life in Review
## August 28

Behold, the Christ of Calvary,
His life is in review.
Go back to Galilee.
Many miracles performed there, too.

He is a man
Marked by sufferings.
Nail prints in His hands,
His life bears the imprint of pain.

His back is torn.
With a whip He was beaten.
He was ridiculed and scorned.
Even the priest had forsaken.

His name is Jesus,
A man that could endure
Pain and suffering for us,
A life that is holy and pure.

He stands alone,
A man of sorrow and grief.
This is God's Son.
He is our hope for eternal life.

His life was one of faith.
For our sins He hung on a cross.
A man obedient to the death,
He came to save the lost.

Let's go deeper into the review.
From the cross He was taken down.
He was the faithful and true.
His body was placed in the ground.

On the third day the grave was open.
From the dead He was revived.
Jesus Christ has risen!
He is alive.

He was resurrected from earth to heaven.
No one knows the day or hour
He will come again.
The dead and the living will rise by His power.

# The Stream Is Flowing Again
## August 29

God's many wonderful blessings
Are like a mighty stream.
The banks are overflowing.
The current moves downstream.

Perhaps you remember the days gone by.
The mighty stream was flowing.
A promise to the Lord you would never deny.
The cup of salvation was overflowing.

But, somewhere along the way,
The rain ceased to fall.
No time to pray.
The stream was once full.

What happens if there is no rain?
You may be looking at a dry bed of sand.
The trees are bare on the mountain.
Where are the blessings for man?

Well, let me tell you, my friend.
The stream may be dry.
But it's certainly not the end.
Look up; a blessing will come from on high.

It's beginning to rain.
Can you feel the touch of the Master's hand?
Let the spiritual rain descend.
A wave of glory spreads across the land.

The stream is flowing again,
Swiftly down the mountainside,
God's blessings for man.
The current of His love is deep and wide

I am happy to say
The stream of God's mercy
Is flowing today.
It is the main stream to eternity.

If the earthly stream is dry,
Look up; receive a blessing.
God will send a spiritual rain from the sky.
The mountain stream of his love is flowing again.

# Too Late for Heaven's Flight
## August 30

A trip has been planned.
The people will meet at the airport.
All of the luggage will be scanned.
Passengers are required to have a passport.

Security is very tight.
It is best to get at the airport early.
If we are late, we will miss the flight.
The plane will leave on time; we had better hurry.

Travel information was acquired in advance.
Many days were allowed for preparation.
The day of departure is near; please don't take a chance.
Another plane will not be available for transportation.

The day has arrived
For that peaceful journey in the sky.
A few members have not yet arrived.
The plane has been inspected and is now ready to fly.

Once the plane leaves,
The unprepared person will be left behind.
There will be many distressful pleas.
This flight to a vacation resort is of the earthly kind.

Now we are ready for a spiritual flight.
We need a certain amount of preparation.
We will leave only by God's power and might.
Heaven will be the place of our destination.

God will only accept I.D.'S of a sinless heart.
Sin stains removed.
It is just about time to depart.
A blood washed life is approved.

A flight to glory will take place.
God help us to be ready.
Just believe in Jesus; salvation is by grace.
The blood of Jesus is our passport to glory.

We had better hurry; time is wasting.
The time of His coming is near.
When He comes there will be great rejoicing.
In the clouds of glory, Jesus will appear.

# The Storm Is Over
## August 31

Storm clouds move across the sky.
Darkness covers the land.
The birds try to fly.
The wings flutter in the whirlwind of sand.

Finally, to make shelter
From the torrents of rain,
Hopefully the storm will be over.
But the wind is unrestrained.

The end is not in sight.
The storm continues day after day.
All morning and throughout the night,
The ship at sea is tossed by the mighty waves.

The cries of distress
From the sailors on board,
Many prayerful requests;
All of them were heard.

When the storm is raging,
There seems to be no end.
But my friend, keep on praying.
The sun will shine again.

Sometimes a storm will come and leave.
Maybe to last a day or two,
To leave behind a gentle breeze,
Dark clouds turn into skies of blue.

On life's stormy sea,
The rain descends.
Dark clouds hover as far as the eye can see.
Will the storm ever end?

Look up, my friend.
Radiant beams from above,
The sunshine from heaven,
It comes down with His love.

God answers prayer.
Before His presence kneel.
Listen and you may hear
Softly spoken words, "Peace be still."(Mark 4:39).

# A Broken Vessel
## September 1

A vessel is broken.
Upon the ground it lay.
Never to be used again.
It's best to throw it away.

Many broken pieces
Scattered all around.
Particles of glass hide in dark places.
Only fragments can be found.

A vessel crafted and formed by man.
A beautiful vase indeed!
Tiny particles in the sand,
They lie in the shadow of the evergreen tree.

It is a broken vessel now.
It will never be the same.
But let me tell you anyhow,
Why the Master Craftsman came.

To heal the brokenhearted,
He works with a vessel in despair.
In Him the love of God is revealed.
Broken pieces of a life, He knows how to repair.

Many lives were shattered and broken.
But when Jesus came,
Life was restored with sins forgiven.
A permanent bond is made in Jesus' name.

A broken vessel is worthless for sale or trade.
Please don't cast it away!
Christ gave His life; the ultimate price was paid.
One drop of His blood will restore a life made of clay.

"Old things are passed away;
Behold, all things are become new" (2Cor. 5:17).
See what happens when we pray.
A vessel of a broken life is mended, too.

The old vessel made by man,
It is an object to be adored.
But when crafted by God's mighty hand,
A life that is broken will be completely restored.

# Road to Destruction
## September 2

The road to destruction:
If you fail to pray,
A truthful realization
You've gone the wrong way.

The same road to travel
Each and every day.
I know it wasn't intentional,
But you traveled anyway.

Just a normal routine
Down the road of corruption,
Over the bridge of sin,
Just past the exit of salvation.

I know you should have turned
Onto the road of glory.
There seemed to be no concern,
So you continued on your journey.

I was just wondering
How far you would have to go
Down the road of sin
Before you would know!

You have missed heaven's highway,
All the glory of eternity,
There is still time to pray.
Receive God's mercy.

Just a little time before the end,
A quick decision to make.
Turn from a life of sin,
Or it will be a terrible mistake.

Ask Jesus to save.
Turn from the road of transgressions.
Follow the straight and narrow way.
He will honor a sincere confession.

Peace will come, now is the time to pray.
Follow Jesus without interruption.
Keep on the glory land way.
This is the road of incorruption.

# The House of Neglect
## September 3

The house of neglect,
A temporal dwelling place,
Just a few moments to reflect,
Think about God's grace.

Remember when
The old house was about to be torn down.
This was a life of many sins,
God's grace had just been found.

I know many days have passed.
Do you remember the day
The love of God was expressed,
When you knelt to pray?

There was rejoicing in the Holy Spirit.
Glory and honor to the King,
Peace and joy, you could feel it.
God forgave your sins.

Remember when
On the rock of ages you would stand.
Sins were forsaken,
You were obedient to the Master's command.

Well, the days gone by,
Where is the joy and peace?
When the Lord walked by your side,
Your heart was filled with praise.

A little bit of neglect,
It can bring a house to ruin.
It can fill a whole life with regret.
A life unrestored will end in ungodly living.

No time to pray
Or read His Word,
Church can wait another day—
And you wonder where is the Lord?

When life is void of devotion,
The spiritual house will come down
And the heart will be filled with corruption.
By daily fellowship with God, grace will abound.

# Drifting Away
## September 4

Drifting away,
Far out to sea,
A little more each day.
Where is the hope of eternity?

The vision of heaven fades out of sight,
The bright horizon
Covered by the night.
The hope of glory disappears in the evening sun.

If you turn away from the Rock of Ages,
The vessel of life will be on a collision course.
Faith and hope will fade as the storm rages.
Peace will come when you meet Jesus at the cross.

The faithless ride the waves of corruption.
No captain on board.
Jesus offers salvation.
Eternal peace is an everlasting reward.

Far out at sea,
Jesus has a lifeline to throw.
A sinner can find mercy.
The love of God is a good thing to know.

Reach out and take the line.
I'm sure it will hold
The strength of glory divine
When Jesus Christ is your Lord.

Live for Him today.
Keep holding the rope,
Or you will drift away.
It is possible you will lose all hope.

Commit your heart and soul.
Seek God first and foremost.
Let heaven be your goal.
He is able to save to the uttermost.

No longer drifting away
Or far out to sea,
But closer to God each day,
The kingdom of God you will see.

# An Old Fire Escape
## September 5

An old fire escape,
Construction began many years ago.
The metal workers so craftily shaped
And placed the frame next to the window.

It was painted with a nice black finish.
They wanted it to last a long time.
Over the years the structure began to diminish.
The metal was weakened with rust and grime.

I know it was very strong
When it was first constructed,
But a lot of things have gone wrong.
The fire escape needs to be restructured.

If we had to use this unit
As a means to escape a fire,
I don't believe we could make it.
The reliability has expired.

This is not a safe retreat.
The equipment is too dangerous for the family.
Is there another exit
That can prevent this terrible tragedy?

The fire escape we built for the Lord
Many years ago
When we committed to live by His Word,
To follow Jesus anywhere He would go.

Well, do we still have a safe fire exit,
One that we can depend on,
A fire-escape strengthened by the Holy Spirit?
Jesus is the only one.

He will deliver from the fire,
But first our souls must be restored.
We may need some maintenance and repair.
Repentance is needed just as before.

How shall we escape
If we neglect our salvation?
Maybe we have a fire-escape to remake
Before God will give us a divine transformation.

# In the Fire
## September 6

The king gave a command.
Every person shall worship a gold image.
Obedience was required throughout the land.
What would be a good response to His message?

If we were told to bow down
Or else we would die
When a flute or harp make a certain sound,
To live or die, now is the time to reply.

To bow down is to live.
If we disobey
Our conscience of what we believe,
A fiery furnace awaits this day.

Three young men—
Their devotion would be found.
Not in an earthly thing
Or in a statue built upon the ground.

The king asked, "Who is that God
That shall deliver?"(Daniel 3:15).
Soon, the king and the world
Would see God's mighty power.

Our God will deliver.
But if not, we will not bow down.
To obey God is divine deliverance.
God's grace, forevermore, abounds.

Smoke from the furnace filled the air.
The furnace was heated seven times more.
The three Jews would be thrown into the fire.
Three in the fire, but now there are four.

 "The fourth is like the Son of God"(Daniel 3:25).
The three Jews would not bow down.
Their story is told throughout the world.
The love of God abounds.

With the conscience of faith, God is first.
It is our belief that will sustain us.
We are required to stand fast.
Resist the commands and be faithful to Jesus.

# A Runner Has Fallen
## September 7

In just a little while,
The race will end.
That last long mile,
Soon it will be time to ascend.

A heavenly home to win,
So run with all your might,
Lay aside the heavy weight of sin.
The finish line is in sight.

With a made-up mind,
Keep pressing on.
It's only a matter of time;
The race will be won.

In the victory lane,
All those who believe in God's Son,
A crown of life to claim,
Run with patience; it won't be long!

Endure to the end;
Time on earth will soon be gone.
On the grace of God depend.
Keep pressing on to that heavenly home.

The finish line will be a sight to see.
A crown of life to adorn.
By God's wonderful mercy
A glory crown will be worn.

But a runner has fallen by the way.
Unable to finish the race,
The saints of God pray
That he will be restored to grace.

Look back, my friend,
Remember the unfaithful times
When you were overcome by sin
And could not cross the finish line.

God is not willing that any should perish.
Do not let the sins of disgrace
Keep you down when there is a race to finish.
God gives an abundance of grace.

# Oil for the Lantern
## September 8

The supplies run low at the camp.
Go back to the store,
Carry the old lamp,
Just like before.

While you are there,
Purchase a loaf of bread for the hungry.
We need plastic dinnerware
And water for the thirsty.

To satisfy the natural desires
Of all the comforts of home,
We will put wood on the fire,
So don't take too long!

Let us patiently wait
For our friend's return.
I know it is getting late.
I'm really quite concerned.

The camper from the store returns—
No more oil in his lantern.
It is very easy to trip over the vines.
The rocks and the cliffs are hard to discern.

The man who went for supplies,
He had to walk in the darkness of the night.
No lantern to rely,
A flameless lamp held no sparks of light.

I am afraid for my friend,
But it appears to be too late.
A terrible tragedy to contend,
He met his fate.

No oil for the lantern,
The pathway of life is dim.
If the fire of faith does not burn,
How can we expect to see Him?

To see the lights of that heavenly home,
A flame burning bright keeps joy in the camp.
Let the glory light shine on.
Make sure there is oil in the lamp.

# Throw out the Lifeline
## September 9

"Man overboard,"
The sailor shouts to the captain.
"Call for the lifeguard.
We have to rescue the man."

"Throw him a rope."
The life preserver is thrown into the sea.
"Let down the lifeboat."
I know he is talking to me.

The boat splashes into the water.
I hear his cries for help!
Suddenly he goes underwater.
I try to reach him by myself.

It seems to be too late.
His face I no longer can see.
A watery grave may be his fate.
He has vanished in the raging sea.

There seems to be no hope.
I felt great despair!
I held onto the rescue rope.
Suddenly I saw the man gasping for air.

He was rescued just in time.
A life had been restored.
Thank God for the lifeline.
We were both safe on board.

Now, just to let you know,
This story is not true,
But I wanted to show
What you and I need to do.

Souls are perishing each and every day.
We need to throw out the lifeline.
Their souls can be saved.
Let us redeem the time.

No time to despair,
Help someone today.
The cries of desperation are in the air.
Lives are saved when they pray.

# A Thief Comes to Destroy
## September 10

Many valuables are left in the home.
Some of them have sentimental value.
It is a terrible tragedy when a thief comes.
He will take away the things that belong to you.

A thief comes to destroy.
He will take watches or gold rings.
These items were a pleasure to enjoy.
The house is ravaged of many wonderful things.

The emotion of the heart is extreme distress.
Take a quick look around the room.
There are no words to express.
The sorrow is for a broken home.

"The thief cometh not, but for to steal,
And to kill, and to destroy" (John 10:10).
Grief is a terrible thing to feel.
A heart of sadness is void of joy.

Satan comes as a thief
To steal and to kill.
Jesus comes, and He offers life.
The presence of God is so real.

Satan comes to take away.
Jesus is here to give,
To restore the joy in a heavenly way.
The blessing of life is to live.

People of all nations have been robbed.
Their valuables taken away.
The joy can be restored
If in Christ they pray.

A life is very precious indeed.
It is purchased with a high price.
Above all earthly treasures it exceeds.
A thief cannot get past the sacrifice.

He will cut chains of steel,
But is powerless against a heart of love.
Those who are obedient to God's will:
Are safe from any intruders by faith in Him above.

# Little Foxes Spoil the Grapes
## September 11

A small family working in the garden,
Unaware of the danger
Close by; little foxes live in a den.
They love grapes that are tender.

Well, these grapes are ripe.
The workers have gone home for the evening.
Harvest will begin at daylight.
The labors will rise very early in the morning.

While the family is sleeping,
Little hungry foxes invade the field.
From the vines mangled grapes hang.
Disaster comes to the harvest yield.

Ruin occupies the crop of grapes,
The vines are broken down.
Foxes retreat back into their holes.
The waste of the vineyard lies on the ground.

The laborer, early to rise,
He looks upon the garden of devastation.
Truly this is a terrible surprise!
Grief and despair fill the heart with frustration.

The field is completely ravaged.
No grapes on the vines,
The crop has been damaged.
All of the work is in vain.

In the great harvest field,
The little foxes of sin
Destroy and turn us away from God's will.
They separate us from the true vine.

To the Lord let us draw near.
Build stronger fences.
It is quite clear
We need stronger defenses!

Little foxes can spoil.
Just like little sins,
They can corrupt the soul.
Please don't allow them to enter in.

# Through the Grapevine
## September 12

The things you hear through the grapevine—
It's not a good source of communication.
The bridge of hearsay will be a poor design.
It will not be safe for transportation.

Be careful the information.
A bridge that you build
On a weak foundation,
The strength may be concealed.

Through the grapevine,
Many things to hear,
False information comes down the line.
An unstable bridge is a thing to fear.

Rumors are quick to destroy.
Would you safely commit
All your family
To a bridge that is poorly built?

In your quest for glory divine
If you follow lies and false instructions,
The misleading words through a grapevine,
Your bridge is doomed for destruction.

God has given His plan.
Don't dare accept another!
The nail prints in Jesus' hands,
There is no salvation by any other.

A line of communication
To build a bridge to eternity,
Hear the truthful words of salvation:
A lasting foundation is built on mercy.

Open up the Bible.
It is God's blueprint to heaven,
Read and believe the Gospel.
The bridge of faith ascends.

A grapevine bridge will fall.
It is built on false information,
The bridge of life stands tall.
The truth is a safe passageway for all generations.

# Depart from Me
## September 13

What would happen
If you heard Jesus say, "Depart from me"(Matthew 7:23)?
Well, you would miss the kingdom of heaven.
Please don't deny the Christ of Calvary.

Perhaps you can remember
When Jesus said, "Follow me."
Now this is just a reminder;
Jesus offered you mercy.

You may not remember the day
When Jesus stretched out His hand,
But you so casually walked away
And refused the glories of the Promised Land.

Jesus offered you pardon,
The love of God to know;
Now the earthly race is run.
Just maybe today God requires your soul.

Jesus offered His love,
Peace, and joy, forgiveness of sins,
Grace that abounds from above.
He wanted to be your friend.

He was denied,
No fellowship with the Lord,
The blood was not applied.
No time to read the Word.

Now your fate is sealed.
Eternal separation:
Your destiny is revealed.
For eternity there was no preparation.

The time will come to stand before the King.
Far above the earth-borne clouds.
If your life could be lived all over again,
Would you cry aloud?

Lord Jesus, have mercy!
At heaven's gate, what will the Lord say?
Enter in or depart from me.
Before life ends, take the time to pray.

# Slow the Wagon Down
## September 14

Work while there is day.
Hook up the old wagon.
Soon it will be time to haul the corn away.
Be careful; the horses may want to run.

Halfway through the harvest field,
The wagon should be full.
Fresh produce from the harvest yield,
The laborers have many ears of corn to pull.

Slow the horses down.
Walk a slower pace.
After a while you can go to town.
Take a wagon of corn to the marketplace.

But for now gather the Lord's harvest.
Labor till the work is done.
Make sure you give your very best.
Work while there is day; soon the Lord will come!

Slow down the wagon,
It will fill up faster.
Soon the day will be gone.
Too much work can be a disaster.

Too many things to do,
Your labor of love will suffer.
If it all depends on you,
An empty wagon shows no help from any other.

Laborers in the field,
God has placed them there for a reason.
The harvest of souls will be a productive yield.
More people will be saved in the final season.

Work today while there is light.
Don't run, more can be done with a slower pace.
An overworked servant will have a restless night.
An empty wagon may be a sign of wasted grace.

The day of laborers is done.
The wagon is full and headed to the market place.
God is pleased because no one worked alone
And all depended on His grace.

# A Walk in the Dark
## September 15

I know you cannot see.
Try walking in the woods;
Feel the hardness of a tree
Or stumble over a few roots.

Don't bring a flashlight.
Then you could see.
But in the darkness of the night,
Tell me where you would be.

There is a path that leads home,
But you have to find.
Now you are all alone.
It is hard to walk a straight line.

There are dangers all around,
Overhanging cliffs,
Jagged rocks on the ground.
Be very careful of your life.

Without a light,
Doomed to stay
In the darkness of the night,
The only hope is the light of day.

It shines from above.
The darkness fades away.
The sunrays of God's love,
They shine upon a bright and glorious way.

The pathway of life to find,
No stumbling in the night,
A light from heaven to shine,
Everything is all right.

No longer to walk alone.
With Jesus by your side,
Now you can see the lights of home.
The glory of God abides.

A walk in the dark,
Stumbling in the night,
You will miss heaven's mark.
Unless you repent, please, walk in the light.

# Time to Repent
## September 16

A life of a servant,
Jesus is Master, Lord, and King.
He waits patiently for souls to repent.
Forgiveness is granted for sin.

Remember when there was no obedience to Him.
Unrighteousness and corruption,
It was easy to yield to them.
No joy or peace, only deception.

Every person has committed sin.
In the old days punishment was by stoning.
Cast the first stone if you have not sinned.
No sins, start throwing.

The stones flew through the air.
That's not true.
No one was standing there.
The accusers, they all withdrew.

The time is now to pray.
Ask God to forgive.
No one is promised another day,
But Christ has a pardon to give.

Lay the stones down.
No need to pick them up again.
God's grace abounds
And sins are forgiven.

You do not have to continue in sin.
Walk away!
Just invite Jesus to come in.
Peace with God is every day.

Thanks be unto God.
Sinners of disgrace,
There is redemption in the blood,
Souls are saved by grace.

A life of a servant,
Jesus is Master, King, and Lord.
Friends, there is still time to repent.
A crown of life in Heaven is the reward.

# In the Lions' Den
## September 17

On the glory road,
From the path of sin,
Walk with the Lord.
Be strong in the lions' den.

Be very courageous,
Many lions to contend.
Hungry and ferocious,
The flesh of man they will rend.

The door is shut and sealed.
A righteous man stands.
The power of God is revealed.
Deliverance is by a strong and mighty hand.

Through the channel of prayer,
With the proper communication,
A victory was there.
God honored one man's dedication.

He saved Daniel
By His mighty power.
Yes, my God is able.
He hears and answers prayer.

In the lions' den,
Satan has come to destroy.
Keep your eyes on heaven.
God will restore the joy.

In a lions' den,
When no one seems to care,
God's holy arm to extend,
He will answer your prayer.

When Satan as a hungry lion
Comes to devour,
He has to run.
He remembers God's resurrection power.

The enemy is like a roaring lion.
In the name of Jesus he has to go.
Satan's deceptive way is lying.
Deliverance is promised by the God you know.

# Take Away the Pain
## September 18

Take away the pain,
The suffering and the shame.
But if the suffering remains,
Keep the faith just the same.

Grace for the trial,
Strength for the day,
In just a little while,
We will be called to glory far away.

Take away the pain.
Be faithful to the end.
Bring forth the spiritual rain.
A blessing will descend.

If the healing does not come,
The pain we must endure.
One day Jesus will take us home.
A divine healing is coming, I'm sure.

Keep believing in Jesus' name.
Be strong and of a good courage.
There is a crown of life to claim.
Think about the eternal ages.

One day we are going to a beautiful place
Where the soul never dies; the angels fly.
Give God the praise, thank Him for divine grace.
Hold the cross up high.

Never give up, never quit!
When the pain is hard to bear,
The hand of the Lord, keep holding it.
Soon we will meet Jesus in the air.

Now I don't know when.
Jesus will split the eastern sky.
From heaven He will descend.
To glory we shall fly.

He that endures to the end,
Maybe through suffering and pain,
But with Christ we shall ascend.
Our faith is not in vain.

# Oil in the Lamp
## September 19

A little bit of oil,
Not very much light.
In just a little while,
The sun fades into the night.

Time to set up camp.
The lantern has gone out.
No oil in the lamp—
More oil needs to be bought.

Now it is very hard to see,
To gather the firewood,
The small branches from the trees.
Some of the campers are in a distressful mood.

When the Lord comes to our camp,
Maybe at midnight,
Will He find oil in the lamp?
The flame of love, is it burning bright?

He has told us to watch and pray.
Let us keep the oil burning
Each and every day.
The Lord is soon returning.

He will come without warning,
His children to take away.
Our light is shining,
It will be a glorious day.

If the lamp is running low,
Maybe it is time to refuel.
The love of God to know,
Make sure the lamp is full.

Now is a good time to prepare.
At the cross, when we kneel,
Jesus will meet us there,
The oil lamp to fill.

Oil in the lamp every day,
No room for any more.
He will come without delay.
Be ready, He will open heaven's door.

# This Old Train
## September 20

This old train has jumped the track.
It no longer runs down the railroad line.
The train carried the mail sacks.
It was almost always on time.

Passengers would come from all around.
They would look out the windows
And wait for the train to come to town.
No matter if it was a storm or heavy snow.

Old faithful would come rolling in.
The smoke looked like thunderclouds.
The train came around the bend.
Noise from the engine was too loud.

The train would come to a screeching stop.
A conductor would announce, "All aboard."
The train would start up the steep slope.
It would climb slowly on the old railroad.

Passengers on the train were headed home.
This was the only way they could get there.
Some of the people traveled alone.
Thick puffs of smoke filled the air.

The train has jumped the track!
Will the residents get home?
Men work on the rails; soon the train is back.
Now the journey will resume.

Is there a train named Old Faithful?
This poem came from my imagination.
On the track of life, be thankful!
God is in charge of the train station.

He will set a derailed soul back on the rail.
When God is near, we are never alone,
By His power and might, we will not fail.
This old train is going home.

The rails have been repaired.
The work has been done in Jesus' name.
We are going to meet the Lord in the air.
Get on board the gospel train.

# Lion on the Prowl
## September 21

Thoughts of the mind,
Make sure you shut the gate
From a roaming hungry lion.
It's been a while since he ate.

He seeks his prey
Early in the morning light,
Throughout the day,
Even in the darkest night.

A lamb in the field,
The lion is on the prowl.
Here is a free meal.
Hear the lion's growl.

The shepherd draws near.
He takes the lamb in his arms.
A small lamb trembles in fear.
The shepherd protects from all harm.

Sometimes a shepherd's staff
Or even a small fire,
It will keep the sheep safe.
A lion has a hungry desire.

At the sound of a man's voice,
The lion leaves its prey.
It is time to rejoice.
The lamb is safe another day.

Our enemy Satan,
He seeks whom he may devour.
He is like a roaring lion,
Hungry, and he is on the prowl.

He is hungry for the lamb.
He has come to destroy and kill.
When he hears Jesus' name,
He retreats back into the hills.

Lion on the prowl,
He seeks a lamb gone astray, too.
God will not allow.
Satan has no power over you.

# Thin Ice
## September 22

A heavy blanket of snow,
It lay upon the ground.
The north wind began to blow.
Trees with fresh snow are crowned.

Icicles hang below.
Tree limbs crack and break.
Power lines way too low.
Ice covers the lake.

A young, adventurous man,
He steps outside in the bitter cold.
With ice skates in his hand,
This imaginary story is told.

At the lake he stands.
All alone in the morning light,
I know it is hard to understand.
But for thin ice you need a little foresight.

Remember, he is alone,
No one else in sight.
Now he will not stay long.
He loves to skate; that is his delight.

Well, I'm sorry to say
About midway in the lake
A terrible tragedy happened that day.
The ice began to crack and break.

His life came to an end.
On the lake of thin ice,
Death came without warning.
This is a good place for some advice.

If on the lake of sin,
It's not too late to turn back.
Let Jesus bring you safely in.
If you venture on, the ice may crack.

The lure of sin, the duration is long.
Get up early and stay late.
The days of life will soon be gone.
An unrepentant heart will meet its fate.

# Abandoned
## September 23

An old house on a hill,
No doors or windows
To stop the winter chill.
Nothing can hinder the gently falling snow.

A place called home
Many years ago,
But now it stands alone.
No windows aglow.

The family moved away
From their small dwelling.
Now the house is in decay.
The snow keeps falling.

The home was abandoned.
It was left to the mercy of the elements.
Soon it will fall to the ground,
A home safe and secure is now vacant.

If a house is left in disarray,
The wind and the storm
Will gradually destroy day by day.
It was a nice family home.

Let us make a home and life as one.
The main problem is neglect.
They both need attention.
No special care will be a time of regret.

Life is a dwelling place.
If abandoned, it will end in despair.
Restoration comes by grace.
The chief architect is needed for the repair.

God's grace is sufficient
To keep us all the day long.
It is more than efficient.
A life in Christ is good and strong.

My God will never abandon
Where the house of faith stands,
A life built by His Son.
Behold the nail-scarred hands.

# Too Close to the Edge
## September 24

Let us take an imaginary trip
High upon a mountain ledge.
Be careful, or you may slip
And fall from the rocky edge.

Now look out across the land.
Tell me what you see.
But be cautious where you stand.
Down below the river flows free.

Truly it is a beautiful waterfall.
The water splashes upon the ground.
Trees grow strong and tall.
Please be aware—jagged rocks all around.

A warning I give,
You need someone to lead.
Follow Jesus, He will give you a new life to live.
Let Christ be your guide; His blood I plead!

On the mountain high
Near the rocks of sin and corruption
It's best to have the Lord by your side.
Stay away from the cliffs of destruction.

In your walk with the Lord
High upon the mountain ledge,
Heed the warning of God's Word.
Don't walk too close to the edge.

A fall would be drastic indeed.
Away from God's love and mercy,
But Jesus Christ, He intercedes
That He might save you and me.

Take hold of the Savior's hand
Before sin drags you down.
Obey His command.
A faithful servant will wear a glory crown.

He will keep you from falling.
The cliffs of sin will lead to the grave.
Hold His hand, tightly clinging.
He has the power to save.

# Self-Inflicted Wound
## September 25

Self-inflicted wound,
There is no one to blame.
This is my very own.
I have to endure the shame.

I gave a false impression.
It was brought into view.
It was a bad representation.
A self-made picture is the clue.

Well, let the mystery be broken.
I had no picture for Memorial Day.
My heart's desire was to honor the veteran.
A self-portrait was used to my dismay.

A lesson I learned.
No picture to show,
It is better than a photo that was falsely created.
I am sorry; I want you to know.

I know that I did wrong.
Sometimes our pain is self-inflicted.
We have to endure the suffering alone.
But our Lord, He cares for the afflicted.

He will give a spiritual blessing,
Let Him wrap the wound.
Good intentions can be distressing.
Healing will come; His grace will abound.

It may take a few days,
The soul takes time to heal.
God works in mysteries ways.
Be patient; His love will be revealed.

The healing has begun.
God's love continues to flow.
Keep pressing on!
His divine healing is beginning to show.

If by chance you have a self-inflicted wound,
God knows how to treat it.
With His love to completely surround,
He gives peace and joy in the Holy Spirit.

# This Old House
## September 26

This old house is coming down.
A life that is built on a weak foundation
Will soon fall to the ground.
Let us examine the materials of construction.

A life that is built on the sand,
The deceitfulness of riches
Will not help it stand.
A spiritual house will not be built by the faithless.

This old house full of sin,
For many long years
A life was wasted within.
But now it's coming to an end.

Let me tell you, my friend,
At an altar of repentance,
A new construction begins.
Peace is made with God without resistance.

"Old things are passed away,
Behold, all things are become new"(2 Cor. 5:17).
The foundation has already been laid.
Now the building process is up to you.

The old house of unrighteousness,
Replace the framework with God's Grace.
A new house of holiness
Will soon take its place.

The construction continues day by day.
The wall of eternal love,
It is fortified when you pray.
Build on the rock of ages, God will approve.

Holiness unto the Lord,
A new life begins.
The development is by the Word.
The end result is a home in heaven.

On a weak foundation,
The building will fall in the sand.
When you build on the plan of salvation,
The house will stand.

# Too Close to the Fire
## September 27

When wood is added to the fire,
There is intense heat.
As the flames reach higher,
The best escape is to retreat.

So don't stand too close to the fire.
It may scorch your eyebrows
Sometimes flames will singe the hair.
But most certainly the wood it will devour.

If the fire is almost out,
Add another branch.
But always have an escape route.
A wildfire—you may not have a second chance.

The danger is to stand idly by.
A burning, raging fire is out of control.
Sparks ascend into the sky.
The dry brush is extremely flammable.

Run for your life, no escape to stay there.
Maybe you will be badly burned
By standing too close to the fire.
Move quickly and you will be unharmed.

There is another fire.
Make sure you turn and run.
Go to Jesus; the only escape is to go there
He is God's Son.

So don't stand too close to the fire.
You may be badly burned.
As the flames reach higher.
From your sins don't hesitate to turn.

Move away from your sins.
Take hold of Jesus' hand.
Let a new life begin.
From the flames you'll be glad you ran.

Escape to the arms above.
Flee from the everlasting flame.
Thank God for His great love.
Rejoice in Jesus' name.

# Drifting Away, Not Anymore
## September 28

Drifting away,
Faraway from the peaceful shore.
No time to pray,
Or seek God anymore.

On life's boundless sea
The ship is tossed to and fro.
The current of life is a terrible place to be.
Sin is the high tide; go with the flow.

No cares or worries on your journey,
Now God is in the distance
And you are a long ways from eternity.
You are in a perilous sea without any resistance.

To ride the waves of sin is your delight.
No concern about tomorrow,
Just live as you please, day or night.
Without God your life will end in sorrow.

For a life of sinful pleasure,
You decided to sail the ocean blue.
Your fulfillment of life is just an earthly treasure.
Many sailors have died; death is coming for you too.

Ride the strong current of sin; it leads to despair.
No peace or joy when you come to the end,
A lifeless ship lies in ruin on the sandbar.
Your fate will be worse if you continue in sin.

Drifting away!
You took up the anchor long ago.
What if you took the time to pray?
Kept your ship anchored in the God you know.

Well you would be closer to heaven.
The raging sea becomes the calm waters of the soul.
The sinful treasures would all be forsaken.
The Lord is coming back for the faithful.

Drifting away, not anymore!
Now you are living the heavenly way.
Soon you will step on to heaven's shore.
Prayer is the lifeline of hope every day.

# Fire on the Mountain
## September 29

It was a hot and dry day.
There was no moisture in the air.
The earth was like hardened clay.
It was perfect conditions for a wild fire.

The Warden comes by.
He warns the campers of the impending danger.
There's not a cloud in the sky.
Also there is a warning from the forest ranger.

Be careful with the fire!
But to his dismay,
Black smoke soon filled the air.
It was about midday.

The entire forest was ablaze,
Flames devouring the mountain,
Vision was poor in the cloudy haze.
The fire was almost impossible to contain.

The campers ran for their lives.
Oh, to be saved from this fiery inferno.
Children, husbands, and wives,
Escape for thy lives; go down to the valley below.

Now, my friend, this is a make-believe vision
I told of a wildfire on a mountain.
But certainly it is for a very good reason.
It concerns the salvation of man.

How can anyone be saved
And escape the eternal flames?
May I suggest that you pray!
Believe on Jesus' name.

Tell Him that you are a sinner.
He is on the mainline.
God is a great forgiver.
Think about the fire on the mountain.

It's time to run!
Flee for thy life; escape the fire.
Believe on God's Son.
Soon your time will expire.

# what would we do?
## September 30

If we could save a man—
He is on the cross dying,
The nails pierced deep into His hands,
His pain was excruciating—

Would we walk away
Or watch Him die?
If we were in the crowd that day,
What would have been our reply?

"Let Him go free,"
Or did we say, "Crucify, crucify?"
Behold the man of Galilee.
On a cross that day He would die.

Many people crying
As they watch the Son of God.
He was on the cross dying.
There was a great loss of blood.

Would we dare to take His place
If His life we could spare?
When we saw the agony on His face,
To set him free would we hang there?

Well, I don't know about your reaction.
Neither do I know my own.
I just know of His passion.
On the cross of Calvary, Jesus stayed on.

For our sins He died.
He took our place.
On the cross He was crucified.
We have freedom from sin by divine grace.

His love is great toward us.
Behold the Son of God.
His name is Jesus.
The soul-cleansing power is in the blood.

He will not walk away
From a soul He came to save.
My friend, it's time to pray.
Don't wait another day!

# Tomorrow's Victory
## October 1

The leaves are gently falling,
Red, yellow and gold.
A strong wind is blowing.
Be prepared for the bitter cold.

Go to the shelter.
Lay your coat in the chair.
Have a little talk with God the Father.
There is peace and tranquility by the fire.

Offer a few words of praise.
This is a good time for a peaceful devotion.
With holy hands to raise;
Thank Him for His wonderful salvation.

Precious minutes in the presence of God.
The sweet Holy Spirit comes down.
Speak reverently; Jesus Christ is Lord!
God's grace will always abound.

Stay there for a while.
You will need strength for the journey.
Peace and contentment for that last long mile,
A crown of life will be given in glory.

Many trials will come your way.
Seek God earnestly in prayer.
He will answer without delay.
The burden is not too heavy for Him to bear.

Today with God,
Rejoice in the hour,
Meditate upon His Word,
He has the power.

He is never late,
Love Him with heart, soul, and mind.
Patiently wait!
He is always on time.

A day to prepare
For tomorrow's victory,
Cast upon Him all your care.
The battle will be won triumphantly.

# Dig a New Well
## October 2

The old well is nearly dry
When once the well was full,
An abundance of water supply.
The bucket was easy to pull.

Enough water for the family;
Even the neighbors could share.
The water container is empty.
There is nothing left to spare.

The water was used to irrigate the fields.
The wheat would grow
Always a good harvest yield,
But now there is nothing to show.

Look out across the land.
Tell me what you see.
The earth is bare, just empty sand.
No leaves on the trees.

The well no longer supplies
The channels to fill;
Even the grass has withered and died.
No need the garden to till.

Don't give up hope.
Just dig a new well.
Down the steep slopes,
The ponds and streams begin to swell.

Open up the channels of your heart.
The well of life overflows.
Salvation and mercy He will impart.
His love and grace is a continuous flow.

The old well is void and empty.
Just an empty shell,
No water for the family.
Dig a new well!

God will send a blessing.
The waters of life rising,
A sweet Holy Ghost refreshing,
God blesses a sinful life confessing.

# God Will Bless
## October 3

A special prayer today,
I asked the Lord to use me
In his own special way
That I may tell of His love and mercy,

To show His goodness,
Concern for all mankind,
His grace and loving kindness.
They are the works of glory divine.

God heard my heartfelt pleas.
I wanted His love to flow through me
So others could be blessed.
A glimmer of hope it is for eternity.

Just a glimpse into the Samaritan story,
Visualize with me a man who was beaten.
Robbed of his money,
He was in great pain.

His need of help was for that day.
He was in great sorrow and distress.
On a cold wet ground he lay.
Now don't be like the others and just pass

To leave him in his pain,
To walk on by
In the cold bitter rain.
Possibly he will die.

Remember, when we asked God to bless,
To use us in His own special way.
This is the answer to our request.
Time is wasting; don't delay!

God's love is expressed
If we find today,
A poor, weary soul in distress,
Please, don't turn away!

God answers prayer.
But where there is a need,
A blessing for today,
It will come when we perform the deed.

# Tear the Old Fence Down
## October 4

Tear the old fence down.
All the barriers of the heart,
Let God's love surround.
With the Holy Spirit He will impart.

There are many things to separate,
To keep us apart,
He will open heaven's gate.
If our sins, we depart.

Commit our heart and soul,
He gives a strong embrace.
His love we know
He gives us grace.

Sin is that wall,
It is a great divide.
Repent, the enclosure will fall
When the blood is applied.

The middle wall is broken down.
We have fellowship with God above.
His arms will wrap around.
He is a God of love.

Tear the old fence down.
Go to God in prayer.
Forgiveness at the cross is found.
Tears of joy will flow like a mighty river.

A fence fortified by sin,
It will separate us from the God of creation.
In His presence, how can we enter in?
Just believe in Jesus, His life, death, and resurrection.

A repentant heart, the wall of sin cannot stand.
Faith breaks apart all barriers of resistance.
Oh, for a touch of the Master's hand.
The gates of heaven will open for a grand entrance.

Tear the old fence down.
We will enter into the presence of God above.
One day soon we will wear the glory crown.
Saved by grace, let us continue in His love.

# Prepare to Meet Thy God
## October 5

I have a very important message.
It requires an urgent reply.
It has been preached down through the ages
In every town and city, all along the countryside.

It's time to get ready!
Put on your garments of white.
Approach the throne on bended knee.
Enter into the presence of His glorious light.

My friend, you are about to meet
The God of all creation.
Do you have your blood-washed garment?
Will heaven be your final destination?

Whatever your answer may be,
The time has come.
Where will you spend eternity?
I hope heaven is your home.

But one thing is for sure—
It's time to meet thy God.
Holy and righteous and pure,
He is the creator of the world.

Come into His divine presence.
Feel the power of His might.
Only God can claim eternal existence.
Be very sure your garment is white.

"Thou your sins be as scarlet,
They shall be as white as snow"( Isaiah 1:18).
Your garment must be washed in the blood of Christ.
This salvation is for your soul.

Prepare to meet thy God!
The angels cry, "Holy, Holy, Holy" (Revelations 4:8).
Oh, to hear those blessed words.
Make sure your soul is worthy.

The time is now to repent.
Let Him touch you with His love.
Put on your holy garments.
Come into the presence of God above.

# Search Diligently
## October 6

It is cold outside.
Please go and search one more time.
Walk down by the riverside.
I know the hills are steep to climb.

It is a matter of life and death.
Perhaps a few hours remaining,
A wayward soul will soon take his last breath.
Don't give up; keep searching!

Go into the towns.
Search diligently!
Inquire of the people all around.
If any news, return home quickly.

Compel others to help you find
The Great Physician.
The backslider may say, "He was a friend of mine."
He knew all about my condition.

It's been a while since we talked.
We parted company many years ago.
We used to go for morning walks.
The way of life He would show.

Now the days have come and gone.
There is a need for the doctor's care.
A blood transfusion is needed of God's Son.
Without the blood a life will soon expire.

Jesus is the only one who can save.
To heal a poor lost soul,
The prescription for life He gave.
Repent; He will make you whole.

Ye shall seek me and find
When you search with all of your heart.
Love God with all of your strength and mind.
The death hold of sin breaks apart.

Search diligently!
Salvation for the soul, a repentant heart will find
God forgives sin if you will seek earnestly;
The blood of Jesus can be applied just in time.

# A Little Kindness
## October 7

Just a little kindness
Can help you throughout the day.
A tremendous amount of peace,
It will come when you pray.

Praise, honor, and glory
Belongs to God above.
Your fellowman needs a little mercy.
Most certainly he needs a lot of love.

If you want to be a blessing,
The riverbanks to overflow,
Tell others with words expressing
Of the great God you know.

Sometimes just a little smile,
A frown can be turned to joy.
It will most certainly last awhile.
Kindness is a good thing to employ.

Goodness and mercy go together.
They work in the harvest field.
You will not find one without the other.
It is time to go home, up the golden hills.

Your work on earth is done.
It may be hard to realize
The many souls you have won
Just because you were kind and nice.

Receive peace, mercy, and grace
From God's holy throne,
A blessing for the entire human race.
What you give is a reflection of God's Son.

It may be hard to understand
But the only Bible some people read.
It is a life crafted by God's mighty hand.
Perhaps, it is the work of a good deed.

Show a little kindness,
Christ life to reflect.
Live a life of righteousness;
Someone's soul it will affect.

# Never Thirst Again
## October 8

Come and go with me
To a well of water pure and find.
Drink all you want; the water is free.
Leave the bucket behind.

Now let me tell you.
The water supply is divine.
It depends on whom you know.
A surrendered heart will give peace of mind.

This well is of a different kind.
It can satisfy the soul.
The longing in the heart of mankind,
It is a refreshing flow.

Where can this water be found?
Water so pure and divine
In the country or the cities all around
No place can confine.

Living water abounds
In the heart of those who believe.
At the altar on holy ground,
The blessing of God is to receive.

Drink of this well;
Never thirst again.
A yielded life to God's will,
He offers forgiveness of sin.

As I said before, it all depends
On whom you know.
Drink from God's holy fountain,
Where living water will forever flow.

To satisfy the longing thirst,
Drink of the living water.
Believe on the Lord Jesus Christ.
Have fellowship with God the Father.

Never thirst again.
When you find the main water supply,
Drink till your heart is content.
Your spiritual thirst only Jesus can satisfy.

# In God We Trust
## October 9

Let us carve a wooden nickel.
This is a project for the Master Artist.
Only He can cut the intricate details.
In the creative process He will assist.

There are very small words to cut,
One of the words is Liberty.
So let us use a piece of walnut.
The knife cuts away the wood so easily.

But now we come to the word In.
It is a much smaller word.
To remove from our life is sin.
Truly this is the work of the Lord.

So continue to carve.
The word following In: it is God.
Think about His great love
When He created the world.

Our lives God would mold and shape.
Let us now cut the word We.
Certainly our sins we must forsake.
God's creative art we shall see.

The last word in that line,
Let us carve the word Trust.
Now we have just a little time.
But God commands us to love Him first.

In God We Trust.
We just carved a wooden nickel.
God is first and foremost.
He is the Master Craftsman for the eternal.

In real life they say,
"Don't take any wooden nickels."
But if it's our sins to take away,
Let God translate the infinite details.

We are His workmanship,
Created in His image and His likeness.
He can remove the sinful chips
And restore a life of righteousness.

# Return unto Me
## October 10

Think about these words:
"Come unto me" (Matthew 11:28).
This was the call of the Lord.
Those who went to Jesus were set free.

Joy and peace was felt.
The love of God was so real.
Multiplied thousands have knelt.
The Holy Spirit they could feel.

But time is gone.
At one time the Savior was close by.
It is a terrible thing to stand alone.
Sins of an unfaithful heart abide.

Sins of the world call for a return.
Walk away from God's grace.
Life after death there is no concern.
They no longer seek His face.

At one time Jesus was near.
He speaks to each one's heart
With words ever so clear.
He is deeply saddened for those who depart.

The invitation from the Lord,
Return unto me!
According to His divine Word,
God will forgive and have mercy.

Where is God?
It is not so hard to find Him.
At the cross where Christ shed His blood,
Sins confessed; He will forgive them.

"Come unto me."
Remember the first call.
Jesus set them free.
He has power over all.

Return unto me, He calls those who walked away.
God is faithful and just to forgive.
Death is in the shadows, it may be too late to pray.
Forgiveness is promised; only believe!

# Keep the Home Fires Burning
## October 11

Keep the home fires burning.
A light in the window,
Our Savior is returning.
I hope you are ready to go.

Oil in the lantern,
Wood on the fire,
Jesus will return.
Will you meet Him in the air?

He is coming back like He said.
But if your candle is under a bushel
His coming will be a time to dread.
A light on a hill is the lamp of the eternal.

If the fire of faith grows dim,
The shadows of darkness move in.
Without faith it is impossible to please Him.
Brighter is the flame when you turn from sin.

On your knees in prayer
Call upon the Lord.
See how the flame grows brighter,
A faltering life is now restored.

Keep the home fires burning.
Hold the cross up high.
Be ready! Jesus is coming
In the clouds of the sky.

Let the light of His glory shine on.
Help one another.
Many souls need to be won.
Tell them Jesus is Lord and Savior.

The flames burning bright,
Plenty of fuel to spare,
The love for mankind is in the lamp light.
God's grace will ignite faith's fire.

Are the home fires burning?
Living the Christian life daily,
Embers of love constantly glowing,
Give God all the glory.

# Lost More Than Was Won
## October 12

The end of life's journey,
Many miles were run.
The hope of the faithful is a home in glory.
A crown of life will be won.

The gates of heaven will open.
They will swing wide.
God welcomes the forgiven.
With Christ they will forever abide.

Life eternal is the promise.
Run to win.
No shortcuts, please.
Runners will be disqualified for sin.

Some people have turned from grace
To a life of sinful pleasure.
They cross the finish line with disgrace.
No crown will be given to the unholy or impure.

Lost more than was won.
A terrible tragedy in this earthly race,
No victory is claimed without God's Son.
The unfaithful are unable to look upon His face.

Crossed the finish line, completed the course.
But lost all hope of glory divine.
An earthly run will end in remorse.
The runners ran without a made up mind.

Run to win, lay hold on life eternal.
When a race is well run,
God will give His approval.
The glory crown will be won.

Shortcuts will not avail.
Cross the finish line,
Only by grace will a runner prevail.
Faithful to the end will be heaven's gain.

Won more than was lost.
Keep the faith and never stop running.
Love God foremost.
A life in Christ is rewarding.

# I Will Answer Thee
## October 13

God is on the throne.
The mighty God, everlasting Father,
He is the Holy One,
Access to Him is by prayer.

Call upon Him today.
He listens attentively to each request.
No one is turned away.
Every day His love is manifest.

He said, "Call unto me,
And I will answer thee"(Jeremiah 33:3).
He is the God of all mercy.
Reverence Him on bended knee.

Come into His presence.
He is a holy and righteous God.
Experience the power of His deliverance.
He is faithful to His word.

Whatever the need,
God said to call.
Prayers and petitions to plead,
He speaks to one and all.

If the request is for healing,
He is the great physician.
With all power revealing,
He can heal any health condition.

Even while we are yet speaking,
He is answering our prayers,
A miracle is in the making.
Receive a blessing from God the Father.

His love and grace are special gifts, too.
God will show great and mighty things.
Worship Him; He is faithful and true.
He will answer the request we bring.

"Kind and gracious heavenly Father,
Lay your holy hand upon us.
We give you the praise, glory, and honor.
Bless the name of Jesus."

# God Answers Prayer
## October 14

Upon the parched ground,
The grass has withered.
The color has changed to a hazy brown.
No food for the cows to feed.

For many a long day,
The earth was thirsty for rain.
Fields were full of seedless hay.
Dry conditions still remain.

There's not a cloud in the sky.
Oh, that the people would pray
Before they perish and die.
If only rain would come today.

There's no place to go.
Lakes and ponds are dry.
The streams cease to flow.
Many residents will die.

But what is that I see in the distance?
Why, it seems to be a small cloud,
About the size of a man's hand.
Could it be a thundercloud?

The clouds gather overhead.
Lightning flashes across the sky,
The dry streams will soon be fed.
The power of God no one can deny!

It's beginning to rain.
The riverbeds overflow.
Banks cannot contain
The raging water as it flows.

God answers prayer.
Heart felt pleas are not in vain.
This could be the hour
When you hear the abundance of rain.

Don't fret or turn away!
Keep on praying.
The answer to your prayer may come today.
By faith receive a blessing.

# Stir Up the Coals
## October 15

The fire has not gone out
As some might suppose,
There is a little doubt;
A bright ember will expose.

Turn the coals over.
A gentle fire is burning.
A new faith to discover,
A passionate fire is consuming.

Stir up the coals.
Move them around a bit.
Revive the flames of old.
A new wave of glory He will transmit.

A live, enriching flame,
A glorious light to shine,
The gospel of Christ to proclaim,
A new life will redefine.

Just a small spark,
A fire will rise.
From the shadow of the dark,
The flames reach high into the skies.

Add a few coals to the fire.
It will last throughout the night.
A strong potential desire
You can see the morning light.

If in your life the embers lie,
The fire has grown dull,
It's not too late to revive.
The fire of faith ignites the flame of the soul.

Just a little talk with Jesus,
The flames begin to grow.
They spread across the field of service.
The gospel message is aglow.

Stir up the coals.
A strong fire returning.
In the depth of the soul,
A passionate fire is burning.

# Unload the Wagon
## October 16

Many bushel baskets to fill,
We must carry each one
Through the harvest field.
Load up the old wagon.

Go get the horses from the barn.
They have a job to do.
The wagon will be drawn.
Slowly it begins to move.

Now the wagon is full.
It is a heavy load.
The horses most certainly can pull.
They walk down the winding road.

The wagon is drawn across the ground.
The farmer likes to buy and trade.
Soon he will be in the little town.
Many deals are made.

With an empty wagon,
He is homeward bound.
All of his produce is gone.
His home is in the foreground.

Let me emphasize
How we are drawn.
We all need to realize
The power is not our own.

The wagon of sin is full.
Our life is loaded down.
It is most certainly too hard to pull.
We need to unload the wagon.

If we want to go
To that heavenly town,
The love of God to know,
Then we must be drawn.

This is the work of the Holy Spirit.
He brings conviction.
He draws us to Jesus, our sins to remit.
Unload the wagon by faith in the resurrection.

# In His Presence
## October 17

Two or three gathered together;
Jesus is in the midst.
He abides forever.
All hope and joy is in Christ.

When two or three are talking
And having fellowship in Jesus' name,
Along with them another is walking.
I know it is very hard to explain.

They may not see Him
Along the path as they walk,
But Christ is most certainly with them.
He listens to them as they talk.

Upon this earthly road,
The Son of God is with us.
On our behalf He intercedes to God.
Let us walk with Jesus.

The Lord is always near.
He stands in our midst.
No need to worry or fear,
Our journey to heaven He will assist.

Just to know He is there,
His presence we can feel.
He loves us and He cares.
The closeness of God is so real.

He meets with us each day.
Our hearts overflowing
As He guides us along the way.
We know He is never leaving.

Let us talk and pray in Jesus' name.
Read the holy Word,
The kingdom of God to acclaim.
We have sweet fellowship with the Lord.

The Son of God will appear
If with a friend we are talking.
Don't be surprised if Jesus draws near!
Along the pathway of life, we are walking.

# What does God require?
## October 18

What shall I bring
Into the presence of the Lord,
Before the throne of the King,
When I bow before the most high God?

A lamb less than a year old?
Shall I give burnt offerings?
The best lamb of the fold?
Perhaps I will give a golden ring.

What about silver and gold?
All of which I have none.
Maybe "ten thousands of rivers of oil"(Micah 6:7)
Or my best gift, "my firstborn."

Many things to offer,
But what does He require?
Let's start with a love offering.
The firstborn is not His desire.

Nor the riches of the world
Or a sacrificial lamb
To come before almighty God.
No need for a thousand rams.

Well then, what does He require?
"To do justly"(Micah 6:8, KJV).
A faithful servant He admires.
He wants us "to love mercy" (Micah 6:8),

"To walk humbly with thy God" (Micah 6:8).
Now I see what He wants me to bring.
A commitment to the Lord
Is far better than any earthly thing.

To love Him with all,
A complete surrender
Of heart, mind, and soul,
In His divine presence, we may enter.

What does God require?
"To do justly, to love mercy."
Let these things be our heart's desire.
We will receive a crown of glory.

# Stay on Course
## October 19

Travel with me
Across the ocean blue.
It expands as far as the eye can see.
I know you have other things to do.

Many miles can be traveled
Imagination brings the trip into view.
The sails have been unraveled.
You are the captain of the crew.

On the weather-beaten map.
An x marks the location.
No time to take a nap;
Soon you will arrive at the destination.

There is a time limit,
But you must stay on course.
Be determined, never give up or quit.
Stay away from the rocks of remorse.

Keep right on sailing.
Don't stop at the pleasure-seeking towns.
Just keep on moving.
Continue the journey until heaven is found.

Follow Jesus every day.
Give a full commitment
To go all the way.
If sin appears, repent.

There is a certain way
That leads to the promised land.
Keep your eyes on Jesus; take time to pray.
Be faithful until the very end.

If your faith and love is in Him,
The destination can be found.
Keep your hand on the helm.
Allow the grace of God to abound.

Travel with Jesus in this journey.
God is waiting for your arrival.
A short stay on earth will end in eternity.
Life in Christ is eternal.

# In His Hands
## October 20

In His hands a sparrow
From the tree had fallen.
Upon the ground so low,
The baby bird, safe in the nest again.

If God so loved the sparrow,
Think about His great love for you.
When in the valley of sorrow
You're feeling mighty blue.

A fall from grace will not keep you down.
Take hold of His hand.
He will lift you to higher ground.
One day you can enter the Promised Land.

In His hands a lamb,
It strayed from the fold.
Just like the lamb, the Lord calls your name.
In His arms, a loving embrace will hold.

With Him you'll forever be.
Safe and secure in His hands,
Even the wind and the sea
Obey His commands.

See the nail prints in His hands.
Thrust your hand into His side.
When Jesus died, darkness covered the land.
Now the Son of righteousness forever abides.

In His hands, the heart of faith will see.
He arose from the grave.
Eternal life for all who believe,
Thank God for His amazing grace.

There is a special place to be.
Where the nails were deep,
The scars of love to see,
His hands can hold with a promise to keep.

A poor defenseless soul,
Yes, in His hands, peace with God you know.
He has the power to hold;
He will never let go.

# High Calling of God
## October 21

What would you have me to do?
As I walk the Christian way
That I may draw closer to you,
I know you want me to pray.

Perhaps you would have me to preach,
My time spent
In a Sunday school class the Word to teach.
I know there are many souls that need to repent.

Could it possibly be
The high calling of God a poem to write?
I know you're talking to me
Words from the heart; it will give a lot of light.

When blessed by the Lord,
The light can show the way.
By the power of the Word,
God receives glory and honor every day.

A word rightly spoken,
The time and the place,
The door to heaven will open.
A soul will be saved by grace.

So whatever we do,
The Lord has many different callings,
The light to shine all the night through.
He wants to keep someone from falling.

Use the talent given,
So keep the light shining.
God continues to bless His chosen.
Go and rescue the perishing.

When we reach out to others,
I am quite sure we draw closer to you.
When we help one another,
Heaven comes into view.

The high calling of God,
Anointed by the Holy Spirit,
Lives are touched by the Word.
The best gift of grace is to live it.

# It Is Only a Tree
## October 22

It is only a tree,
With branches and limbs,
But let me tell you what I see.
The branches climb

Toward the sky.
Each limb has its own style.
A message to the birds that fly,
"Come and rest awhile."

With arms lifted high
To give God the glory and the praise,
A gentle breeze passes by.
Soon all the limbs rise.

I see the beautiful leaves.
Just a glimpse of all God's blessings,
Many wonderful, beautiful trees,
God's wonderful love expressing.

A tree of such splendor,
I wonder how it can stand.
It has strong roots in the ground floor.
But it must be by God's divine hand.

The power of His love,
It will never lose its hold.
Grace and mercy come down from above.
The tree stands with many stories untold.

Upon the ground I see
The leaves cover like snow.
God's divine love and mercy
Are the shadows of my soul.

It's only a tree,
"Steadfast, unmovable, always abounding"(1Cor.15:58).
Tell me what you see.
Perhaps limbs of praise are rising.

I believe God wants us to be the same.
Just like a tree, arms lifted high.
Strong and secure in Jesus' name,
Lift up holy hands, the Son of God to magnify.

# Unlock the Door
## October 23

Call upon the Lord.
Pray with a sincere heart,
Read His holy Word.
His love He will impart.

The Lord stands at the door, gently knocking.
Time is running out for the unbeliever.
Please don't keep Him waiting.
Those who repent know Jesus is the Savior.

He will not force His way in,
Or offer a temporary reprieve
For the multitude of sins.
Eternal life is promised to those who believe.

He is preparing a home in glory.
Think about the place.
Open the door; you won't be sorry.
Salvation comes by grace.

His love extends to the uttermost.
Even to a person who is the worst sinner.
Jesus is the Lord of host.
God is a great forgiver.

Unlock the door!
Do you want Him to leave or stay?
Decide today or He may depart forevermore.
This could be the last chance to pray.

He is patiently waiting.
Salvation He will impart.
Jesus will be your Savior.
It depends on faith in the heart.

Please don't turn Him away.
Sins will be forgiven.
No time to delay,
Repent! The gates of heaven will open.

Faith turns the key.
Only you can unlock the door.
The power of God to see,
Go and sin no more.

# Strike the Match
## October 24

On a cold wintry night,
The snow is coming down.
Upon the mountain height,
Ice crystals sparkle all around.

Sleet and freezing rain
Falling upon the ground.
The survival of man,
He will die unless a shelter is found.

Inside a mountain cave,
Safe from the threatening storm,
It is surely a time to pray.
A fire can keep him warm.

The body aches in pain.
How can he escape the bitter cold?
Only a couple of matches remain,
And they are difficult to hold.

Live or die, maybe this is his last breath.
A small fire can revive.
He can escape the stronghold of death.
Strike the match; the fire of hope may save a life.

In answer to his prayer,
There is a small spark in the wood.
The heat and warmth of a small fire,
Beside the flames this young man stood.

Always in life keep a watchful eye on the fire.
It may dwindle and even die,
But the fire of faith God requires.
See the flames, how they reach into the sky.

If the fire has gone out
And the wood is covered with snow,
Be up and about.
Strike the match of faith; the embers of life will glow.

Those who believe will see
A spiritual flame rising.
The prayer of faith, God will answer thee.
Eternal life to claim, please keep the fire burning.

# God Will Supply
## October 25

He supplies all our needs,
According to His riches.
Many souls to feed,
A hungry soul He blesses.

When in need of a blessing,
A spiritual thirst to satisfy,
The cup of joy refreshing,
He sends a sweet shower from the sky.

When there is hunger,
Sit down at the table.
It's time for supper.
A fresh filling comes from the Bible.

My God supplies.
When in need of guidance,
On the Lord Jesus, we can rely.
On Him, there is complete reliance.

From a sincere, searching heart,
He gives a wonderful blessing.
Love, joy, and peace, He imparts.
Salvation is worth confessing.

When the dark clouds form,
He sends the sunshine.
A new life to transform,
The hope of glory is divine.

He supplies according to His riches.
With a holy hand He reaches down.
Even in the miry clay, a sinner to reach,
The grace of God abounds.

Now if we want something material,
we may have to go to town,
But if we're in need of the eternal,
We had best turn our lives around.

According to His riches in glory,
He will supply our needs.
The blessed hope of eternity,
My Jesus will intercede.

# Go Back to the River
## October 26

The blessings from above,
They will satisfy the thirst.
At the river of His love,
God has commanded to love Him first.

To love Him first and foremost,
With all the heart and soul,
He is the Lord of host.
The love of God you know.

Fill up the empty vessel,
Patiently wait at the river of His grace.
There is peace and joy in the words of the Bible.
It is an eternal resting place.

A few drops of water will not satisfy
The longings of a thirsty soul.
A sincere searching heart He will not deny.
Remember when the spiritual container was full.

Come and partake of the water.
Fill up all of your vessels.
Drink from the flowing river.
God performs mighty miracles.

Fill up the empty pail.
Drink to your heart's content.
God's love and mercy will never fail.
Jesus wants you to repent!

Sins will be forgiven.
Sometimes the need is to go back to the river,
The holy place where you have been.
Fill up the vessel with pure water.

Go back to the river
Where the love of God forever flows.
Drink of the living water.
The cup of salvation overflows.

Jesus will meet you there.
A soul He will revive.
He loves you and He cares.
A refreshing drink He will supply.

# Hold On, My Friend
## October 27

Many men at sea,
Angry waves splash over the ship's side.
A most dangerous place to be,
To save the crew, all must abide.

Let the boat go,
Or else many will die;
Even now the ship overflows.
The raging water continues to rise.

All the people will be saved
If Paul's command they obey.
God spoke to him as he prayed.
It was a promise for the day.

No one would lose his life.
The empty boat drifted away,
Their only hope to save their lives.
All would be saved if on the ship they would stay.

The mighty vessel drew closer to land.
Everyone knew the ship was going down.
But at the Lord's command,
All would be alive on solid ground.

Some were able to swim.
Others found a board or a plank.
All were saved without loss of life or limb.
I believe it's time to give God thanks.

By His love and mercy,
No matter where the place,
He saved Paul from a perilous sea.
A greater blessing still, he was saved by grace.

The Lord came to rescue the perishing,
So get on the board of anticipation.
In the water of life to cling,
Rejoice; this is the day of salvation.

Hold on, my friend!
The hand of mercy I see.
Take hold of His hand.
Jesus came to save you and me.

# Keep the Faith Lines Open
## October 28

In my home I have a water faucet.
The water satisfies my thirst.
Sometimes I fill up a bucket.
A good drink is hard to resist.

The water is almost always available
Unless I have frozen lines.
The water flow is not very reliable;
Gradually the pipes thaw as the sun shines.

I turn the handle of the faucet.
Patiently I wait!
But no water yet.
I know it is getting late.

The sun is beginning to set.
Little drops of water start to drip.
I open all the faucets.
The water flows through the pipe

So bountiful and free.
Next time I'll leave the water running.
It truly was a refreshing sight to see.
Frozen lines need a good warming.

In our quest for heaven,
Let us keep on moving,
Keep the faith lines open.
There is peace in believing.

God wants us to be available
Whenever He needs us.
A servant that is dependable
God will use in His service.

Faith is like an open faucet.
An active life is ever flowing.
With a gentle move of the Holy Spirit,
God gives a special blessing.

He wants us to be consistent
In our daily living.
God's grace is sufficient,
But we must keep the faith lines open.

# Meet Me at the Cross
## October 29

Meet me at the cross of the crucifixion.
Our spiritual journey will begin.
A quick visit to the grave reveals the resurrection
And the power of God to forgive sin.

Jesus is alive!
At the cross, He will meet us there.
Wait patiently for Him to arrive.
He gives peace and joy to share.

The faith of the heart is the meeting place.
Tears of repentance will bring Him running.
Believe in Jesus, God gives an abundance of grace.
Sins forgiven, sure is a good reason for rejoicing.

Our heart's desire is to see Jesus.
Well, listen to what He said.
He will be with us
In our midst when the Word of God is read.

Where two or three
Are gathered together in the name of the Lord...
Do you remember where the Lord said he would be?
In our presence—this is a promise from His Word.

All heaven comes down.
Jesus is in our midst.
The glory of God abounds.
He is the holy one; He is the Christ.

At the altar of His love,
All of our sins to remit,
Be touched by the hand above.
Rejoice in the presence of the Holy Spirit.

Meet me at the cross,
Where Jesus died for our sins.
He came to save the lost.
On the cross His arms extend.

Visit the grave if we desire.
Grave clothes folded in a pile.
We'll find He's not there.
Jesus is coming back to earth in a little while.

# Would you follow Jesus?
## October 30

Jesus said,"Take up the cross, and follow me"(Mark 10:21).
Now the cross of Jesus
Was quite heavy indeed.
With love He carried it for us.

Would you follow a man
That could speak to a storm?
The raging wind stops at His command.
There is peace and a great calm.

Would you walk with Him
If He would pay the price?
Your soul to redeem,
His life He gave as a sacrifice.

Would you follow
A man who was beaten?
Oh, the pain He felt as the blood began to flow,
His back was smitten.

Would you follow
The pathway of life
Led by "a man of sorrows
And acquainted with grief" (Isaiah 53:3)?

Up Calvary's hill,
With a wooden cross on His shoulders,
In obedience to God's will,
Jesus was crucified; death came by the soldiers.

Would you follow all the way,
Even to the grave,
Or would you turn and walk away
From the sacrifice He gave?

Would you follow without reserve
If all of your sins could be forgiven?
Repent, Jesus will forgive.
Sins forgiven when you believe Christ has risen.

"Follow me;" Jesus is calling.
He came to save all sinners' of disgrace.
Christians around the world are following.
Forgiven sinners' are thankful for the saving grace.

# A Made-Up Mind
## October 31

We have a mountain to climb.
Sometimes we will slip and fall.
Let us follow Jesus all the time.
Even now can we hear the Master's call?

This way, my daughter and son,
The Lord is leading.
He commands us to march on.
Every day keep following.

He will lead us safely home.
Don't return to the valley of sin.
No one wants to be all alone,
A mountain to climb all over again.

When Jesus calls us by name,
Don't be so far away,
Salvation is unclaimed.
Heaven is waiting if we pray.

He will show us the way,
The pathway to Glory.
Walk with Him, day by day.
The Lord is rich in love and mercy.

Take hold of His hand.
Receive power, strength and might.
Walk across the land.
Climb the mountain heights.

Leave the past behind.
With a new dedication
And a made-up mind,
Receive from God a divine inspiration,

An anointed determination
To live for Jesus.
Let us resist temptation.
Follow the one who came to save us.

With a made-up mind
Never to quit or walk away,
Be faithful to Him all the time.
Follow Jesus every day.

# Early in the Morning
## November 1

Early in the morning
At the beginning of the day,
When the clouds are forming,
It is a good time to pray.

Jesus comes to visit.
The dark clouds to take away,
He gives a refreshing of the Spirit,
Peace and joy all along life's way.

Let us rise with the morning sun.
Talk with God in prayer.
Sweet fellowship with Him has begun.
It is all right to call Him, Father.

What a blessing!
To begin the day with Jesus,
Early in the morning,
He calls us for service.

He gives us a longing
To walk in the light,
A deep heart felt burning,
Let us rejoice in the power of His might.

He will never leave or forsake.
Occasionally in our lives, storm clouds rise.
The sun of righteousness will radiate.
He will place a rainbow in the skies.

Early in the morning
There is a special meeting place.
A touch from the Lord is always refreshing.
It's always good to begin each day with grace.

A day of grace for the believer,
Let every searching heart find
Sweet peace with the Savior.
Rejoice in the Spirit all the time.

Fellowship begins on our knees.
A day bright and fair, someone is praying.
God listens attentively to our pleas
And He always meets with us early in the morning.

318

# Lovest Thou Me?
## November 2

"Lovest thou me?"(John 21:16)
Jesus asked that question.
"Thou knowest that I love thee."
This is a time for meditation.

What would be our reply?
Search the heart deep.
Abounding love, God's Son is magnified.
A truthful evaluation is His honor to keep.

The blessing is to serve Christ with love.
He has commanded us to forgive.
Mercy comes from above.
His promise is eternal life to give.

Reverence Him with Godly Living.
I can tell you more.
Christ has risen.
He's alive forevermore.

We have a high calling of God.
Go forth in Jesus' name.
Tell sinners there is life in His blood.
The message of hope, gladly proclaim.

Tell the gospel story,
Their lives can be forgiven.
They will have the hope of glory.
Use the talents given.

Help others along the way.
If the calling is to preach,
No time to delay,
There are so many souls to reach.

The hungry are crying.
Please take the time to pray.
Loved ones are dying.
Show love and kindness every day.

Do we love Jesus?
This question is for you and me.
His love will prevail as He depends on us.
Lord you know that we love thee.

# Keep Going
## November 3

As we look toward heaven,
Our home is beyond the skies.
Keep on walking!
The Lord forever abides.

Keep pressing on!
We are almost home.
Our faith in God's Son
Will help us to overcome.

The obstacles of the day,
Hold the cross up high.
As we walk the narrow way,
A repentant heart He will not deny.

From the valley to the mountain,
Press onward!
The height of glory is yet to attain.
God will give a reward.

To have life everlasting,
Don't look back or even down.
Keep on going!
A crown of life will be won.

The way is steep,
Danger on every side.
Jesus will show us each step
If in Him we confide.

Look up and beyond,
To step on the eternal shore
Keep pressing on!
We will be with the Lord forevermore.

We have a vision to pursue.
Up ahead is the glory land.
Heaven is in view.
Keep holding His hand.

Keep going,
By faith in Christ we will abound.
Heaven is waiting.
Soon we will wear the victory crown.

# Live for Today
## November 4

Live for today
As time is quickly passing.
Follow Jesus all the way.
Worship Him with a joyful heart expressing.

Sing a new hymn.
Let the praises ascend.
All glory and honor belong to Him.
A blessing from heaven will descend.

Our life on earth is temporary,
No promise of tomorrow.
Live each day for the Christ of glory.
Joy in the heart will replace the sorrow.

Seek earnestly God's will.
Walk the straight and narrow way.
The pathway of life He will reveal.
Take the time to pray!

Life in Christ is joy unspeakable.
Live for today,
With God all things are possible.
He will make a way.

Rejoice in the morning light.
Praise God every hour.
Sweet peace comes at night.
A new day dawns with resurrection power.

Live for today as if there were no other.
Heaven is waiting.
His command is to love one another.
On the streets of glory, oh what rejoicing!

The heavenly choir will sing.
Holy, holy, holy,
The faithful believers will join in.
Let every joyful heart give God the Glory.

Live for today,
Love God with heart, soul, and mind.
Eternity is just a breath away.
Life on earth, It is only a matter of time.

# A Light on a Hill
## November 5

A light on a hill,
Radiant beams will glow.
Oh, what a thrill;
A Reflection of God's love will show.

His love and mercy is a constant flow.
A dark path is made clear.
A life in Christ is to know
Jesus is always near.

His glorious presence,
Don't try to hide.
His eternal existence
Will forever abide.

Now a light in the valley,
The way is dark indeed.
It is easy to fall into the gulley
Or maybe walk into a tree.

If the light is on a hill,
It will show the way to glory.
Those who are obedient to God's will,
They live a life that is holy.

Cover a candle with a basket.
There is not much light to give,
Not enough for anyone's benefit.
A light on a hill is a godly life to live.

Radiant beams of His love,
He has chosen this remarkable place,
On a hill far above.
A life in Christ is one of grace.

When the light is dim,
Dark shadows move in.
The lantern needs a good trim.
A strong flame is reviving.

A light on a hill is godly living.
Grace shines bright in a dark valley.
Faith keeps the light shining.
Give God the glory.

# Till We Meet Again
## November 6

Last word from a friend, goodbye!
When the parting days have come,
God will wipe away the tears in the eyes.
One of His children is going home.

It is time to lay the old cross down.
A Christian soldier fought the battle and won.
The reward in heaven is a glory crown.
Faithful to the end, the race is run.

A sinner of disgrace
In the race could not compete.
But a child of God saved by grace
Will not accept defeat.

Onward, onward!
Never give up or quit.
Keep your eyes on the Lord.
Yield your life to the Holy Spirit.

Be strong in the Lord and the power of His might.
Love God with heart, soul, and mind.
Always do what is right.
Hear the call of the Master; it is time.

To be forever with Him,
The days on earth are past.
The family will rejoice and sing a new hymn.
Soon he will be in heaven at last.

No sorrow to leave behind,
He held the cross high.
With the Savior He walked the fine line.
Behold, Jesus is coming in the sky.

Please give a few words of encouragement
Before you leave.
His best advice is to repent.
Life eternal is promised if you will only believe.

The time has come and gone.
Pearly gates swing wide, goodbye!
Peace will come when you believe on God's Son.
Watch and pray; Jesus is coming in the skies.

# No Turning Back
## November 7

The athletes have gathered on the track.
The judge fires the gun.
No use to look back.
The race has already begun.

If you look at the crowd,
Other athletes will pass you.
Victory does not belong to the proud,
But of humbleness of spirit and grace too.

To cross the finish line,
A new home to win,
Some things you need to leave behind,
Heavy burdens and the weight of sin.

This race is not the ordinary kind.
It all begins with sinners of disgrace.
Lives are changed as grace comes from behind.
A crown will be given at the end of the race.

 What if you fail to run?
Will the glory land be in sight?
Our hope is in God's Son.
Receive strength, power, and might.

There are many obstacles in the way,
Many hurdles to overcome.
In order to win, you must pray.
Keep the faith; you are almost home.

You may be tired, weary, and worn,
Keep running; up ahead is the victory lane.
A crown of life to be adorned,
A race will be won in Jesus' name.

There's no turning back to the ways of the old.
Don't be satisfied until the race you have won,
And with Jesus walk down the streets of pure gold.
Don't turn back; keep going on.

The race has begun.
Give God the praise.
Victory is promised in His Son.
Run to win with grace.

# One Thing Is Needed
## November 8

Lord, I know there are many deeds to do.
I know the most important thing:
First and foremost, we should worship you.
Let our joyful hearts sing.

From a heart of praise,
Let the well of joy overflow.
With holy hands raised,
Our love to God will show.

Time spent with God, He will show the way.
Other things occupy the mind
When we kneel to pray,
We do not give Him our time.

I know I asked you to bless,
But I ran out the door
Before you could open the treasure chest.
Now I have to wait another day or even more.

So many things to do,
Yet so little time for the Lord,
I'm sorry to say I'm as guilty as you.
God, inspire us all to read your Word.

To be faithful and true,
Diligent in our prayer life throughout the day,
Consecrated in our worship of you,
Wait upon the Lord; take the time to pray!

Before we rush off, as if on eagle's wings,
We should hear what the Lord has to say.
Don't worry about other things,
A blessing is coming our way.

One thing is needed,
To love Him with all our hearts,
The Lord would be pleased.
Wait at the cross before we part.

Kneel at the feet of Jesus.
He will give a blood transfusion.
He wants us to give our lives in service.
Don't rush out the door without the instructions.

# Let Everybody Know
## November 9

The call is to the faithful.
Go and labor in the field.
God is merciful.
The harvest will be an abundant yield.

Wherever we go,
Whatever our position,
Always someone needs to know
God's plan of salvation.

Christ gave His life to set us free,
Our sins to forgive,
Mercy for you and me,
We have a new life to live.

Good news to bring
That everyone may hear.
He is Master, Lord, and King.
Proclaim the gospel message loud and clear.

Give us a burning desire,
With heartfelt emotion,
Glorious news of a Savior, we need to share.
Be fully committed without reservation.

Jesus died on a cross
So our sins could be forgiven.
He came to save the lost.
The supreme sacrifice was given.

He was laid in a grave.
Death held Him as a prisoner.
He had no intentions to stay.
On the third day He arose as our Savior.

This is the gospel story.
To be saved, just believe!
God is waiting to hear, "I'm sorry."
He honors a repentant heart; He will forgive.

Everybody needs to know
He was dead, but now He lives.
The high calling of God is for us to go.
Good news to share, He forgives.

# Be Ye Kind to One Another
## November 10

A little kindness,
A sweet melody of a lark,
Mix in a handful of gladness;
You will have a joyful song in the heart.

If in the garden
You perform a good deed;
Treasure is laid up in heaven
If a hungry mouth you feed.

Just a little love
Can cover a multitude of sins.
Grace comes from above.
Loving kindness always wins.

A hand extended in forgiveness
Can set the guilty free.
Time to rejoice for the release
And thank Him for the mercy.

A forgiving heart will not fail.
Sins are so graciously forgiven.
Love and mercy will always prevail.
The gates of heaven are open.

If you are in the miry clay,
Sinking deeper in sin,
I believe it is time to pray.
The hand of mercy He will extend.

In stormy conditions give peace,
An anchor that holds in the storm.
The rain and the wind cease.
A soul will be transformed.

It's all right to be kind.
From the river of His goodness,
Throw out the lifeline.
A soul will be saved by grace.

Be ye kind one to another.
Rescue the perishing.
Kindness is the lifeline to the Father.
Love is never failing.

# In a Faraway Land
## November 11

In a faraway land,
The American soldier,
He fights upon the desert sand.
His little child, he would love to hold her.

He would love to be with his family
And celebrate Veteran's Day.
At a moment's notice, he would leave.
On a plane he would fly away.

But until his time comes,
He continues to fight for you and me.
Someday to return home,
But first he must set the captive free.

My friend, if you happen to pass a flag today,
In honor of our veterans give a salute.
Across the land the American flag waves.
It is a strong and lasting tribute.

Soldiers have fought under the banner
Of the red, white, and blue.
Faithful to bring honor,
Their commitment is loyal and true.

Hold the flag up high.
Remember the soldiers in a faraway land.
Some soldiers will die
As they fight on the desert sand.

The hope of all the nations,
Whether it is in peace or war,
Our most sincere expectations,
Freedom is worth fighting for.

America, the land of the free,
It is the home of the brave.
The soldiers fight for our liberty.
See the flag as it waves.

To all veterans, honor is due.
Freedom is not free!
All the sacrifices belong to you.
Thanks for your service to our country.

# How much do you love me?
## November 12

Jesus of Nazareth,
How much do you love me?
On a cross He took his last breath.
The answer is really plain to see.

His arms stretched wide
On a cross made of wood.
For your sins and mine, He was crucified.
A love so strong, it would require His blood.

But Lord, if I were the only one,
Would you die for me?
The cross held God's only Son.
This is the answer to my plea.

The wounds in your side,
The thorns and the nails--
Would you brush me aside,
Or would your love prevail?

But Lord, I would like to know,
How much do you love me?
See the blood dripping from His brow.
He hangs lifelessly.

Jesus is on the cross,
Dying in my place.
Death for my sins, see what it cost.
His life so I could be saved by grace.

A love so strong
To die for one or all,
God's beloved Son,
He answered heaven's call.

Lord, how much do you love me?
The answer to my appeal,
On a cross made from a tree.
God's love He came to reveal.

He spread His arms wide.
A loving embrace to give,
This much for me He died.
His life for mine, so I could live!

# Just a Little Closer
## November 13

On a journey very far away
In a distant land,
No time to pray,
God was reaching down His hand.

More effort was needed to reach it.
Perhaps on a boat, far out to sea,
Still not yielding to the Holy Spirit,
Salvation is a gift so free.

This trip led to the mountains high.
There was no peace.
Even though Christ walked by,
There could have been grace.

It is possible to be in the wilderness,
Far away from God,
Living a life of unrighteousness,
Sin holds onto the ways of the world.

Stop walking away.
There is no place to run.
Take a little time to pray.
Get acquainted with God's Son.

He has been following every day.
Always with love compelling,
His hope and desire was to save a stray.
He knew all about the rebelling.

Grace will not be found by hiding.
A way of escape was not found.
Start a new life with Him abiding.
His love will always abound.

God is not very far away.
Can His hand be reached yet?
Now is a good time to pray.
Salvation to impart, only believe it.

Just a little closer,
His loving arms embrace.
A little bit nearer,
A sinner is saved by grace.

# A Day of Haste
## November 14

Early to rise,
Many things to do today,
Get up before sunrise.
There is not enough time to pray.

Fellowship with God can wait.
An appointment has been made.
Please hurry or you will be late.
Time with God begins to fade.

Every day the same routine,
Always in a hurry,
Left behind a cup of coffee with caffeine,
Days pass without saying, "I'm sorry."

No apology was given.
The day has begun without His presence.
A new life began when sins were forgiven,
It seems to have ended with negligence.

It's bad enough to leave the morning hour
Without so much as mentioning His name,
But throughout the day, absolutely no power.
Every day without prayer is the same.

Satan comes in his own defiant way.
He loves to attack the weak.
No time to pray
Or fellowship with God, expect defeat.

Let's start all over again.
Fellowship with God is comfort for the day.
Sins have been forgiven.
The Savior will be with you all the way.

Stand strong and vibrant,
Begin the morning with God's Son.
A prayer a day can keep you triumphant.
The victory will be won.

Early to rise,
Strength and grace for the day,
Just before the sunrise.
Take the time to pray.

# Be Still
## November 15

Come into His presence,
Talk with God in prayer.
Honor Him with reverence.
At the family altar, He is there.

He listens attentively to the request
The windows of heaven are open.
He knows what is best.
A blessing will be given.

Truly it is a wonderful time
To have fellowship with God,
Love Him with heart, soul, and mind.
He will bless according to His Word.

He has heard all the talking,
But now it is time to be still.
It is like a gentle breeze blowing.
God reveals His will.

This is when the heart is overflowing.
A touch from heaven is so real.
The Holy Spirit is gracefully moving.
Tell me what you feel.

In the room all alone
God came down.
He left the throne.
His holy arms wrap around.

Fellowship with Him in prayer,
There is something special
When God is there.
The soul is emerged in revival.

When He makes a personal visit
To come and be with me in my home,
I can feel the Holy Spirit.
I'm not alone.

What does God require?
Silence fills the room; be still!
A touch from heaven will transpire
When we yield to His will.

# Keep Running
## November 16

How strong the anticipation
For the runners of a race,
Heaven will be the final destination.
The finish line is in sight; quicken the pace.

On the track of life, tired and worn,
Burdens seem to be heavier.
The winner will receive a crown.
Closer to the end, the willpower is stronger.

If you must look back,
Just do it for a brief moment!
Continue on down the track,
The race began at the word repent.

Salvation by grace was the beginning.
The hope of glory is to cross the finish line.
So keep on running!
A reward will be given in glory divine.

The pace is fast.
This may be the last long mile.
Finish the course, home at last.
Go to be with Jesus in just a little while.

Keep your eyes on the goal,
A strong determination to win.
A sight of glory, a vision to behold,
God will open the gates of heaven.

Be faithful to the end.
In life's race always abound.
Stay away from sin.
Behold the victory crown.

The finish line is in sight.
Pick up the pace.
By the power of His might,
Receive a crown won by grace.

Heaven is the destination.
The Lord is coming!
He is looking for dedication
And for those who are still running.

# Onward, Christian Soldiers
## November 17

The battle rages on.
Oh Christian, take a stand.
There is victory in God's Son.
The faithful will inherit the Promised Land.

Don't turn and run.
Be victorious on the battlefield.
The war is nearly won.
Keep the faith; be obedient to God's will.

God will keep us from all harm.
Seek the glory of His face.
To be sheltered in His mighty arms,
Oh, how wonderful it is to be saved by grace.

I know the enemy is strong,
More powerful than you and me.
Defeat is certain if we stand alone.
The Lord has promised us the victory.

Let us go forth to conquer.
Be strong and brave.
Our trust and reliance in the Savior,
He has the power to save.

A committed soul He will not turn away.
God is pleased when our lives we yield.
Fight and be strong today;
We are crossing the battlefield.

Greater is He that is in us.
We can defeat the enemy.
Hold the flag high; we are marching through.
Victory to claim, it will be for eternity.

Strength and power and might,
When Jesus dwells within,
To be victorious in the final fight,
The war against sin, we will win.

Onward, Christian soldiers.
Sing the battle hymn.
It is just about time to cross over.
The battle won, give the glory to Him.

# My Debt Is Paid
## November 18

The price of redemption,
Look at the cost.
A man would die for our salvation.
He was crucified on a cross.

Oh, how great the love!
Jesus of Nazareth came
To offer pardon from above
I'm so glad there is forgiveness in His name.

Who could pay so great a price
So our souls would be blessed?
One man gave the ultimate sacrifice.
Behold, God's Son, Jesus Christ.

My debt He forgave.
The price for sin was paid.
On a cross His life He gave
So our souls could be saved.

His precious blood was spilled.
The pain was so severe.
He accomplished God's will.
His love for mankind would persevere.

Remember the words crucify, crucify.
From the grave He would rise.
Death, grave, and hell, He would defy.
The angels escort Him to the throne in the skies.

The Lord is coming again.
We are listening for that trumpet sound?
Look up, my friend.
Soon we will be heaven bound.

The gates of heaven are open.
Be patient, it won't be very long.
The record shows forgiveness of sin.
A crown of life we have won.

Christ paid the debt we owed.
He paid it all.
Life eternal is promised.
Please answer the Lord's call!

# Locked in the Past
## November 19

Locked in the past,
Where is the key?
Many days have passed.
Oh, to be set free.

A new day has begun.
My only hope is to flee.
Many times I tried to outrun.
Always the past catches up to me.

No matter how fast I run,
I know the past is following me.
Like a shadow in the evening sun,
Will it follow me to eternity?

God will set me free if I pray.
When I look to the Lord above,
The shadows of the past fade away.
They are replaced with His love.

Don't look back, my friend!
The past is gone.
The Lord has forgiven.
It is time to move on.

God forgives, and He forgets.
He wants us to do the same.
Leave the past behind. No regrets!
Press onward in Jesus' name.

Where is the key
That will help me forget the past?
I found it on bended knee.
God answers prayer, free at last!

The Lord set me free.
From the things that come from behind,
He has the eternal key
That can open and unlock the mind.

Sins are gone!
The past is forgotten.
Thank God for His Son.
The gates of heaven are open.

# Just a Drink of Water
## November 20

A drink of water to give,
A revived spirit will show.
Without water no one could live.
Fail to share, who would know?

Those who did not receive
Would become very weak.
Thirsty for life, help others believe.
Talents are not given for you to keep.

No need for sharing
Or any water to spare.
A soul may perish for lack of caring.
Show them that you care.

Use the talent given.
Thirsty souls will live.
They will have the hope of heaven.
Faltering spirits, God will revive.

He will give them strength to go on.
A drink of water is for survival.
The weak become strong.
Give and God will bless with His approval.

Souls are crying.
They need a drink of water.
Many of them are spiritually dying.
This is not the will of God the Father.

The anointing is from above.
A talent is given, please use it.
Others need to know of His great love.
Yield to the Holy Spirit.

Water for a thirsty soul in a barren land,
Everyone needs to know:
Love one another is still the great command.
A revived spirit will most certainly show.

Just a drink of water,
Is that too much to give
For a soul to come to the Father
And have a new life to live?

# Give What You Keep
## November 21

Many things in life to keep
In the heart's treasure chest;
Some are classified as antiques.
God wants the very best.

Choose something from the heart
And now give it away.
This will be a special gift to impart.
It will come back to stay.

If you want to keep love,
Compassion is the gift for today.
A blessing comes from above.
God touches lives in His own way.

The good news of the gospel.
It is a wonderful thing to give.
Words from the Holy Bible
Will help others to live.

A terrific message to proclaim
I am sure you will discover.
If you give to drink in Jesus' name,
The fountain overflows many times over.

Give a little sunshine
Of deep emotional concern;
Offer friendship of the heavenly kind.
Into the treasure chest, it will return.

In a dark, stormy night,
On life's troublesome sea,
Godly living will shine bright.
It will show the path of mercy.

If you give peace,
The burdens of life to calm,
The torrent of rain will cease.
It's time to go home.

The things you want to keep,
Give them away.
In the treasure chest, dig deep!
What you give is coming back to stay.

# A Divine Connection
## November 22

A powerful storm moves across the land.
The power lines are down.
A small family is stranded.
Live electrical wires are on the ground.

The snow keeps falling,
Sleet and freezing rain.
Soon it will be evening.
The residents bring some wood in.

They all gather around the fire,
Each one trying to keep warm
In the cold damp air,
Cuddled together in each other's arms.

The storm continues throughout the night.
The fire burns low.
Only a small glimmering light,
Just a few embers glow.

Several days in the freezing cold,
About to give up hope,
Life is about to lose its hold.
A lifesaving crew will climb a steep slope.

A rescue team is on the way.
Will they be on time?
Or maybe they are too far away.
A decision is made to restore the power line.

The connection is made.
The family is alive.
All of the residents were saved.
They received the hope of a new life.

Imagination fades, in reality a life to be saved.
Jesus Christ is the lifeline.
An eternal connection can be made.
A life can be restored before the end of time.

Just call upon the Lord.
Ask Him to save.
Believe the Holy Word.
A divine connection is made.

# He Inhabits the Praise
## November 23

My God inhabits the praise.
He knows each person by name.
Rejoice with hands raised.
His glory we can proclaim.

Let us share the love of His Son
From a heart of adoration
Sing a new song.
Express words of admiration.

Glory to God above,
Let the praises ascend.
Thank Him for His great love.
A sweet blessing will descend.

Let the glad hosannas ring.
A joyful noise throughout the land,
A sweet melody of praise let us sing.
God inhabits the praise of man.

Glory to the King!
From the sanctuary of the heart,
Good tidings we bring.
A special blessing He will impart.

Praise the Lord!
Sing a new hymn.
He can hear every word.
Let us worship and honor Him.

From the depths of the soul,
A love so intense,
Let the whole world know
Faith in God will bring deliverance.

Offer the sacrifice of praise
He fills our hearts with love.
His joy and peace
We receive from above.

He inhabits the praise.
Blessed is the name of Jesus.
Worship Him with hands raised,
He comes down and walks among us.

# Any Good Thing in Nazareth?
## November 24

"Can there anything good
Come out of Nazareth? Come and see" (John 1:46).
Let us take a quick look.
Listen closely; I want to tell a new story.

If I could ask the multitudes,
Now I know that is not possible,
Imagination brings us to the neighborhood.
The words we gather will be very profitable.

The born-again believer,
Did any good thing come out of Nazareth?
I'm sure he would speak of a Savior.
His love was stronger than death.

Good deeds Jesus performed
From that day until this;
Many lives have been touched.
A soul in need the Lord would bless.

Any good thing
From such a small town,
I mean, is there anything
When hate is all around?

Yes, I'm aware Nazareth was a little place,
But His love extends throughout the world.
No one is out of the reach of grace,
Life is in His blood.

There is a constant flow.
Can any good thing? Come and see.
Sins are forgiven; we know.
Don't go very far, just believe.

When the Lord Jesus is revealed,
Mighty deeds are performed.
The sick are healed.
Sinners are transformed.

Nazareth is a little place.
Is there any good thing?
All can be touched by grace.
Faith in Christ is by believing.

# Tell Me What You See
## November 25

The story is told of a blind man.
His sight was restored
By a touch of the Lord's hand.
He had a brand-new world to explore.

Bartimaeus, tell me what you see.
"I see men as trees, walking"(Mark 8:24).
Each image was hard to perceive.
Soon he would see everything.

Once more Jesus touched his eyes.
The blind man could see, now without fear!
The crystal-blue sea
And the beautiful sky, it was all so clear.

He was touched by the Master's hand.
Everything came into focus.
He marveled at the beauty of the land.
But most importantly, he could see Jesus.

Oh, to look upon His face.
The glory of God to see,
Thank Him for His wonderful grace.
Jesus heard his plea.

Perhaps Jesus is waiting to hear,
"Have mercy upon me."
All things will be clear,
Salvation is so wonderful and free.

He extends the hand of mercy.
From darkness to light,
Behold the glory,
Receive your spiritual sight.

The eyes open wide.
Peace in the heart
And Jesus stands beside,
His love and mercy to impart.

Tell me what you see.
Perhaps a sinner of disgrace,
But after you received His mercy,
Your life was changed by grace.

# A Broken Cistern
## November 26

The cistern is broken.
Once it was a good water supply.
The gutter was always open
To catch the rain from the sky.

The pump was old.
Hot water was used to prime
It in the bitter cold.
Water drips a little at a time.

Soon it was flowing.
The bucket was slow to fill up.
The water was no longer frozen.
Now for a refreshing drink from the cup.

Let's go back to the beginning.
The cistern is broken down.
Mechanical parts are not working.
A fresh water supply cannot be found.

The thirst of a longing heart
Can only be satisfied from above.
With His grace to impart,
Lives are blessed by His love.

Don't turn away
From God's wonderful blessings,
Satisfy your thirst today.
Sometimes faith needs a gentle warming.

The heart is in need of thawing.
Love God with heart, soul, and mind.
Prayer keeps His blessings coming.
Be faithful to Him all the time.

A broken cistern needs repairing
For a good water supply.
So does a broken heart need reviving
To meet Him in the sky.

Whosoever will, let him come!
The water is freely given.
Fill up your cup, all you can consume.
Sins are so graciously forgiven.

# No Warning
## November 27

Life is so precious.
Hold onto each hour.
Live by faith in Jesus.
A storm may come with power.

It was so peaceful in the morning.
Dark shadows hid from the light.
Suddenly there were screams and weeping.
The unexpected happened in the night.

A giant tornado came with vengeance.
There was no place to hide.
The strong winds came without resistance.
Cars and trucks were thrown aside.

There was no warning
Of the impending danger that day.
Fierce winds began blowing.
Homes were carried away.

No one knows when life will end.
It is as a vapor
And will perish in the wind.
Repent! Jesus will be your Savior.

No warning will be given
When He comes in the sky.
He is coming back for the forgiven.
Those who are repentant, He will not deny.

Jesus is coming.
No one knows the day or hour,
The time of His appearing
Will be with power.

The sun may be shining
Or you may be a sleep at night.
He is returning.
Keep the lamp burning bright.

He is coming in the clouds of glory.
There will be no warning.
Those who are ready
Will find the gates of heaven are open.

# Overcoming Hurdles
## November 28

Run in a race,
Obstacles to overcome.
The power of God's Grace,
A life it will transform.

Hurdles of life to ascend,
The big and the small,
Now if you want to win,
Don't worry about a fall.

Just get up and try again.
If you turn and run,
How can you expect to win?
The race of life needs to be won.

The hurdles are high.
More strength is needed.
I know if you try,
The high jump can be completed.

There is strength in the Lord.
Power for all, I'm sure.
In His soul-cleansing blood,
There is victory to all who endure.

Never quit or give up!
"Press onward."
Receive the victor's cup.
A crown of life is a wonderful reward.

"Be ye steadfast, unmovable" (1Cor. 15:58).
A crown of life you will receive.
Remember all things are possible,
But you must believe.

A hurdle has fallen.
Don't look back!
Keep on running.
Stay on the glory track.

Many hurdles have been overcome.
Keep pressing on!
You are almost home.
The last hurdle, the race will be won.

# Picking up Pebbles
## November 29

Picking up pebbles,
Down by the riverside.
God will take away our troubles,
For in Christ we abide.

Down at the altar,
When in need of salvation,
I met God the Father.
His Son gave me a blood transfusion.

Jesus is my Lord and Savior,
Blessed be His holy name.
God is a great forgiver.
His love is always the same.

Picking up pebbles,
One by one,
Be diligent in the study of the Bible.
We have a battle to be won.

Pebbles in the sand,
Salvation we received.
Hold on to the nail scarred hand,
For in Jesus we believed.

Pebbles on the ground,
Faith in the heart,
God's grace will always abound.
His promise is never to depart.

Picking up pebbles,
Life's battle is won.
For God is able;
There is victory in His Son.

A few pebbles along the way,
We may face a giant
Before the end of the day.
The faithful will be triumphant.

The enemy likes to boast.
Let us take a stand
In the name of the Lord of host.
Faith in the heart is pebbles in the hand.

# Wings as an Eagle
## November 30

Look out across the land—
The many beautiful trees
Planted by God's holy hand.
The forest is a glorious sight to see.

The birds take shelter there,
Surrounded by many colorful leaves.
An eagle flies in the air.
Graceful is the flight in a gentle breeze.

Over the vast domain,
It searches for its prey.
By no means will it remain.
It sees the catch of the day.

Maybe a fish in the sea
Or a small rabbit in the field,
The eagle flies from the tree.
Soon its victim will yield.

From the mountain heights,
The eagle will descend.
Its prey will most certainly fight.
But usually the eagle will prevail in the end.

The eagle flies high above the earth.
It is triumphant in its victory.
Oh, that Christians would apply their faith
So they could conqueror their eternal enemy.

Mount up with wings as an eagle.
Keep heaven in sight.
Fight on until you prevail.
Deliverance is by His power and might.

Be steadfast, unmovable, always abounding.
Keep the faith that last long mile.
Never stop praying.
Jesus is coming in just a little while.

In the clouds of the sky
You will be carried away.
In the sweet by and by,
Rejoice He could come today.

# A New Life Living
## December 1

Think about the days of summer,
Life is in full bloom.
Smell the fragrance of a flower,
Rest in the shadows in the afternoon.

A time to remember,
The autumn season comes to an end.
Everything seems to be lifeless in December.
The harsh weather will soon begin.

A Tree stands alone.
Once there were colorful leaves.
Now they are all gone
Carried away by a winter breeze.

A cold wet snow covers the ground.
Icicles hang
In the trees all around.
Is it too early to think about spring?

When the flowers begin to grow
And the birds so cheerfully sing.
Buds on a tree begin to show,
Small baby birds a chirping.

A new life is formed.
God's creation is breathtaking.
It is more spectacular when a soul is reborn,
Well that is simply amazing.

When the old sinful ways are gone,
A new life in Christ takes its place.
The heart is transformed by God's Son.
There is nothing like His grace.

A new life living,
Old things are passed away.
A life in Him is all about believing.
His forgiveness is the only way.

When does life begin?
Faith in the heart,
Sins are forgiven.
Salvation He will impart.

# A New Candle
## December 2

The candle is burning low.
Dark shadows creep in.
Melted wax below,
It is in a candleholder of tin.

Once the room was bright,
A brilliant red glare.
The flame flickers in the night.
Now darkness fills the midnight air.

Just a small glimmer,
The fire will soon be gone.
Even now it begins to tremble.
Once the candle was tall and strong.

The shadow grows larger still.
Deeper and deeper they grow.
The oppression of guilt
Takes away the joyful glow.

This is the power of darkness.
Let us light a new candle,
The glory of God to express.
A new life will be rekindled.

With the flames reaching high,
Shadows leap back in fear.
The darkness runs to hide.
The Son of God is near.

Let us light a new candle, my friend,
A candle that burns low.
The shadows of dismay will come again.
Sorrow and despair we will know.

If the flame is of the glory kind,
Faith and hope in God's Son,
Shadows disappear; joy and peace return.
Keep the faith; let the fire burn on.

Place a new candle in the window,
A strong defense against the night.
The dark shadows have to go.
They have no power in the light.

# Confidence
## December 3

A day at the park,
Some athletes were in training
Just a few hours before dark.
Well, God gave me a special blessing.

As I watched the players run,
I saw them kick the ball.
I could see how the game could be won
No matter if the person was short or tall.

A little confidence,
Victory we can claim.
With a small amount of self-assurance,
We are looking at a brand new ball game.

Confidence comes by knowing
If we keep our eyes on the goal,
The crown of life is worth winning.
A good prospect: We already know.

The Lord gave me the word confidence.
My heart was open to receive
A lesson of trust and reliance,
The goal of life is to achieve.

Confidence is faith in believing.
If in the quicksand of doubt,
Every day sinking,
God will lift us out.

We have the ability to compete,
On the solid rock to stand.
We don't have to accept defeat.
Victory comes at the touch of His hand.

Trust is the hope reassuring
Whatever we do
The Lord is keeping,
And He is watching over us, too.

What is confidence?
We most certainly know,
The God of reliance,
He is with us everywhere we go.

# Praise, Glory, and Honor
## December 4

The God of all glory
Worship Him,
For He is worthy!
Sing a new hymn.

Let the praises ascend
To the most high God,
Upon our souls to descend.
Let us receive His gracious and wonderful love.

His love is like a mighty river
That has no bounds.
My God is bigger.
His love abounds.

Upon every mountain peak
And every valley below,
Each waiting heart to seek.
The cup of mercy will overflow.

A touch of His hand
And oh, to hear His voice,
A wave of glory across the land.
Let every heart rejoice.

Praise, honor, and glory
Bless His holy name,
For Jesus is worthy.
I'm glad He came!

He saved a wretch like me
And gave salvation for my soul,
Thank God for His mercy.
The love of God I know.

Give Him praise and honor
From a heart that overflows;
He is a wonderful Savior.
The whole world needs to know.

Praise, honor and glory
We give to Him,
For our God is worthy.
Let us all worship and sing a new hymn.

# Faith Comes by Hearing
## December 5

Where does faith come from?
Well, I would like to know.
Psalms is a book of wisdom.
Surely the answer is there for my soul.

Perhaps we should look in the book of John.
"God so loved the world,
He gave His only begotten Son" (John 3:16).
I am very sure faith comes from God.

There are many books;
Our search for faith is not hard to find.
Let us take a quick look,
Open up the eternal pages to the mind.

We know what faith means,
To believe and trust in God.
Jesus came our souls to redeem.
He came to preach the everlasting Word.

But what about the church?
Can faith be found there?
The preacher with many pages to search,
He speaks of God's love and care.

Hear the words as the preacher speaks,
The blessing for us is to receive.
God has called some people to teach.
Remember, faith in God is to believe.

Where does faith come from?
We have faith by hearing.
Listen carefully, the Lord may say, "come."
Oh, what a wonderful blessing

When we hear God's holy Word
Spoken from the pulpit
Or anywhere that it can be heard.
Faith comes when we believe it.

"Faith comes by hearing,
And hearing by the word of God" (9 Romans 10:17).
So if we are listening,
Faith comes when we hear the Word.

# Praise God Today
## December 6

In the presence of God,
Let us worship Him.
We receive inspiration from His Word.
Sing a new hymn.

The time is now to give honor and praise.
Rejoice in His great love.
Reverence Him with hands to raise.
Thank Him for the blessings from above.

Enter into the holy place.
Kneel at the altar.
Seek the glory of His face.
Give praise and honor to God the Father.

Come before His presence.
Rejoice and sing today.
Feel the power of deliverance
When we kneel to pray.

His love is great toward us.
He hears the heart's cry.
God's only Son, Jesus,
He comes walking by.

Touch the hem of His garment.
The virtue flows.
From a sinful heart repent!
The love of God we will know.

He will not turn away.
God loves us and He cares.
He hears when we pray.
All of our burdens He will bear.

Talk to God in prayer.
Find that special place.
I know He will meet us there.
Feel the spirit of His grace.

Jesus prayed, "Our Father and our God."
Let us worship Him with holy hands raised.
Lift our voices in one accord.
Our God is worthy to be praised.

# My Father
## December 7

Begin the day with prayer.
A kind and loving Savior will appear.
Draw a little bit closer.
The presence of the Lord is near.

It is a family affair,
Sisters and brothers,
Oh yes, Jesus is there.
We have a special visit of the Father.

Well, I would like to know,
Whose father is there?
He is very well known
By His love and care.

He has many wonderful children.
I can't name each one.
I don't know where to begin.
So let us listen to God's Son.

Let us hear the words of Jesus.
As He speaks of a loving Father so kind,
The words He speaks to us,
It will bring peace of heart and mind.

To know who the father is,
Hear His glorious words,
I am sure we will be blessed.
Listen reverently to the Lord.

"My Father, and your Father," (John 20:17)
They are the same.
We meet together in prayer
And have fellowship In Jesus' name.

Allow Jesus to finish,
"My God and your God," (John 20:17)
Let us pray in earnest.
We are joined together by His blood.

Our Father and our God,
Bless us with peace every day.
Fill our hearts with thy Word.
Visit us daily as we pray.

# Peace Be Still
## December 8

The storm is coming;
You can see it in the clouds.
Sometimes it comes without warning.
The sound of the thunder is so loud.

The storm may start as a light rain
Falling from the sky.
Upon the earth it came.
Shelter from the storm, the birds did fly.

The wind grew strong,
And the trees began to sway.
Raging winds became stronger.
The people began to pray.

You could feel the raging winds
And see the limbs come crashing down.
The storm—will it ever end?
The streams and creeks their banks did overflow.

Several days went by.
Gradually the storm came to an end.
The people gathered together outside.
They went looking for their friends.

Everyone has to endure a storm,
Maybe not in the torrents of rain.
Storms may come in many shapes and forms.
Often they will leave a trail of pain.

Remember the storm at sea,
When each disciple feared for his life?
The storm was raging for all to see.
The Lord brought peace in the midst of strife.

Come into God's presence with prayer,
Think about those blessed words "Peace be still" (Mark 4:39).
In the storm of life, Jesus is there.
The sweet spirit you will feel.

Christ is the master of the storm.
When there is turmoil in the troubled soul,
He will lift you up in His everlastings arms.
To be with Him all is peaceful.

# Peace in the Shadows
## December 9

On a nice summer day,
Find a large tree.
Go and rest in the shade.
A peaceful place is by the sea.

Feel the summer breeze.
Close your eyes
If you please!
Or watch the birds in the sky.

A moment of tranquility and peace,
A gentle wind blowing.
The cares of life cease,
No troubles bothering.

A good time to meditate,
To think about God's goodness.
A few minutes to appreciate.
Enjoy the magnitude of His loving kindness.

God is great and greatly to be praised.
Remember the day
All of your sins were erased.
The blood of Jesus washed them away.

The way of life was open.
The showers of mercy,
A new life was given.
Now you have the hope of glory.

Rest peacefully
In the shadow of the Almighty,
Live for Him daily.
In Him there is hope of eternity.

"My peace I give unto you:
Not as the world giveth"(John 14:27).
You'll find that it is true.
Salvation is for all who receiveth.

As you lie in the shadow,
Rejoice in the hour.
The blessings of heaven will follow.
Enjoy a refreshing spiritual shower.

# Peace on Earth
## December 10

Where can I find Him?
The Savior of the world,
Is He in the town of Bethlehem?
I am looking for Jesus Christ our Lord.

Let us search till we find
The Prince of Peace,
The King of glory divine.
Look upon His face.

Mary's arms held
A little baby boy,
The story is told.
He is God's glory.

A child is born
To set the captive free.
Yes, it is God's Son.
He is our hope for eternity.

He lay in a manger.
Just a small infant,
A message from the angels,
They made a wonderful announcement.

Peace on earth,
Glory to God on high.
Let us tell others of His birth
Just like the angels in the sky.

In every city and town,
From the manger let us run.
All over the world it may be known.
Let us proclaim the birth of God's Son.

So if we want to find,
Call upon the Lord on bended knee.
Commit soul, heart, and mind—
He will hear the heart's plea.

We will not find Him in a manger of hay,
Nor in a heart of corruption.
He is not in the grave of dismay.
Jesus is near when we believe in the resurrection.

# Peace in the Storm
## December 11

When the dark clouds roll in,
The sun fades away.
The torrents of rain descend.
Howling winds continue throughout the day.

The thunder and the lightning
Break up the tranquility of peace.
The storm is raging.
High waters increase.

The riverbanks overflowing,
Devastation and destruction,
Hour after hour, it keeps on raining.
The earth takes on a new transformation.

The raging waters overflow.
Trees fall by the wayside,
Power lines hanging low.
No place we can run or hide.

From the fierceness of the storm,
A glimmer of hope shines,
A new life to transform.
The raging river declines.

When we are in one of life's storms,
Listen to the Lord as He speaks.
There is peace and a perfect calm
If God we will seek.

Tranquility in the soul,
Blessings from heaven descend,
The love of God to know.
A violent storm comes to an end.

The sun shines brighter still,
And the troublesome waters cease.
The waters recede from the mountains and hills.
We have perfect peace.

A soul to reclaim,
A new life He will transform.
Peace and joy in Jesus' name,
We have peace even in the midst of the storm.

# My Peace I Give unto You
## December 12

The rain is coming down.
It is falling from the sky above.
It splashes upon the ground.
We can feel God's great love.

Raindrops falling from the sky,
There's something special about this day.
No teardrops in the eyes,
A sweet spirit enters the room as we pray.

It's such a peaceful day,
Though it is cloudy and hazy outside.
The clouds block the sun's rays.
But God's love we can feel inside.

He gives us peace.
As the gentle rain falls upon the ground,
Our lives are blessed with grace.
Hear the raindrops…what a beautiful sound.

Yes, there's something in the air.
We can feel God's divine, holy presence
And know that He is always there.
He has given to us a blessed assurance

That He would never leave nor forsake us,
He would be with us all the way.
"Come unto me." Hear the words of Jesus.
Let the rain from heaven fall upon us today.

It comes down gently from the skies above.
Yes, this is a special day,
For we can feel God's great love
As we walk the straight and narrow way.

Jesus said, "My peace I give unto you" (John 14:27).
So let the rains from heaven descend.
Peace in the heart, we know it's true.
Let the praise and worship begin.

Precious rain falls from the sky.
Oh, for a heavenly touch.
The Lord Jesus walks by.
The presence of God means so much!

# A Brand-New Slate
## December 13

Come and see what the heavens will bring.
He may give a lightly covered snow.
Or even a gentle falling rain.
Peace is what I want to know.

From the depths of sadness,
A heart that is broken,
To the throne room of gladness,
He will heal with words unspoken.

Upon the Lord I wait.
For soon He will give
A brand-new slate,
For the Lord told me to forgive.

The past is forgotten,
To remember no more,
He has forgiven.
Jesus Christ is my Lord.

So if you'll turn the paper over,
You'll see what God has done for me.
You won't find a four-leaf clover,
But a clean slate you'll see.

My sins were a crimson red.
Transgressions deep as a river,
I met the man whose blood was shed.
For my sins He came to deliver.

Thou our sins are as scarlet,
They shall be white as snow.
A life yielded to the Spirit,
This is the only way to go.

Without spot or blemish,
The slate is clean.
Nothing to contaminate or tarnish,
Jesus said, "Ye must be born again!" (John 3:7)

"Old things are passed away:
Behold, all things are become new" (2 Cor. 5:17).
Oh, take a little time to pray.
A sanctified life comes into view.

# This Gift Is for You
## December 14

It is a white Christmas.
Joy bell's ringing.
We hear of the birth of Jesus.
Heavenly angels sing.

Now you already know
I like to imagine,
I see the earth covered with snow.
A bright light is shining.

A baby wrapped in swaddling clothes,
God's gift to adore,
No fancy ribbons or bows,
But who is this gift for?

Well, it is a gift for the wealthy.
But it is much more!
The sick and the healthy,
It is a gift for the poor.

God's gift to mankind
For all who will receive
A blessing of the heavenly kind,
Forgiveness of sin comes when you believe.

Truly it is a wonderful present.
Let me reveal the cost.
God's Son was sent.
He came to save the lost.

To forgive your sins,
His life He had to give.
In His hands the nails were driven.
He died so you could live.

This gift is freely given.
God's only begotten Son,
Sins can be forgiven.
For unto you God's Son is born.

This gift is for you.
Won't you receive it, please!
Joy and love, His merciful kindness too.
God's gift is for peace.

# A Reflection
## December 15

The mirror of life will show
A born-again believer.
Jesus Christ, I know.
He is my Savior.

My sins are forgiven.
Transgressions are gone.
Blessings from heaven,
The love of God is shown.

A new image to behold
From the dark shadows of the night.
There is a new command of the Lord.
He wants us to walk in the light.

There was a reflection in the mirror.
I saw a sinner of disgrace.
God is a great forgiver.
Now I'm saved by grace.

Let me tell you what I see.
Well, the blood is flowing
Salvation for you and me.
Peace comes in believing

Take a good look, my friend.
Step up to the glass.
The old life of sin,
It quickly fades into the past.

If the old sins remain,
Give your heart to Jesus.
Believe on His name;
He came to save us.

Come and walk with me;
Jesus will show the way.
He opens the door of mercy.
Take the time to pray.

A reflection in the mirror,
The image is not yet in focus.
He is my Lord and Savior.
The blessing of all is to be like Jesus.

# The Gift of God's Love
## December 16

There are many wonderful gifts,
The gift of love and family,
A glorious new life.
God gives us faith, hope, and liberty.

The gift of God's love,
A child was born.
He came down from the heavens above.
He was laid in a manger, God's only Son.

God gave His very best,
A gift to all mankind.
God has a special request;
He wants us to love Him all the time.

God gave us the gift of peace.
To Him confess our sins.
With a new heart, we can rejoice;
Let a new life begin.

Jesus said, "My peace I give unto you:
Not as the world giveth" (John 14:27).
His gift is not in a box, red and blue,
But it is in every heart that receiveth.

Receive the gift of peace.
Take away the sadness.
When we speak to Him, say please.
He will fill the heart with gladness.

I'm sorry; please forgive me!
Give Him the gift of your heart.
My God will forgive.
Abide in His love, never to depart.

Receive Him today,
God's gift to mankind.
Receive His gift without delay.
Love Him with soul, heart, and mind.

The greatest gift of all,
The gift of life, we shall receive.
Not from the mall,
But in each heart, only believe.

# What can I give?
## December 17

What could I give
If I were to repay
For the sacrifice He gave,
The price He had to pay?

God gave the very best.
See what it cost:
His Son He loved the most.
He died for the lost.

A supreme sacrifice,
God's only Son,
He paid the price.
For our sins He would atone.

What would God accept
From our earthly treasure chest
To pay the debt
And give honor to Jesus Christ?

A huge debt we owe.
What can I give?
For the love bestowed,
What would He receive?

As a final payment
To satisfy the debt in full,
Jesus said to repent!
He requires us to love Him with all

Heart, mind, and soul.
Receive His payment for sin.
Then we will most certainly know
What we can give Him.

Love, honor, and praise,
All my heart to give,
Thank Him for His grace.
We have a new life to live.

A debt to repay,
A committed life to impart,
He will not turn away.
Let us give Him our hearts.

# An Open Window
## December 18

An open window,
God's creation to behold.
The ground covered with snow.
Feel the bitter cold.

Holiday decorations appear
In the darkest of night.
Everyone knows Christmas is near;
Many trees adorned with bright lights.

This is a special time of year.
Family members come from far and wide.
But sometimes there is a tear.
Loved ones no longer abide.

Sweet fellowship passes us by.
Some family members called away to glory.
Now I can't tell you why.
Occasionally there is another sad story.

Every Christmas I look for my son.
Many years have passed,
But I stand alone;
There is no way to erase the past.

But, I keep hoping
Someday my son will come home.
My heart is overflowing;
Only God's grace can atone.

So I keep the window of my heart open.
This may be the season
For the doorbell to start ringing.
Welcome home, my son!

Keep the love overflowing.
Your daughters and sons,
You may find them missing.
Keep the door open for their return.

An open window,
Keep the light burning.
The flame in the heart will forever glow.
This may be the year of their returning.

# The Birth of God's Son
## December 19

A child was born many miles away.
Wrapped in swaddling clothes,
He came to save.
Sins of the world He would expose.

God's gift to mankind,
A love strong and free,
I know words cannot define
What salvation means to me.

"For unto you is born this day" (Luke 2:11).
You mean Christ was born for me.
He lay in a manger of hay.
I know the world cannot see

The miracle of the birth.
For all those who believe,
They know why Jesus came to earth.
He came to give salvation for all who receive.

Glory to His name,
A Savior is born.
Let the world proclaim
Good news to tell: the birth of God's Son.

The greatest gift ever given,
A gift for you and me,
Receive Him; sins can be forgiven.
Thank Him for His divine mercy.

We celebrate Christmas,
The birth of Christ,
His name shall be called Jesus.
Receive Him; your life will be blessed.

Joy unspeakable and full of glory,
Christ is born in Bethlehem.
This is the Christmas story.
Let us bow down and worship Him.

"For unto you is born...
A savior, which is Christ the Lord" (Luke 2:11).
The birth of God's Son.
He is God's gift to the world.

# God's Gift to Us
## December 20

On that first Christmas day,
A wonderful gift to give,
A baby boy lay in a manger of hay.
A child is born, oh, the joy of a new life.

The gift from above,
He came down to earth
To reveal His great love.
He came to give us a new life, a rebirth.

Yes, the Bible tells us
We must be born again!
Believe on Jesus,
He forgives sin.

God gave us His Son,
The greatest gift of all mankind,
But He wants something in return.
Love Him with heart, soul, and mind.

Jesus was born that day.
The gift of salvation
He gives to us when we pray.
A home in heaven is our expectation.

From a small baby boy,
He grew to a fine young man.
Always His life revealed God's glory.
At the cross the nails were driven into His hands.

His life He gave
On an old rugged cross
That all might be saved
He died to save the lost.

We have a choice, my friend.
A gift to receive,
"Ye must be born again" (John 3:7).
Salvation is for all who believe.

We celebrate Christmas.
The birth of God's Son,
God's gift to us,
Jesus Christ was born.

# Countdown for Christ
## December 21

Let's say we start with ten.
We're still in our sins.
How about nine?
Leave our sins behind.
Don't forget about eight.
It's not too late.
Let's think about seven.
We can go to heaven.
What about six?

Remember the crucifix.
But, now we come to five;
In Christ we can be alive.
Now there is only four.
Decide for Christ before He shuts the door.
Then we come to three;
The Son of God can set us free.
Hope we didn't forget the number two.
He can make the heart brand new.
Then, there was one.
Say yes to Jesus before there is none.
Since we still have a zero,
Believe in God's Son.

Tell your child today.
Tomorrow, it may be too late!
Jesus Christ is the way.
Turn to Him without delay.

For God so loved the mother,
He gave His only Son.
He also loved her brother.
He promised one day He would return.

Let us also remember the father,
A hard-working man was he.
Down at the altar,
He was praying on bended knee.

The countdown for Christ has begun.
Let us start with the number ten,
Counting back until there is none.
We can go to heaven if in Christ we depend.

# Let's Say We Start with Ten
## December 22

Start with the number ten.
This is the first day of the countdown.
Sins have not been forgiven.
Ungodly living abounds.

Imagination reveals an ocean of despair,
Alone and without God,
The ship is in need of repair.
There is no food.

Many miles from the shore,
No ships on the horizon,
You may have to stay nine days more,
Or this could be the last one.

There is a huge hole in the side of the ship.
Water is gushing in.
The sails in the strong winds begin to rip.
The water is bailed with a bucket made of tin.

All efforts fail.
Unable to save yourself from an angry sea,
A sinful life is a rough ocean to sail.
A vessel in sight is a glorious thing to see.

Lives will be saved unless the ship sails away.
Without Christ you are sinking in the perils of sin.
Repent! The Lord can still save.
There is still time to invite Him in.

The sins of corruption
Overflow the boat.
They will drag a vessel of life to destruction.
Faith in Christ will keep you afloat.

It is impossible to save yourself.
Jesus is the only one, who can.
He responds quickly to the cries for help.
He will reach down His hand.

Sins can be forgiven.
Ten days and counting,
Life's journey, you are so close to the end.
Jesus is waiting.

# How about nine?
## December 23

How about nine?
We are counting the days.
Leave your sins behind.
There is still time to pray.

A race to be won,
Lay the heavy burden down.
There is victory in God's Son.
God's grace always abounds.

The race has begun.
You came on the track
With a horse and wagon.
Other riders are riding horses bareback.

What are your chances to win?
A horse and wagon against a racehorse,
They are rather slim.
There is not much hope of finishing the course.

Unhook the wagon,
The heavy weight the horses have been pulling.
The race can be won.
Leave the extra burdens behind.

In the race for the glory land,
Sin is too heavy to carry around,
Unrighteousness is a very steep mountain.
Someone else will receive the victory crown.

There is hope, my friend.
Let Jesus remove
The heavy weight of sin.
Your pace will most certainly improve.

In fact, you are promised the victory.
Only nine days remain.
The wagon of sin can be history.
The crown of life you can claim.

Leave the sins behind.
Turn from a life of disgrace.
Nine days—will you cross the finish line?
Just a little time left to receive God's grace.

# Do Not Forget Eight
## December 24

Do not forget eight.
Another day has passed.
It's not too late!
But the clouds are overcast.

There was a trip to plan.
A time to go to the station,
The schedule was for the evening train.
Each person had to have a reservation.

At home there is some work to do.
There is plenty of time,
But eight is just a few.
Remember there was ten and nine.

The days are gone.
You had better hurry.
Wait too long,
Well, it would be a sad ending to this story.

Finally, the baggage is packed.
Listen very closely; you may hear!
The train is coming down the track.
The time of departure is near.

The train is at the station.
You had better run!
The wheels are already in motion.
A missed train will be your misfortune.

At heavens train station,
The place of departure,
Late and without a reservation,
It is possible to miss the Rapture.

You still have a little time
To make that final preparation.
Commit your heart, soul, and mind.
Christ opens the way for an eternal destination.

The Lord is coming!
He will not be late.
It's Christmas Eve; will He find a soul repenting?
The countdown is eight.

# Christmas Past, Think About Seven
## December 25

Friends and loved ones gather around,
Kind words spoken.
The Christmas tree is taken down,
No more gifts to open.

The story of Christ birth
Will be told in another year.
Same day, December 25th.
As always Christ will appear.

He is the honored guest.
Remember, no room in the inn.
A manger was chosen as His place of rest.
Well, Christmas is past and the angels still sing.

"Glory to God in the highest,
Peace on earth, good will towards men."
The Bethlehem star shines the brightest.
Our fellowship with Him has no end.

Glory bright, the stars in the night,
You can put away the earthly treasure.
Take down all of the Christmas lights.
These gifts were made for your pleasure.

Their joy is for a reason.
Soon the satisfaction will grow dim.
Peace in Christ is a continual season.
It is a wonderful blessing to know Him.

Christmas past!
The days are gone.
Only what you have in Christ will last.
Give praise and honor to God's Son.

His gift God gave
For the world to receive.
In the grave His body was laid.
Now is the time to believe

In the resurrection.
You will have the hope of heaven.
Please don't put off your salvation.
The countdown is seven.

# What about six?
## December 26

What about six?
The days are gone.
Remember the crucifix.
Think about God's Son.

Go back to the cross.
Recall the pain and suffering.
Jesus came to save the lost.
He is slowly dying.

It is a terrible, agonizing death.
Do you remember the nails?
Can you see Him gasping for breath?
I do not like to use so much detail.

But we all need to know
They placed on His head a crown,
Not made of gold and silver for show,
But it was made of sharp thorns.

They pierced His brow.
The pain no ordinary man could bear.
His precious blood did flow.
His side was cut with a spear.

A sacrifice to give
For your sins and mine,
He gave His life so we could live
And be with Him all the time.

The price for sin was paid
On a cross by crucifixion.
In a grave He was laid.
Remember three days later, the resurrection.

This message is very important,
Especially for you:
A call to repent
Before another day you pass through.

What about six?
The days are disappearing.
Remember the crucifix.
You still have a little time; the Lord is waiting.

# Now We Come to Five
## December 27

Now we come to five.
The countdown continues.
In Christ you can be alive.
Your commitment is overdue.

The days dwindle away
As quickly as smoke or vapor.
You still have time to pray,
But you must earnestly seek the Savior.

He will forgive.
God will grant you favor.
Salvation comes when you believe.
The punishment for sin, He will waiver.

A life of sin brought you shame.
Soon the door will close.
Faith opens the heart, His peace to claim.
Jesus Christ arose!

But only five days to give,
Still living a life of sin,
Not many more days to live.
Life is coming to an end.

It is not God's will for you to perish.
Jesus came to save.
His love, a wonderful thing to cherish,
On a cross, His life He gave.

He hears the cries for mercy.
It's not too late to respond.
Believe and receive; give God the glory.
Grace from heaven will abound.

"Old things are passed away;
Behold, all things are become new"(2 Cor. 5:17).
He will hear you pray.
Heaven comes into view.

A warning to you, my friend:
It's the fifth day. Have you noticed the countdown?
You are very close to the end.
Soon the curtain of darkness will come down.

# There Is Only Four
## December 28

Now there is only four.
You can't bring back the other six days.
Decide for Christ; He stands at the door.
Only a little time left to pray.

Christ has given you another opportunity.
The choice you make—
It determines where you spend eternity.
It is getting late!

Soon it will be night.
The sun may not come up in the morning.
Turn off the light.
Please be aware of the warning.

Punishment for sin or life everlasting:
You have a choice.
One way leads to heaven,
The other is one of remorse.

Turn from sin.
The Bible says "to repent."
Open the door of your heart; let Jesus in.
He will come in only by consent.

He does not force the door open.
The doorknob is on the inside.
It will be your decision
Please don't keep Him on the outside.

This is the day of grace.
You are not promised another.
The time is now to seek His face.
Confess your sins to the Father.

A decision for Christ,
An entrance into heaven,
A soul is most certainly blessed.
Jesus is knocking at the door; please open!

You are living the last four.
Turn to Christ without delay.
Soon there will be no more.
Just a little time left to pray.

# Then We Come to Three
## December 29

Then we come to three.
Security is on high alert.
The Son of God can set you free.
He will grant a pardon to convert.

The prison guards stand watch.
There are rumors of an escape.
Check the time on your wristwatch.
It is getting late!

More guards are brought in.
All security guards bear arms.
For safety and to defend,
They will protect themselves from harm.

An escape has been planned.
The inmates wait for instructions.
Their orders come from a higher command.
They will escape the jaws of perdition.

Jesus walks the corridor.
He is searching the dark shadows.
A soul is in need of a Savior.
The man of Galilee is the one to follow.

Over in the corner of despair,
A man on his knees,
Jesus walks over there.
He hears the heartfelt pleas.

"Lord, forgive me!"
The Savior hears a sinner cry.
God opens the cell door of mercy.
Jesus will not turn away or deny.

This was an imaginary prison.
If you want the whole truth,
There is pardon for sin by God's Son.
Freedom comes by faith.

You are on day three.
The alarms are sounding.
The Son of God can set you free.
Soon there will be no more counting.

# Don't Forget the Number Two
## December 30

Hope you didn't forget the number two.
Look at the crowd, all the sinners.
Jesus died for them, too.
Heaven's gates will open for the believers to enter.

The days are numbered,
So you had better hurry!
You don't have time to take a nap or slumber,
Two days remain to make it to glory.

Jesus died for the unmerciful.
He gave His life for the unforgiving.
All the people who are unthankful—
He was crucified for the evil speaking.

Do you want to know more?
Jesus died for the person who does good,
Or a kindhearted person who helps his neighbor
And one who shares with the poor a little food.

The list goes on.
A sinner at his worst,
None is excluded, not even one.
Jesus died for a sinner who was at his best.

Jesus died for all; read the Word.
"For all have sinned,
And come short of the glory of God" (Romans 3:23).
Jesus forgives sin.

If you haven't sinned, throw the first stone.
The men would walk away.
No rocks were thrown.
God is waiting for you to pray.

This may be your last notice.
He is not willing that any should perish.
Give your heart to Jesus.
Two—days please don't let another day vanish!

Today is the day of salvation.
A very important decision to make,
You can still make heaven's reservation.
Tomorrow it may be too late!

# Then There Was One
## December 31

Then there was one.
Only one day remains,
Say yes to Jesus before there is none,
Just a little time, salvation to claim.

I know Jesus has been pleading.
He can see the conviction.
The Lord is still waiting.
Your last hours require a decision.

He can feel the sorrow.
Many times you walked away.
The Lord continued to follow.
He waited patiently every day.

There is rejoicing in heaven.
When a lost soul
Repents, sins are forgiven,
The journey of life is so peaceful.

For someone this is the last day!
Prepare to meet thy God.
It's not too late to pray,
Even though this is the end of the road.

The light from a candle, it flickers in doubt.
Hear the call of the Savior.
Give your life to Christ before the fire goes out.
Say yes to Jesus; receive God's favor.

Would you commit your life?
All your sins and cares,
Ask Him to forgive
Before life on earth expires.

He prays, "Yes, Lord Jesus, I give you my all."
At that moment, a new candle was lit.
A sinner heard the Savior's call.
He responded to the drawing of the Holy Spirit.

Salvation, a new life begins.
Well, this is the end of the poetry road.
For real peace and joy I would gladly recommend
A daily walk with the Lord.

# Epilogue

I have begun a new adventure in the world as a new writer. My book, a Daily Walk with the Lord offers hope and encouragement for a new life in Christ. As you walk with me on the straight and narrow way, you will find many times that you are in the presence of Jesus. When two or three people talk about the Lord, soon He will be in the midst.

This book is about many encounters with the Lord. There are poems of spiritual inspiration. The reader will be inspired to live and serve God. Jesus will be introduced as Lord and Savior. The gates of heaven will open for the repentant sinner. The weary traveler will stop at the cross and make peace with God. The born-again believer will have the hope of life eternal. There are poems about the crucifixion, the burial, and the resurrection.

I know that the friends I meet along the way will come from all walks of life. We will gather Together in the name of Jesus and offer praise unto God. I believe that through the pages of this book, Souls that are lost will find the way in Jesus. The sacred pages of the Holy Bible will become the treasure of the heart. I know that God's love will prevail and lives will be transformed by the conviction of the Holy Spirit.

Pardon me, my friend! There is a time for spiritual edification.It is only proper that I end this presentation of A Daily Walk with the Lord. I need to give God the praise, the glory, and the honor.

# Praise Ye the Lord

I want you to join with me in this journey of a Daily Walk with the Lord. I know that the way of salvation, faith in Jesus is the correct path to follow. As we walk the path together, soon we will be in the presence of God the Father, God the Son, and God the Holy Spirit.

The poems in this book were written from my heart. As you join with me, I'm sure the Lord will meet us along the way. For where two or three are gathered together in Christ's name, Jesus is in the midst.

# About the Author

David L. Hurst was born in 1949 in Chilhowie, Virginia. He served his country in the military in the years 1969-1971. After his service in Vietnam, he was married and had one son. In the early seventies, David received Jesus Christ into his life.

The Lord has led him into many wonderful places. He shared the gospel with the little children in Sunday school class. Later, he worked with youth and brought the good news of salvation to the elderly at a nursing home.

David attends the Dublin Church of God in Dublin, Virginia. In 1982, he received a very special award by the State Layman's Board of Virginia. He was recognized as layman of the year.

The Lord blessed David through his endeavors and gave him a gift of telling recitations. David and the Gospel Lights, a singing group, would go to various churches to magnify the name of Jesus and glorify the Lord God of Heaven.

God has given him a new talent; he has called and anointed him to write poems.

David lives in Radford, Virginia. He works for the United States Postal Service. He knows that life is short; he is only passing through. All the good he can do he wants to do now, for he will not pass this way again. Tomorrow will take care of itself. While he walks with the Lord, his heart's desire is to be a faithful servant and a witness for Jesus Christ.